Routledge Revivals

Into Another Mould

It is widely agreed that the period from 1625 to 1700 witnessed radical shifts in English life and thought. For historians of politics, science, religion, and philosophy, it is a time when the intellectual bases of modern thought and modern institutions were in the process of formation: divine monarchy gave way to contractual monarchy, the 'truths' of received authority gave way to those reached by inductive reasoning.

Although the year 1660 to some extent marks a turning point, this comprehensive and fascinating book, *Into Another Mould* (originally published in 1992), demonstrates an underlying *continuity* within the period of Stuart rule. It presents thinkers and writers before and after 1660 responding to similar dilemmas, albeit with different attitudes, methods, and conclusions.

Central to this volume are the related concepts of authority and reason. By looking at the changing attitudes to these two concepts in all spheres of life, it examines the crucial developments of the period and their bearing on the literature. Within this framework, the authors examine social and political history, religious belief and scientific knowledge, and painting, sculpture, and architecture as contexts for the literature of the time. This book will be a beneficial read for students and researchers of English literature, history, and cultural studies.

Into Another Mould

Change and Continuity in English Culture 1625–1700

Edited by T. G. S. Cain and Ken Robinson

First published in 1992
by Routledge

This edition first published in 2024 by Routledge
4 Park Square, Milton Park, Abingdon, Oxon, OX14 4RN

and by Routledge
605 Third Avenue, New York, NY 10017

Routledge is an imprint of the Taylor & Francis Group, an informa business

© 1992 Collection, T. G. S. Cain and Ken Robinson; individual essays, © the contributors

All rights reserved. No part of this book may be reprinted or reproduced or utilised in any form or by any electronic, mechanical, or other means, now known or hereafter invented, including photocopying and recording, or in any information storage or retrieval system, without permission in writing from the publishers.

Publisher's Note
The publisher has gone to great lengths to ensure the quality of this reprint but points out that some imperfections in the original copies may be apparent.

Disclaimer
The publisher has made every effort to trace copyright holders and welcomes correspondence from those they have been unable to contact.

A Library of Congress record exists under LCCN: 90008705

ISBN: 978-1-032-84627-9 (hbk)
ISBN: 978-1-003-51420-6 (ebk)
ISBN: 978-1-032-84629-3 (pbk)

Book DOI 10.4324/9781003514206

Into Another Mould

Change and continuity in English culture 1625–1700

Edited by
T.G.S. Cain and Ken Robinson

London and New York

First published 1992
by Routledge
11 New Fetter Lane, London EC4P 4EE

Simultaneously published in the USA and Canada
by Routledge
a division of Routledge, Chapman and Hall, Inc.
29 West 35th Street, New York, NY 10001

© 1992 Collection, T.G.S. Cain and Ken Robinson;
individual essays, © the contributors

Typeset in 10/12 pt Times by
Selectmove Ltd, London
Printed in Great Britain by
TJ Press (Padstow) Ltd, Padstow, Cornwall

All rights reserved. No part of this book may be reprinted
or reproduced or utilized in any form or by any
electronic, mechanical, or other means, now known or
hereafter invented, including photocopying and
recording, or in any information storage or retrieval
system, without permission in writing from the publishers.

British Library Cataloguing in Publication Data available

Library of Congress Cataloging-in-Publication Data
  Into another mould: change and continuity in English culture,
  1625–1700/edited by T.G.S. Cain and Ken Robinson.
  p. cm.
  Includes bibliographical references and index.
  1. Great Britain – Civilization – 17th century. 2. English
  Literature – Early modern, 1500–1700 – History and criticism.
  I. Cain, T.G.S. (Thomas Grant Steven) II. Robinson, Ken, 1946–. III. Series.
  DA380. I59 1990
  941.06 – dc20   90–8705

ISBN 0–415–01083–7 (HB). – ISBN 0–415–01084–5 (PB)

Contents

	List of plates	vi
	Notes on contributors	vii
	Preface	ix
	Table of dates	xi
1	**Introduction** *T.G.S. Cain and Ken Robinson*	1
2	**English politics 1625–1700** *Ivan Roots*	18
3	**From faith to faith in reason? Religious thought in the seventeenth century** *Margarita Stocker*	53
4	**The book of nature** *Ken Robinson*	86
5	**The visual arts and architecture in Britain 1625–1700** *T.G.S. Cain*	107
6	**Conclusion: another pattern. Seventeenth-century Britain revisited** *P.W. Thomas*	151
	Index	187

List of plates

1	Inigo Jones, Banqueting House, Whitehall (1619–22)	118
2	Sir Roger Pratt, Coleshill, Berkshire (1649–61)	119
3	Sir Christopher Wren, St Paul's Cathedral, West Front	120
4	Antonio Canaletto, *The Thames from Somerset House Terrace*	121
5	Sir Christopher Wren, Hampton Court Palace, Fountain Court (1689–1702)	122
6	Sir John Vanbrugh, Seaton Delaval, Northumberland (1720)	123
7	Nicholas Hawksmoor, The Mausoleum, Castle Howard (1732)	124
8	Nicholas Stone, *John Donne*, St Paul's Cathedral (1631)	125
9	Edward Pierce, *Sir Christopher Wren*	126
10	Daniel Mytens, *Algernon Percy, 10th Earl of Northumberland* (*c.* 1620)	127
11	Sir Anthony Van Dyck, *Algernon Percy, 10th Earl of Northumberland* (*c.* 1640)	128
12	Sir Anthony Van Dyck, *The Five Eldest Children of Charles I* (1637)	129
13	William Dobson, *The Artist with Sir Charles Cotterell and ?Nicholas Lanier* (*c.* 1646)	130
14	Samuel Cooper, *Oliver Cromwell* (*c.* 1650)	131
15	Samuel Cooper, *James Scott, Duke of Monmouth and Buccleuch* (*c.* 1664)	132
16	Sir Peter Lely, *Self-Portrait* (*c.* 1660)	133

Notes on contributors

T.G.S. Cain is Head of the School of English at the University of Newcastle upon Tyne.

Ken Robinson is a Senior Lecturer in English Literature at the University of Newcastle upon Tyne.

Ivan Roots is Professor Emeritus of History at the University of Exeter.

Margarita Stocker is a Fellow of St Hilda's College, Oxford and a Lecturer in English at the University of Oxford.

P.W. Thomas is Senior Lecturer in English at the University of Wales College of Cardiff.

Preface

'The only end of writing', said Samuel Johnson in the greatest of all book reviews, 'is to enable the readers better to enjoy life or better to endure it.' Our aim in this book is to enable our readers better to enjoy the writing of seventeenth-century England. Anyone who feels that the reading of *Paradise Lost* or *The Pilgrim's Progress* is more a duty to be endured than enjoyed will, we hope, read with more sympathy when those books are seen not as classic milestones on the long haul through Eng. Lit., but as features (however prominent) in a wider landscape, products of an age whose other contours – its politics and religion, its painting, architecture and philosophy, something of its *mentalité* – we have tried to set out.

For in one sense the culture of this, as of any age and society, is a seamless garment. *Paradise Lost*, Newton's *Principia* or St Paul's Cathedral are stitches in it – but so is the testimony of a soldier in the Putney debates, a miniature by Cooper, a speech of Strafford's or Cromwell's, the spread of glass windows to ordinary houses, or the evidence we can glean of feelings of parental tenderness or of coping with death. In one important sense, though, the metaphor of a seamless garment is misleading: it does not imply, as books on the 'context' of literature used simplistically to assume, that there was a single Stuart world-view, a set of common values universally acknowledged from which the seventeenth-century Englishman or woman contemplated their common predicament. There was not. This is not to say that a unifying study of English culture at this time comparable to Simon Schama's study of Dutch seventeenth-century *mentalité*, *The Embarrassment of Riches*, could not be written. Indeed, P.W. Thomas goes some way towards such a study in the concluding chapter of this book. But he and the other contributors, each looking at a part of that culture, avoid the old assumption that by describing the reigning orthodoxies we are describing the beliefs of both writers and audience, and so 'explaining' the texts we study. In the end, it is not our hope that through this book readers will be able to understand *the* meaning of *Paradise Lost*; rather, we hope that they will have a stronger sense of its complexity, a recognition that it has a multiplicity of meanings, not all of them intended by Milton, some of them indeed subverting his avowed beliefs and intentions. Above all, we hope, readers will see it and all the other writings of the age embedded in their time, and, seeing it thus, will see it as more alive in our own time.

Several years have passed since the conception of this book, and many debts have been incurred by each contributor, too many, sadly, to list here. We hope that all those who have read or typed drafts or contributed ideas to the various chapters will accept our thanks, and understand that in a collaborative venture such as this book it is impossible to name them all, and so better to name none. It is, however, fitting that as editors we should acknowledge the patience of our fellow contributors, Ivan Roots, Margarita Stocker and P.W. Thomas, of whom it says much that after many trials they are still our friends. That we can say the same of Jane Armstrong, our editor at Routledge, argues that some of the old values and virtues survive in publishing.

T.G.S.C., K.R.
Newcastle upon Tyne

Table of dates

Dates of Shakespeare's plays are not included. In the table *b.* = born; *d.* = died; *lit.* = literature.

DATE	LITERARY EVENT	PUBLIC EVENT
1600	*b.* John Ogilby *d.* Richard Hooker *lit.* Fairfax, *Godfrey of Buloigne* Gilbert, *De Magnete* Jonson, *Cynthia's Revels*	East India Company founded
1601	*d.* Thomas Nashe (?) *lit.* Dekker, *Satiromastix* Jonson, *Poetaster* Marston, *What You Will*	Essex rising and execution. Parliament attacks Elizabeth's right to grant monopolies. Poor Law
1602	*b.* Edward Benlowes, William Chillingworth, Mildmay Fane *d.* William Perkins *lit.* Campion, *Observations in the Art of English Poesy*	Bodleian Library opens
1603	*b.* Sir Kenelm Digby *d.* William Gilbert *lit.* Daniel, *Defence of Rhyme* Florio, *Essays of Montaigne* Heywood, *Woman Killed with Kindness* Jonson, *Sejanus*	Elizabeth *d.* 24 March. James succeeds to throne. Millenary Petition. Plague. Ralegh sentenced for treason
1604	*lit.* Chapman, *Bussy D'Ambois* Marston, *Malcontent*	Hampton Court Conference. Enforcement of conformity. Peace with Spain
1605	*b.* Sir Thomas Browne, Thomas Randolph *d.* John Stow *lit.* Bacon, *Advancement of Learning* Drayton, *Poems*	Gunpowder Plot

xii Table of dates

	Jonson, *Masque of Blackness* Marston, *Sophonisba* Middleton, *A Trick to Catch the Old One*	
1606	*b.* Sir William Davenant, Sir William Killigrew, Edmund Waller *d.* Arthur Golding, John Lyly *lit.* Jonson, *Volpone* Middleton, *A Mad World, My Masters*	Oath of Allegiance. King's right to levy impositions upheld. Charter for Virginia
1607	*lit.* Beaumont, *The Knight of the Burning Pestle*	James imposes bishops on Scottish Church. Conflict between Coke and Bancroft over authority of Church. Bacon becomes Solicitor-General
1608	*b.* Thomas Fuller, John Milton *d.* John Dee, Thomas Sackville, Earl of Dorset *lit.* Fletcher, *The Faithful Shepherdess* Hall, *Characters of Virtues and Vices* Jonson, *Masque of Beauty*	Proposed union with Scotland rejected
1609	*b.* Sir Matthew Hale, Edward Hyde, Earl of Clarendon, Sir John Suckling, Gerrard Winstanley *lit.* Bacon, *De Sapientia Veterum* Beaumont and Fletcher, *Philaster* Jonson, *Epicoene*	Virginian commissioners shipwrecked in Bermudas
1610	*lit.* Chapman, *The Revenge of Bussy D'Ambois* Donne, *Pseudo-Martyr* G. Fletcher, *Christ's Victory and Triumph* Jonson, *The Alchemist*	Commons's Petitions of Right and Grievances. Archbishop Bancroft *d.*
1611	*b.* James Harrington, William Cartwright, Sir Thomas Urquhart *lit.* King James Bible Beaumont and Fletcher, *A King and No King* Byrd, *Psalms, Songs and Sonnets* Coryate, *Coryate's Crudities* Donne, *Ignatius His Conclave*;	Parliament dissolved. George Abbot created Archbishop

	First Anniversarie Jonson, *Catiline* Middleton, *A Chaste Maid in Cheapside*	
1612	*b.* Samuel Butler, Richard Crashaw, Thomas Killigrew *d.* Sir John Harrington *lit.* Bacon, *Essays* Donne, *Second Anniversarie* Drayton, *Poly-Olbion* I Webster, *The White Devil*	Prince Henry *d.*
1613	*b.* John Cleveland, Jeremy Taylor *d.* Sir Thomas Overbury *lit.* Browne, *Britannia's Pastorals* I Purchas, *Purchas his Pilgrimage* Webster, *The Duchess of Malfi*	Princess Elizabeth marries Frederick, Elector of Palatine
1614	*b.* Henry More, John Wilkins *lit.* Jonson, *Bartholomew Fair* Napier, *Mirifici Logarithmorum Canonis Descriptio* Overbury, *Characters*	Parliament dissolved as result of protests against impositions. Fresh proposals to marry Charles to Spanish Infanta
1615	*b.* Richard Baxter, Sir John Denham, John Lilburne *lit.* Camden, *Annales*	
1616	*b.* Sir Roger L'Estrange, John Wallis *d.* Francis Beaumont, Richard Hakluyt, Shakespeare *lit.* Chapman, *The Whole Works of Homer* Goodman, *The Fall of Man* Jonson, *Works*	James sells peerages to raise money. Coke dismissed as Chief Justice of King's Bench. Jonson granted royal pension
1617	*b.* Ralph Cudworth *d.* Thomas Coryate *lit.* Webster, *The Devil's Law Case*	Negotiations for Spanish marriage
1618	*b.* Abraham Cowley, Richard Lovelace *d.* Joshua Sylvester *lit.* Chapman, *Georgics of Hesiod* Jonson, *Pleasure Reconciled to Virtue*	Thirty Years' War begins. *Declaration of Sports*. Ralegh executed. Bacon created Lord Chancellor and Baron Verulam

1619	b. Richard Allestree d. Samuel Daniel lit. Drayton, *Poems*	Queen Anne d. Frederick of Palatine chosen king of Bohemia
1620	b. Alexander Brome, John Evelyn, Lucy Hutchinson d. Thomas Campion, lit. Bacon, *Novum Organum* Jonson, *News from the New World Discovered in the Moon*	Frederick loses Bohemia. First English newsbooks appear, in Holland. Voyage of *Mayflower*
1621	b. Roger Boyle, Earl of Orrery, Andrew Marvell, Henry Vaughan d. Mary Herbert, Countess of Pembroke lit. Burton, *The Anatomy of Melancholy* Middleton, *Women Beware Women* Sandys, *Ovid's Metamorphosis* I	First Parliament since 1614. Protestation on liberties of the House. Donne created Dean of St Paul's. Newsbooks printed in London
1622	b. Algernon Sidney lit. Bacon, *Historia Naturalis et Experimentalis* Drayton, *Poly-Olbion* II Massinger, *A New Way to Pay Old Debts* Middleton and Rowley, *The Changeling*	Parliament dissolved. Impositions and Benevolence. Completion of Banqueting House at Whitehall
1623	b. Margaret Cavendish, Duchess of Newcastle, Sir William Petty d. William Byrd, William Camden, Giles Fletcher the younger, Thomas Weelkes lit. Daniel, *Whole Works* First Folio of Shakespeare Wither, *Hymns and Songs of the Church*	Failure of Spanish marriage negotiations
1624	d. Stephen Gosson lit. Donne, *Devotions* Lord Herbert, *De Veritate* Middleton, *A Game at Chess* Wotton, *Elements of Architecture*	Marriage arranged between Charles and Henrietta Maria. Recusancy laws suspended
1625	b. Thomas Stanley d. John Fletcher, John Florio, Orlando Gibbons lit. Bacon, *Certain Psalms* Fletcher, *The Chances*	James d. Charles I succeeds and marries Henrietta Maria. War with Spain. Failure of Cadiz expedition

Table of dates xv

Jonson, *The Fortunate Isles*

1626	*b.* John Aubrey, Sir Robert Howard *d.* Lancelot Andrewes, Francis Bacon, Sir John Davies, John Dowland, Samuel Purchas, William Rowley, Cyril Tourneur *lit.* Bacon, *Sylva Sylvarum; New Atlantis* Donne, *Five Sermons* Jonson, *The Staple of News* Shirley, *The Wedding*	Parliament declares tonnage and poundage illegal. Dissolved
1627	*b.* Robert Boyle, John Hall, Dorothy Osborne, John Ray *d.* Sir John Beaumont, Lucy Russell, Countess of Bedford, Thomas Middleton *lit.* P. Fletcher, *Locustae* Hakewill, *An Apology* May, *Lucan's Pharsalia* Massinger, *The Great Duke of Florence*	Resistance to forced loans. Expedition to the Isle of Rhé.
1628	*b.* John Bunyan, Sir William Temple, George Villiers, Duke of Buckingham *d.* Fulke Greville *lit.* Coke, *Institutes* I Earle, *Microcosmography* Ford, *The Lover's Melancholy* Harvey, *De Motu Cordis et Sanguinis* Shirley, *The Witty Fair One*	Petition of Right. Laud created Bishop of London. Buckingham assassinated
1629	*d.* Sir Edwin Sandys, John Speed *lit.* Andrewes, *XCVI Sermons* Davenant, *The Siege* Jonson, *The New Inn* Quarles, *Argalus and Parthenia*	Parliament opposes popery, Arminianism impositions. Dissolved. Laudian censorship of press
1630	*b.* Isaac Barrow, Charles Cotton, John Tillotson *lit.* Quarles, *Divine Poems*	*b.* Charles II. Charles I acquires Raphael cartoons
1631	*b.* John Dryden *d.* John Donne, Michael Drayton *lit.* Jonson, *Love's Triumph*	Laud enforces conformity
1632	*b.* John Locke, Katherine Philips, Anthony Wood, Sir	Van Dyck settles in England

Christopher Wren
d. Thomas Dekker
lit. Donne, *Death's Duel*
Jonson, *The Magnetic Lady*
Massinger, *The City Madam*
Prynne, *Histriomastix*

1633	*b.* George Savile, Marquis of Halifax, Samuel Pepys *d.* George Herbert *lit.* Cowley, *Poetical Blossoms* Donne, *Poems* Fletcher, *The Purple Island* Ford, *'Tis Pity She's a Whore* Herbert, *The Temple*	*b.* James II. Laud becomes Archbishop. *Declaration of Sports* reissued
1634	*b.* George Etherege, Robert South *d.* George Chapman, John Marston *lit.* Donne, *Six Sermons* Milton, *Comus*	Laud re-enforces conformity. Witch trials. Ship money levied
1635	*b.* Thomas Sprat, Edward Stillingfleet *d.* Edward Fairfax, Thomas Randolph *lit.* Davenant, *The Platonic Lovers* Quarles, *Emblems*	
1636	*b.* Joseph Glanvill *lit.* Cowley, *Sylva* Sandys, *Psalms of David*	King held to be above the law. Plague
1637	*b.* Wentworth Dillon, Earl of Roscommon, Thomas Traherne *d.* Nicholas Ferrar, Robert Fludd, Ben Jonson *lit.* Shirley, *The Royal Master* Suckling, *Aglaura*	Censorship of press
1638	*d.* John Hoskyns *lit.* Brian Duppa (ed.) *Jonsonus Virbius* Milton, *Lycidas* Randolph, *Poems* Quarles, *Hieroglyphics*	Scottish Covenant
1639	*b.* Sir Charles Sedley *d.* Sir Henry Wotton *lit.* Fuller, *Holy War* Shirley, *The Politician; The Gentleman of Venice*	First Bishops' War with Scotland

1640	b. Aphra Behn d. Robert Burton, Thomas Carew, Philip Massinger lit. Carew, *Poems* Donne, *LXXX Sermons* Jonson, *Underwoods; Timber*	Second Bishops' War. Long Parliament impeaches Strafford and Laud. Root and Branch Petition
1641	b. Thomas Rymer, William Wycherley d. Thomas Heywood lit. Brome, *The Jovial Crew* Milton, *Reformation touching Church Discipline* Quarles, *Threnodes*	Laud imprisoned. Army Plot. Execution of Strafford. Irish uprising
1642	b. Isaac Newton, Thomas Shadwell d. Sir John Suckling lit. Browne, *Religio Medici* Denham, *Cooper's Hill* Hobbes, *De Cive* Milton, *Reason of Church Government; Apology for Smectymnuus*	Charles tries to arrest five members. Civil War. Edgehill. King makes HQ at Oxford until 1646. Theatres closed by law
1643	b. Gilbert Burnet, Charles Sackville, 6th Earl of Dorset d. William Cartwright lit. Cowley, *The Puritan and the Papist* Milton, *Doctrine and Discipline of Divorce*	Abolition of episcopacy. Licensing of press. Solemn League and Covenant
1644	d. Francis Quarles, George Sandys lit. Cleveland, *Character of a London Diurnal* Milton, *Of Education; Areopagitica* Quarles, *Shepherd's Oracle*	Covenant imposed on adults. Marston Moor. Trial of Laud
1645	lit. Milton, *Tetrachordon* and *Poems* Quarles, *Solomon's Recantation* Waller, *Poems*	Self-Denying Ordinance. New Model Army. Laud executed. Naseby. Use of Book of Common Prayer forbidden
1646	lit. Browne, *Pseudoxia Epidemica* Crashaw, *Steps to the Temple* Edwards, *Gangraena* Shirley, *Poems* Suckling, *Fragmenta Aurea*	Oxford surrenders. Presbyterians and Independents at odds

	H. Vaughan, *Poems*	
1647	*b.* John Wilmot, Earl of Rochester *lit.* Cleveland, *Poems* Cowley, *The Mistress* More, *Philosophical Poems* Stanley, *Poems and Translations*	King put into Parliament's hands. Putney debates, Charles escapes to Isle of Wight
1648	*b.* Elkanah Settle, John Sheffield, Earl of Mulgrave *d.* Lord Herbert of Cherbury *lit.* Bacon, *Remains* Filmer, *Anarchy of a Limited or Mixed Monarchy* Herrick, *Hesperides*; *Noble Numbers* Wilkins, *Mathematical Magic*	Preston. Leveller Petition. Army seizes King and enters London. Pride's Purge
1649	*d.* Richard Crashaw, William Drummond, George Hakewill *lit.* Gauden, *Eikon Basilike* Lovelace, *Lucasta* Milton, *The Tenure of Kings and Magistrates; Eikonoklastes* Ogilby, *Works of Virgil*	Trial and execution of King, 30 January. Rump abolishes Lords and proclaims Commonwealth
1650	*b.* Jeremy Collier *d.* Phineas Fletcher, Thomas May *lit.* Baxter, *The Saints' Everlasting Rest* Anne Bradstreet, *Tenth Muse* Davenant, *Gondibert* Davenant and Hobbes, *Discourse upon Gondibert* Hobbes, *Human Nature; De Corpore Politico* Taylor, *Holy Living* H. Vaughan, *Silex Scintillans*, I	Charles II in alliance with Scots. Acts dealing with adultery, fornication, swearing and blasphemy, and Sunday observance
1651	*lit.* Cleveland, *Poems* Hobbes, *Leviathan* Stanley, *Poems* Taylor, *Holy Dying* H. Vaughan, *Olor Iscanus*	Charles II crowned at Scone. Worcester. Charles escapes. Royalist lands confiscated. Navigation Act.
1652	*b.* William Dampier, Thomas Otway, Nahum Tate *lit.* Benlowes, *Theophila* Crashaw, *Carmen Deo Nostro*	Dutch war

	Heylyn, *Cosmography* Winstanley, *Law of Freedom*	
1653	*b.* Thomas D'Urfey, John Oldham, Roger North *d.* Sir Robert Filmer *lit.* Margaret Cavendish, Duchess of Newcastle, *Poems and Fancies; Philosophical Fancies* H. Lawes, *Airs and Dialogues* Shirley, *Six New Plays* Urquhart, *Rabelais*, I&II Walton, *Compleat Angler*	Rump Parliament dissolved. Barebones Parliament dissolved. Protectorate established
1654	*d.* Nicholas Culpeper, William Habington, John Selden *lit.* Hobbes, *Of Liberty and Necessity* Milton, *Defensio Secunda*	Parliament curtails power of Protector and Council. Peace with Holland
1655	*lit.* Hobbes, *De Corpore* Marvell, *First Anniversary of . . . the Lord Protector* Milton, *Pro Se Defensio* H. Vaughan, *Silex Scintillans*, II Waller, *Panegyric to my Lord Protector*	Rule of major-generals. Penruddock's rising. War with Spain.
1656	*d.* John Hall, Joseph Hall *lit.* Bunyan, *Some Gospel-Truths Opened* Cowley, *Poems* Davenant, *First Day's Entertainment at Rutland House*; *The Siege of Rhodes* Evelyn, *First Book of Lucretius* Harrington, *Oceana*	Second Protectorate Parliament. End of major-generals' rule
1657	*b.* John Dennis, John Norris *d.* William Harvey, Richard Lovelace *lit.* King, *Poems*	Humble Petition and Advice. Cromwell turns down kingship
1658	*b.* Henry Purcell *d.* John Cleveland *lit.* Browne, *Hydriotaphia; The Garden of Cyrus* Davenant, *The Cruelty of the Spaniards in Peru* John Hall, *Emblems* Harrington, *Virgil*	Cromwell *d.* 3 September. Richard Cromwell becomes Protector

xx   Table of dates

	Waller and Godolphin, *Passion of Dido*	
1659	*b.* Thomas Creech, Thomas Southerne *lit.* Davenant, *The Siege of Rhodes* II Dryden, Sprat and Waller, *Three Poems upon the Death of . . . Oliver Lord Protector* Suckling, *Last Remains*	Third Protectorate Parliament. End of Protectorate. Rump Parliament returns
1660	*b.* Daniel Defoe *d.* Sir Thomas Urquhart *lit.* Dryden, *Astraea Redux* Lovelace, *Lucasta, Posthume Poems* Milton, *Ready and Easy Way* Pepys begins his diary	Monck recalls members excluded from Parliament in 1648. Charles II restored. Charles enters London 29 May. Declaration of Breda. Regicides punished. Royal Society founded. Patents granted to Thomas Killigrew and Davenant to establish two theatres
1661	*b.* Samuel Garth *d.* Fuller *lit.* Boyle, *The Sceptical Chemist* Cowley, *Cutter of Coleman Street; A Proposition for the Advancement of Experimental Philosophy* Dryden, *To his Sacred Majesty* Glanvill, *The Vanity of Dogmatizing* Waller, *A Poem on St James's Park*	Coronation. Corporation Act. Savoy Conference
1662	*lit.* Butler, *Hudibras*, I Davenant, *The Playhouse to be Let* Dryden, *To My Lord Chancellor* Fuller, *Worthies of England* Petty, *A Treatise of Taxes and Contributions*	Act of Uniformity. Book of Common Prayer reintroduced. Charles marries Catherine of Braganza. Licensing Act. Royal Society granted Charter with Charles as patron
1663	*lit.* Butler, *Hudibras*, II Cowley, *Verses upon Several Occasions* Dryden, *The Wild Gallant*	
1664	*b.* Matthew Prior, Sir John Vanbrugh	War with Dutch until 1667. Conventicle Act

	d. Katherine Philips *lit.* Cotton, *Scarronides* Dryden and Howard, *The Indian Queen* Etherege, *The Comical Revenge* Evelyn, *Sylva*	
1665	*lit.* Dryden, *The Indian Emperor* Hooke, *Micrographia* Marvell, *Character of Holland* Walton, *Life of Richard Hooker*	Plague closes theatres. Five Mile Act
1666	*d.* James Shirley *lit.* Bunyan, *Grace Abounding* Tillotson, *The Rule of Faith* Waller, *Instructions to a Painter*	Theatres reopen. Hobbes's work censured by Parliament. Fire of London, 2–6 September
1667	*b.* Jonathan Swift *d.* Abraham Cowley, Jeremy Taylor *lit.* Dryden, *Annus Mirabilis; Secret Love* Marvell, *Clarendon's House Warming; Last Instructions to a Painter* Milton, *Paradise Lost* Sprat, *The History of the Royal Society*	Dutch sail up the Medway. Peace with United Provinces and France. Clarendon impeached
1668	*d.* Sir William Davenant *lit.* Denham, *Poems and Translations* Dryden, *An Essay of Dramatic Poesy; An Evening's Love* Etherege, *She Would if She Could* Sedley, *The Mulberry Garden* Shadwell, *The Sullen Lovers* Wilkins, *Essay towards a Real Character and a Philosophical Language*	Triple Alliance between England, Netherlands and Sweden. Dryden becomes Poet Laureate
1669	*d.* Sir John Denham, Henry King *lit.* Dryden, *Tyrannic Love* Shadwell, *The Royal Shepherdess*	Parliament prorogued. Henrietta Maria *d.*

1670	b. William Congreve lit. Behn, *The Forced Marriage* Dryden, *The Conquest of Granada*, I Shadwell, *The Humourists* Walton, *Lives*	Cabal established. Secret Treaty of Dover
1671	b. Colley Cibber lit. Buckingham et al., *The Rehearsal* Dryden, *Conquest of Granada*, II Milton *Paradise Regained; Samson Agonistes* Wycherley, *Love in a Wood*	Louise de Kerouaille acknowledged as King's mistress
1672	b. Joseph Addison, Richard Steele lit. Dryden, *Marriage-à-la-Mode* Shadwell, *Epsom Wells* Wycherley, *The Gentleman Dancing-Master*	Declaration of Indulgence. Third Dutch War
1673	lit. Behn, *The Dutch Lovers* Settle, *The Empress of Morocco*	Declaration of Indulgence withdrawn. Test Act. James, Duke of York marries Mary of Modena. Shaftesbury goes over to opposition
1674	b. Nicholas Rowe d. Robert Herrick, Edward Hyde, Earl of Clarendon, John Milton, Thomas Traherne lit. Flatman, *Poems and Songs* Lee, *Nero* Rymer, trans. of Rapin's *Reflexions sur la Poétique d'Aristote*	Peace with Dutch. Buckingham joins opposition
1675	lit. Dryden, *Aureng-Zebe* Lee, *Sophonisba* Otway, *Alcibiades* Shadwell, *Psyche* Wycherley, *The Country Wife*	Proclamation to enforce laws against nonconformists. Building of Wren's St Paul's begins
1676	b. John Philips d. Edward Benlowes lit. Cotton, *The Complete Angler*, II D'Urfey, *Madam Fickle* Etherege, *The Man of Mode* Otway, *Don Carlos* Settle, *Ibrahim*	Secret treaty with Louis XIV

	Shadwell, *The Virtuoso* Wycherley, *The Plain-Dealer*	
1677	*d.* James Harrington, Isaac Barrow *lit.* Behn, *The Rover* Dryden, *All For Love* Lee, *The Rival Queens* Marvell, *An Account of the Growth of Popery*	Buckingham, Shaftesbury and other opposition leaders committed to Tower. William and Mary marry
1678	*b.* George Farquhar *d.* Andrew Marvell, Thomas Stanley *lit.* Bunyan, *The Pilgrim's Progress*, I Butler, *Hudibras*, III Cudworth, *The True Intellectual System of the Universe* Dryden, *The Kind Keeper* Rymer, *Tragedies of the Last Age Considered*	Titus Oates reveals Popish Plot, Five Catholic lords sent to Tower. Danby impeached
1679	*d.* Thomas Hobbes *lit.* Burnet, *History of the Reformation* Dryden, *Troilus and Cressida* Oldham, *Garnet's Ghost* South, *Sermons*	Parliament dissolved. Habeas Corpus Act. Exclusion Bill. New Parliament dissolved. Parliament prorogued. Licensing Act lapses. Proclamation against libels on Government
1680	*d.* Samuel Butler, Joseph Glanvill, John Wilmot, Earl of Rochester *lit.* Bunyan, *The Life and Death of Mr Badman* Burnet, *The Life and Death of the Earl of Rochester* Wentworth Dillon, Earl of Roscommon, trans. of Horace's *Art of Poetry* Dryden *et al.*, trans. of Ovid's *Epistles* Filmer, *Patriarchal* Lee, *Lucius Junius Brutus* Otway, *The Orphan* Radcliffe, *Ovid Travestie* Rochester, *Poems* Temple, *Miscellanea*, I	Monmouth makes Progress through West country. Second Exclusion Bill thrown out by Lords
1681	*lit.* Behn, *The Rover*, II Dryden, *Absalom and Achitophel*	Parliament dissolved. New Parliament meets at Oxford. Shaftesbury proposes Monmouth as

	Oldham, *Satires upon the Jesuits*	Protestant heir to throne. New Exclusion Bill and Parliament again dissolved. Shaftesbury tried for Treason and acquitted by Whig jury
1682	*d.* Sir Thomas Browne *lit.* Bunyan, *The Holy War* Creech, trans. of *Lucretius* Dryden, *MacFlecknoe* (comp. *c.* 1676); *The Medal*; *Religio Laici* Grew, *The Anatomy of Plants* Otway, *Venice Preserv'd*	Shaftesbury flees to Holland. Monmouth makes second progress in West and arrested
1683	*d.* John Oldham, Izaac Walton *lit.* Crowne, *City Politics* Dryden *et al.*, trans. of Plutarch's *Lives* Oldham, *Poems and Translations* Otway, *The Atheist*	Shaftesbury *d.* in Holland. Rye House Plot. Monmouth to Holland
1684	*lit.* Bunyan, *The Pilgrim's Progress*, II Wentworth Dillion, Earl of Roscommon, *Essay on Translated Verse* Southerne, *The Disappointment*	Danby released
1685	*b.* John Gay *d.* Wentworth Dillon, Earl of Roscommon, Anne Killigrew, Thomas Otway *lit.* Cotton, trans. of Montaigne's *Essays* Crowne, *Sir Courtly Nice* Dryden, *Threnodia Augustalis*; trans. in *Sylvae* Waller, *Divine Poems*	Charles II *d.* 6 February. James II to throne. Monmouth's uprising and his execution, 15 July. The Bloody Assizes
1686	*lit.* Behn, *The Lucky Chance* Anne Killigrew, *Poems* Sir T. Browne, *Works*	James II appoints Catholics to Privy Council and army
1687	*d.* Charles Cotton, Henry More, Edmund Waller *lit.* Dryden, *Song for St Cecilia's Day*; *The Hind and the Panther* Halifax, *A Letter to a Dissenter* Newton, *Principia* Norris, *Miscellanies*	Magdalen College refuses Catholic President. Fellows ejected

Table of dates xxv

	Winstanley, *Lives of the English Poets*	
1688	*b.* Alexander Pope *d.* John Bunyan, Thomas Flatman, Cudworth *lit.* Dryden, *Britannia Rediviva* Halifax, *The Character of a Trimmer*; *Advice to a Daughter* Shadwell, *The Squire of Alsatia*	Declaration of Indulgence. Trial of Seven Bishops. William of Orange lands 5 November. James flees
1689	*b.* Samuel Richardson *d.* Aphra Behn *lit.* Dryden, *Don Sebastian* Locke, *A Letter concerning Toleration* Purcell and Tate, *Dido and Aeneas*	William and Mary offered crown, Toleration Act. War with France. Bill of Rights
1690	*lit.* Dryden, *Amphitryon* Locke, *An Essay Concerning Human Understanding*; *Two Treatises of Government* Temple, *Miscellanea*, II	William defeats James at Battle of the Boyne
1691	*d.* Richard Baxter, Robert Boyle, George Etherege *lit.* Congreve, *Incognita* Dryden, *King Arthur* Ray, *The Wisdom of God Manifest in the Works of Creation* Wood, *Athenae Oxonienses*	Tillotson succeeds as Archbishop of Canterbury
1692	*d.* Nathaniel Lee, Thomas Shadwell *lit.* Dryden, *Cleomenes*; *Eleonora* Settle and Purcell, *The Fairy Queen*	Nahum Tate appointed Poet Laureate. Thomas Rymer becomes Historiographer Royal
1693	*lit.* Congreve, *The Old Batchelor*; *The Double Dealer* Dennis, *The Impartial Critic* Dryden, trans. of *Juvenal* (with others); *Persius* Locke, *Thoughts concerning Education* Rymer, *A Short View of Tragedy*	
1694	*d.* John Tillotson, Archbishop of Canterbury	Foundation of Bank of England. Triennial Act. Queen Mary *d.*

xxvi Table of dates

	lit. Dryden, *Love Triumphant* Wotton, *Reflections upon Ancient and Modern Learning*	
1695	*d.* George Savile, Earl of Halifax, Henry Purcell, Henry Vaughan, Anthony Wood *lit.* C. Blount, *Miscellaneous Works* Congreve, *Love for Love* Locke, *The Reasonableness of Christianity* Southerne, *Oronooko* Tillotson, *Works*	Whig Junto
1696	*lit.* Aubrey, *Miscellanies* Cibber, *Love's Last Shift* Toland, *Christianity not Mysterious* Vanbrugh, *The Relapse*	Jacobite plot to assassinate William at Turnham Green
1697	*b.* William Hogarth *lit.* Bentley, *Dissertation upon the Epistles of Phalaris* Congreve, *The Mourning Bride* Dampier, *A New Voyage round the World* Defoe, *An Essay upon Projects* Dryden, *Alexander's Feast*; trans. of Virgil Vanbrugh, *The Provok'd Wife*	Treaty of Ryswick. Parliament seeks disbandment of standing army
1698	*d.* Sir Robert Howard *lit.* Behn. *The Histories and Novels* Collier, *A Short View of the Immorality and Profaneness of the English Stage* Farquhar, *Love and a Bottle* Sidney, *Discourses concerning Government*	First Partition Treaty
1699	*d.* Edward Stillingfleet, Sir William Temple *lit.* Dampier, *Voyages and Descriptions* Farquhar, *The Constant Couple* Garth, *The Dispensary*	Break-up of Whig Junto

	King, *Dialogues of the Dead*	
1700	*d.*John Dryden *lit.* Brown, *Amusements Serious and Comical* Congreve, *The Way of the World* Defoe, *The Pacificator* Dryden, *Fables Ancient and Modern; The Secular Masque* Motteux, trans. of *Don Quixote*, I	Second Partition Treaty

Chapter 1

Introduction

T.G.S. Cain and Ken Robinson

> As if his highest plot
> To plant the bergamot,
> Could by industrious valour climb
> To ruin the great work of time,
> And cast the kingdoms old
> Into another mould.
> (Andrew Marvell, *An Horatian Ode upon
> Cromwell's Return from Ireland*)

Henry James once wrote that 'it takes a great deal of history to produce a little literature'. It is the aim of this volume to recover some of the ideas, events and ideologies that lie behind the literature of the seventeenth century in England. The task is not so straightforward as it might seem, for there has been (and still is) considerable debate about the weight that should be given to historical background in literary studies. Some critics would even doubt its usefulness in the analysis and appreciation of literature. The 'New Criticism' of the 1930s (which still has its exponents) chooses to regard literary texts as self-enclosed verbal structures, as autotelic. Its approach is fundamentally ahistorical, as, too, is the synchronic approach of the Structuralism of the 1960s and 1970s. And if humanistic critics value literature in relation to the world outside its words, for the sensitivity with which it explores and realizes the complexity of the human inner life, they are no less ahistorical in tendency. For though that inner life cannot but be affected by historical accident, the humanistic critic (whether the heir of Arnold or Freud) puts special store by texts that transcend their time. For all these critics texts supply their own contexts. History might in a loose sense have produced texts but they do not stand in need of help from historians. At the other end of the critical spectrum Marxist criticism, whatever its specific alignment, regards literature as a strict product of a particular ideology together with its economic infrastructure. Marxist critics are committed to analysing literature's relation to its context.

This is not the place to distinguish the myriad brands of critical perspectives on the relation of literature to its context that lie between these poles; but it is safe to say that no school of critics has sought to outlaw background knowledge entirely. The question for more recent theorists has been less whether we should pay attention to a text's milieu and rather more what sort of attention it is proper to give, or, keeping in mind that key word from James's dictum, in what sense the text is produced by its context. The traditional view is simple: we should try to read through the eyes and assumptions of past periods, jettisoning our modern and personal perspectives so as to understand the text as it really is, or was. Such straightforward historicism has long been suspect, chiefly because the neutral objectivity that it calls for in historian and critic is an unattainable ideal. Without this disinterested objectivity the edifice of historicism crumbles. In its place there has begun to develop a more sophisticated approach that makes a virtue out of the difficulties that beset traditional historicism, out of the fact that there is no absolute arbiter to guarantee a particular view of history and out of the inevitable subjectivity (or limited objectivity) of the critic. Inspired by the investigations conducted by Foucault and others into the perceptual, epistemic structures by which individuals in any given age make sense of their world, it sees the relationship between literature and its background as rather like that between event and structure in linguistics, as two-way and dynamic. Texts both help to shape and are shaped by their social context; they are read by critics who are ideologically self-conscious. This newer historicism leaves critics freer to interpret texts as subversive, whereas the older approach constrained them to distrust such readings as evidence of an anachronistic perspective.

This volume does not prescribe a particular approach. Each contributor was left free to plot his or her own path through the tangled undergrowth of seventeenth-century life. Although they all touch on the literature, they leave individual readers to face the challenge of establishing their own conception of the relationship of the plays, poems and prose of the seventeenth century to their milieu. They leave them, too, to ponder for themselves the relationship between the seventeenth century's outlook and our own three centuries later. The five chapters provide a starting-point. It is impossible to cover every aspect of the background in a single, relatively slim volume. All the contributors have had to remain silent about aspects of their topics that they did not have space to include. One major context that is touched on explicitly or implicitly throughout this book needs to be brought to a focus here – the audience. We can understand a good deal about any text by identifying its target audience and by studying that audience's competence. What were their skills? Were they steeped in the classical tradition or were they closer to an oral tradition of folk tale and ballad? Were they expected to be at home with biblical exegesis and doctrinal debate, or were they inward with the Bible in less academic ways?

The old historicist approach to the study of literature and its background tended to hypothesize a unitary audience with the same assumptions, knowledge and competence. This is now recognized as misleading. Instead it is best to think of a variety of target audiences. The task of identifying these is large and difficult, not least because it needs to be conducted separately for each writer (and sometimes for individual texts). It is often not easy at a remove of three centuries to be precise about the likely audience. We cannot travel back through time to conduct surveys of readership or to monitor sales; but, though it is impossible here to deal in detail with particular texts and their readers, some general pointers should be helpful.

Evidence of a book's immediate readership can be gleaned from several sources. The book might, for example, have a dedication to a patron associated with a particular intellectual or political circle; or it could contain commendatory material from fellow writers and thinkers which might also suggest a milieu (though a degree of caution is necessary because some publishers, like Jacob Tonson, employed writers to puff works by authors with whom they were not acquainted: in one amusing case Tonson approached Dryden to compose lines on Thomas Creech's translation of Lucretius's *De Rerum Natura* and when Dryden refused, Tonson, unwilling to forgo the advantage of using the poet's name, passed off someone else's lines as Dryden's). There might perhaps be references to the writer's circle within the text, possibly in epistolary verses; towards the end of the period subscription lists provide very valuable information. All these types of evidence (and the evidence of letters and biographies) can help to define or confirm the immediate audience and with it the ideology of a text or writer. The subscription list for John Dryden's translation of Virgil (published in 1697), for example, goes some way to supporting the hints of Jacobitism within the text. Such evidence can also play a part in laying bare allusions and references which might otherwise pass unnoticed. It is not uncommon for seventeenth-century writers to indulge in covert allusions meant for an inner group of readers, even though their work might have a much wider appeal. One interesting example of a work which is best understood in terms of the appeal that it makes to a well-defined audience is Charles Cotton's *Scarronides* (1664–5), in its time a best-seller though now very little read. *Scarronides*, a travesty of the first and fourth books of Virgil's *Aeneid*, inspired by Scarron's *Virgile Travestie*, specializes in comically bad poetry. Its irreverence and scatological elements brought it popularity way beyond its target audience, but it was aimed primarily at classically educated Cavalier country gentlemen. Not only would they have been alert to all the jokes played with (rather than at the expense of) the Latin, but also they would have appreciated the travesty as in a line of facetious wit that expressed the Cavalier refusal to be broken by defeat or, even after the Restoration, by debt, a line characterized by the verse of Smith and Mennes in the drollery *Musarum Deliciae: or The Muses Recreation* (1655). Aeneas is made to articulate this refusal after his escape from the storm in Book One. Addressing his men he seeks to 'set a good Face on a bad matter' with a typically Cavalier invitation to drink:

> Here Lads, have at ye, and be merry,
> W'are got at last safe o're the Ferry;
> And though w'ave had but angry wark, yet
> Let's make the best of a bad Market:
> To day let's drink, and hang to morrow,
> A grain of mirth's worth pounds of sorrow;

Recovering the context of a minor work like *Scarronides* is unlikely to reveal it as major, but it does help to breathe fresh life into writing that might seem to be beyond resuscitation.

More general evidence of the target audience is sometimes provided by the details of a work's publication. It can sometimes be important to know who published it. In the later part of the century some publishers, like Joseph Hindmarsh, 'the notedst TORY in the Town', were thought to have particular political sympathies and therefore to be likely to publish writers of the same persuasion (though in retrospect their lists can in fact look more catholic). In other cases it is not the publisher but the timing of the publication that can be significant. The appearance of John Dryden's anonymously published *Absalom and Achitophel* on or just before 17 November 1681 was, for example, precisely timed to influence the outcome of Shaftesbury's trial for high treason on 24 November. Dryden aimed at a particular audience at a particular time, a fact that throws into prominence the satire's forensic rhetoric. Most satire, whether it appeared in print, in manuscript or on stage, needs to be similarly placed. The weapons with which it seeks to defame and persuade need to be seen as appropriate to its context and audience. Thus at the beginning of the century Jonson's *Poetaster*, which attacks his rival playwright John Marston, a member of an Inn of Court, is primarily addressed to an audience from the Inns, who would have not only recognized the portrait of Marston, but also enjoyed the play's frequent references to law and law students.

Different forms of competence were required in different audiences. Sir Robert Stapleton's translation of Juvenal, for example, is aimed at those with classical education. Unlike Dryden's *MacFlecknoe* it asks for no knowledge of contemporary pamphlets or squibs. Dryden's poem draws on an equally strong classical knowledge, but it expects also that its readers will be familiar with a range of racy anti-Puritan and anti-Whig propaganda by reference to which it marks out Thomas Shadwell, its butt, as related to the fanatic sects of the Civil War period who were linked in the popular Tory mind with the emerging Whigs. By contrast Bunyan's *Pilgrim's Progress* plays to an audience closer to an oral folk-tale tradition and to one inward with the Bible but not at home with academic biblical exegesis and doctrinal debate (though elsewhere Bunyan shows himself competent in these skills). We could go on distinguishing more and more different configurations of skills in relation to different target audiences. Instead it is more helpful to concentrate on a broad area of competence which will frequently be drawn on by seventeenth-century literature and which causes difficulties for many modern readers.

The seventeenth-century reader enjoyed a remarkable knowledge of the classics, especially Latin, that was drilled, and sometimes beaten, into pupils in their passage through both free and private schools. The preserve of the merchant, professional and upper classes, the schools catered almost wholly for boys. From 4 or 5 the child began to learn to read and write English until at 8 or 9 it was time to enter a grammar school. Here the classical training began, directed towards the fundamentally humanist end of equipping the child to be eloquent in the service of its country. Starting with *Lilies Grammar*, by the time he left school he would be fluent in reading and writing Latin, in parsing and rhetorical analysis, and he would have an intimate acquaintance with all the major Latin writers. He would also know some commentaries. We can get some idea of the degree of the older schoolboy's skill in Latin from the schoolmaster Charles Hoole's remark in his valuable handbook of seventeenth-century schooling, *A New Discovery of the Old Art of Teaching Schoole* (1660), that having read Virgil's *Eclogues* and *Georgics*, the boy could be left on his own for the *Aeneid*. In addition he would have studied Greek and perhaps a little Hebrew. In the best schools he would have read Homer as well as Pindar, Euripides, Sophocles and Aristophanes in Greek in the sixth form, then as now the final year. Hoole's account of how the master might ensure a firm knowledge of, for example, Horace's works in his pupils indicates just how steeped in classical literature we might expect the seventeenth-century mind to be:

> Their afternoons Lessons may be in *Horace*, wherein they should be emploied.
> 1. In committing their Lessons to memory, as affording a rich mine of invention.
> 2. In construing and parsing, and giving the Tropes and Figures.
> 3. In scanning and proving verses.
> 4. Sometimes in turning an Ode, or Epistle, into other kind of verses, English, Latine, or Greek; sometimes in paraphrasing or enlarging the words in an Oratorial style.

Despite the new spirit abroad in the universities from the mid-century onwards, with its challenge to Aristotle, and despite the so-called Ancients and Moderns debate, the classical competence of readers changed little throughout the century.

Given such intensive training it is not surprising that educated seventeenth-century readers should enjoy literature which drew on their classical knowledge. It is all the less surprising when we remember that it was common to view the classics not just as a source of eloquence and artistic rules but as a repository of wisdom. When Alexander Pope wrote that '*Nature* and *Homer* were . . . the *same*' he gave memorable form to something that had long been thought but never so well expressed. Classical literature offered touchstones by reference to which it was possible to come to place one's own life and times. Such touchstones form the basis of the mock-heroic satire which began to flower in England in the mid-1670s. Three centuries later Thomas Shadwell's reputation has still not recovered from Dryden's uncomplimentary portrait of him in *MacFlecknoe* as a ridiculously inept pretender to the stature of Aeneas. In the educated seventeenth-century mind the classical past lived in dynamic relationship with the present. At about the time that Dryden seems to have written his lampoon, John Wilmot, Earl of Rochester, wrote to his bosom-friend Henry Savile, enquiring whether 'parliament be like to sit any time'. Recovering from illness in the country, Rochester had been reading the Roman historian Livy. 'Livy and sickness', he told Savile, 'has a little inclined me to policy.'

The thorough immersion in the classics that Rochester shared with all those who had benefited from grammar school education left his and his contemporaries' minds charged with classical material and fond of imitation, allusion and translation. The literature of the period is often resonant with classical timbres. Ben Jonson, Robert Herrick, Abraham Cowley, Charles Cotton and John Oldham, among others, could all rely on their readers to be inward with, for example, the 'beatus ille' topos and its *locus classicus* in Horace's epode in praise of country life. And when Dryden composed his sombre elegy on Oldham he called on his audience's intimate knowledge of Catullus's famous elegy on his brother ('Ille mi par esse . . .') as well as on passages from the *Aeneid* to deepen the poem's resonance. It is difficult for a modern reader who does not share the seventeenth-century's intimacy with classical literature to appreciate the art or subtlety of classical resonance in English writings. All too often critics transform the delicate, allusive touch of Herrick or of Milton into heavy-handed analogy. Without a confident inwardness with the classical past we are in danger of approaching the neo-classical poem as a fossil.

Many, if not most, seventeenth-century women readers must have felt as ill equipped as readers in 1992 in this respect. An anonymous tract from 1640, *The Woman's Sharpe Revenge*, complains that

> when a father has a numerous issue of sons and daughters, the sons must be first put to the Grammar School, and after perchance sent to the University and trained up in the liberal arts and sciences, and there (if they prove not blockheads) they may in time be book-learned . . . [whereas daughters] are set only to the needle to prick our fingers; or else to the wheel to spin a fair thread for our undoings, or perchance to some dirty and debased drudgery. If we are taught to read, they then confine us within the compass of the mother tongue, and that limit we are not suffered to pass. . . . If we be weak by nature, they strive to make us more weak by our nurture.

The author of the tract has an axe to grind, but she probably does not exaggerate. It has been estimated that in 1600 90 per cent and in 1640 80 per cent of women in London were illiterate. The projected figures for the country were appreciably higher – almost 100 per cent in East Anglia. Few could expect to be fortunate enough to learn Latin, the passport to scholarly endeavour. Some who strove to do so met with obstructions. In 1650 Sir Ralph Verney advised his goddaughter against learning the classics (though he did not object to her picking up French):

> Good sweet heart, be not so covetous; believe me a Bible (with the Common Prayer) and a good plain catechism in your Mother Tongue being well read and practised, is worth all the rest and much more suitable to your sex.

Aphra Behn spoke for the majority of women who were 'unlearn'd in schools' but who desired intellectual advancement when she noted that if it were not for translations

> The God-like Virgil, and great Homer's verse
> Like divine mysteries are concealed from us.

But there were exceptions: Aphra Behn herself seems to have at least a little Latin. One remarkable figure is Bathusa Makin, who benefited from being born into an extremely learned household. At the age of 9 she was reputed to have some knowledge of Latin, Greek, Hebrew, French and Italian. She was to go on to set up a girl's school in Tottenham, which stood apart from most female academies of the time because of its enlightened academic aims. There she taught her pupils the humanist trinity of grammar, logic and rhetoric, introducing them to languages, especially to Greek and Hebrew, as well as mathematics, geography, music and poetry. Even Bathusa Makin's establishment, it seems, had its shortcomings. If she did not run a seventeenth-century version of today's finishing school, she still placed less emphasis on Latin than might be expected, preferring Greek and Hebrew 'as these will enable the better understanding of the Scriptures'. She was turning out future housewives, learned as well as pious but housewives for all that. By contrast some like Lucy Hutchinson, Katherine Philips or Margaret Cavendish rivalled men in their classical learning. Lucy Hutchinson's Latin was good enough to translate Lucretius; Philips, the matchless Orinda, was widely respected by her male contemporaries; and Margaret Cavendish imitated Lucian in *The Blazing World* (1666). Women such as these, doubly fortunate by accident of birth in being born into a family both well off and enlightened, prove the rule. The best that most could expect was to acquire a smattering of French, the language of romance.

Women would have been less disadvantaged as members of a different audience, that of the theatre. Drama was less of a male preserve, not least because throughout the years when the theatres were open women played an important role in them. Queen Henrietta Maria herself took an active interest in drama, as patron, author and, on occasion, as performer, taking parts herself along with ladies of her court. Their involvement scandalized the Puritan William Prynne, who forfeited his ears for his attack in *Histriomastix* (1632) on the 'wholly impudent' practice of women acting on stage. No doubt something of Prynne's response contributed to parliament's swift action to close the theatres very soon after the end of the first Civil War in 1642, 'to appease and avert the wrath of God'; but with the Restoration women enjoyed an increased involvement in the theatre. When a Royal Grant was issued in 1660 to create new theatres, it ushered in a theatre in which professional actresses appeared for the first time on the English stage. In complete contrast to Prynne's disgust at female acting, the patent granted to Thomas Killigrew in 1662 argued that actresses might help to make the theatre a place of 'harmless delight', a piece of idealism that was soon exploded. As the diaries of Pepys and Evelyn make abundantly clear, actresses used their sexuality to the full, on and off the stage; but the period did produce artists of the calibre of Nell Gwyn, Anne Bracegirdle and Elizabeth Barry, whose impact on their contemporaries suggests that they could stand comparison with Sarah Siddons, Edith Evans or Maggie Smith. If women did not enjoy complete equality in the later seventeenth-century theatre – they were paid less and they were fewer in number – in 1695 they did, at least in principle, become equal sharers in a new company owned by actors, the United Company. It is not surprising that there should also have been an increasing number of women writing for the stage, foremost among them the remarkable Aphra Behn.

Women were also less disadvantaged in terms of their competence as members of the audience. If an important part of the competence of the seventeenth-century reader of creative literature was laid down in the grammar school, the theatre audience found its education in the theatre, learning its essential competence through theatrical experience. Most of what it needed to know it could learn from performances. Men and women alike picked up a generic sense of comedy and tragedy, of the species, the comedies of humours and of manners; of the way that pastoral and heroic drama could contain and dramatize debate, and of much more. Those who knew their Terence might occasionally perceive its relevance to the performance on hand, just as those who were acquainted with the *précieux* writing that Henrietta Maria and her court so valued might find points of correspondence with English drama. And a knowledge of Molière's comic art and values might have brought an additional dimension to much of the comedy of the 1670s. But what matters fundamentally with drama is its performance; skilled appreciation of theatrical performance cannot be acquired in the schoolroom or study. This was particularly true of seventeenth-century drama, which is now widely acknowledged by scholars to have made little pretence to realism. Instead it was proto-Brechtian: performed in playhouses which ensured an intimate relationship between the auditorium and the stage, it drew attention to its own workings. Amidst a rowdy hustle and bustle – in an atmosphere very different from the dimmed and hushed auditorium of today's theatre – companies asked their audiences to exercise their connoisseurship to appreciate the skills of the actors, scenic artists, carpenters and scene-shifters. This dynamic relationship between the audience and company can be imagined most easily before the closure of the theatres in 1642 in the productions of masques with their extravagant scenic spectacle, but it would have existed equally, though in a different way, in a performance of John Ford's *'Tis Pity She's a Whore* (1633). When Thomas Killigrew and William Davenant, who had been influential in the theatre before its prohibition, took on the task of re-establishing the theatre at the Restoration, they recreated a Brechtian atmosphere in which audiences innocent of today's filmic special effects could thrill to swift scene changes which were made possible by increasingly sophisticated stage machinery, or in which they could appreciate the less spectacular but no less captivating uses of disguise and concealment, witty exchange and sentimental set piece; or where they could see contemporary dramatic taste parodied, as they did in Buckingham's *Rehearsal* (1671), which laid bare the artificiality of the rhymed heroic play. If the price of entry to the theatre inevitably restricted the social range of theatre-goers, especially after 1660, theatrical performance was open to a wider audience, in terms of both gender and class. To understand *The Rehearsal* it was necessary only to be a regular theatre-goer.

Such were some of the different kinds of competence of different seventeenth-century audiences, possessed of skills and assumptions often remote from our own, but never forming the monolithic block which historicist critics have traditionally assumed in describing the Elizabethan or Stuart 'world picture'. Nor were the texts themselves the passive reflectors of this or that world-view: they shaped, educated and changed their audiences, creating new ways of understanding contemporary experience and unsettling the preconceptions with which readers approached them. It is in the light of this complicated version of a text's relationship to its times that a modern reader approaches what can no longer be simply called 'the background' against which a writer works. Doing so, what kind of world do we see the writers of this period working in? What generalizations that are not hopelessly flawed emerge from the essays in this book? One of the hardest to accept is that generalizations about this (as about any) period are bound to be misleading, except for the one that says we cannot generalize. To leave the reader with a proper sense of the complicated cross-currents of the time, of the particulars which contradict the patterns beloved of historians of ideas, is one of the most important things a book like this can hope to achieve. This is particularly true of the age of the Stuarts: though almost all periods of history can be seen as pivotal, many of them as ages of crucial change, these labels are more often applied to this century than to others. It is a cliché to say that the seventeenth century sees the death of an old, half-medieval world and the birth of the modern one; while it is as true as such clichés usually are, it is also misleading, not least because exactly the same could be (and has been) said about the fifteenth, sixteenth and eighteenth centuries. By the same token, every period is one of continuity as well as change, and claims that the seventeenth century was exceptionally endowed in either of these qualities have to be viewed with scepticism. Those who wish to find revolution will find it in the seventeenth century, as surely as those who want to find continuity will find their wishes provable.

When all qualifications have been made, however, we have to recognize that in England in particular this was indeed more than usually a century of revolution, a century of change in which we really can see the modern world, the world in which we live now, being forged. It sees the challenging of authority in all fields of activity, the rise of rationalism and of scepticism, and with them the growth of what we would now describe as a scientific approach to the physical world. It sees the dramatic execution of a reigning monarch for treason, and the establishment of a republic, a 'revolution' followed nearly forty years later by another, more peaceful 'Glorious Revolution'. And yet every contributor to this book recognizes that this century of change is also one of deep continuities in social, intellectual, political, constitutional and artistic life. In many ways, the old order was not dead by 1700: Hermetic literature, for example, lives on long after the dating of the mystic works associated with 'Hermes Trismegistus' had been exploded in 1614 by the modern, sceptical scholarship of Isaac Casaubon, and not only among eccentric devotees of the occult: in the 1670s Newton and Cudworth, representatives of different aspects of a new rationalism, are both keen to recognize that there may be some genuine Hermetic writings. In Chapter 6 P.W. Thomas associates Newton with Dr John Dee, the great *magus* of Elizabeth's court, as well as with Einstein. John Milton, too, looks backwards as well as forwards: his values and his involvement with social and political issues of his day may make him seem a very modern figure, but they also remind us that he is the last and greatest of Renaissance humanist writers, exemplar of the tradition of More and Erasmus. Moreover, the reformer Milton, champion of the liberty of the individual, liberty of the press, and liberty in divorce, is driven by a millenarianism which later liberals would regard at best as quaint.

We must, then, register pressures for both change and continuity working simultaneously to shape literature and audience in the seventeenth century. The revisionist view which denies drastic change and looks only for underlying continuities is as distorting as the old picture of the 'Century of Revolution'. To illustrate the extent of change, it is instructive to continue with Milton as an example: he ends his career writing in a period of schism unknown to Donne or Jonson, or to the young Milton of the 1630s. Something akin to party strife, of which there is no serious hint in the 1600s, has entered deep into the world of literature by the 1660s. The schism is much more than literary, with Milton, Marvell and Bunyan on one side, the outside (or in Bunyan's case the inside of Bedford jail) and such writers as Dryden, Sedley and Etherege on the other. That division is the product of changes whose impact was devastating. The execution of the king in 1649 is the most dramatic of them, a symbolic fulcrum for the century. The revolution that it heralded was, typically, a mixed affair, millenarian zeal going hand in hand with the preservation of an idealized concept of ancient English liberties that were largely conceived of as belonging to the property-owning classes, and, more mundanely, with a settling of various personal, local accounts. The upheaval was only partly ideological; yet it was to be the inspiration for the American War of Independence, through that of the French Revolution, and thus, at yet one more remove, of the Russian Revolution. The king's execution was symbolic of an even larger change, one suggested by Barbara Everett's remark that with Charles I died a world 'of ritual, of myth; it was the last Reformation, the final breaking of an icon'. The icon was not just the Stuart claim to a power ordained by God. Not the medieval but the High Renaissance world of sacred and mysterious correspondences and significances died with the king, a world in which magic was the serious science of the *magus*, not only of a fictional Prospero or Faustus, but also of a real-life Agrippa or Dr Dee. The oppositions one makes here must, again, involve generalizations to which there are important exceptions, but it is broadly true to say that in the early years of the century Shakespeare's characters still inhabit this world. Most of his audience would have been awed rather than sceptical at the sight of Lady Macbeth's possession by evil spirits, at the storm which rages in natural sympathy round a crazed and dispossessed king, or the ghost which comes to demand revenge for its untimely death. Donne too, for all his melancholic sense of 'the world's infection', responds to the serious *magia* of Paracelsus at the same time as he sees the 'new philosophy' calling all in doubt. The order that was overturned in the years between 1640 and 1660 had the anointed king at its centre, but it was a more than secular order. When the king's son returned he too was anointed, in a spectacular coronation, but he reigned in the world not of Paracelsus or Dee but of Thomas Hobbes, the great purger of 'superstition' and author of a distinctly secular political philosophy. Many writers of these later years articulate this deep change of attitude, the coolness of the Restoration settlement finding its echoes in the careful rationalism of much of its prose and poetry, in the rejection of insights that depend merely on the 'fancy'.

Here too, though, there is a schism, one which helps to register the extent of continuity. Writers like Traherne, Marvell or Bunyan reject the imposition of such curbs on the non-rational, non-verifiable aspects of experience as Hobbes or the Royal Society would have liked to impose. That profound difference of opinion helps the modern reader to recognize that while much later seventeenth-century literature is significantly different in tone from that of the earlier years of the century, the Interregnum and Restoration years do not stand as a watershed in the period, dividing, as it were, the old world from the new. Many versions of cultural and constitutional history work on the assumption that they do, and that England is in some way or other transformed with the return of Charles II. The year 1660 becomes a convenient date for cultural historians and the devisers of syllabuses: some see the Restoration in terms of maypoles and cakes and ale, a return to an old Merrie England barbarously suppressed for a few years by philistine killjoys. More sophisticated interpretations see the Interregnum as a barren period also, but find the change that takes place at the Restoration more problematic. T.S. Eliot's notion of a 'dissociation of sensibility' taking place during the course of the century is focused implicitly by many, explicitly by some, on the Restoration. Certainly Eliot's examples – Donne and his contemporaries on one side, Milton and Dryden on the other – support this interpretation of his famous phrase. But it is hard to accept his diagnosis, brilliantly penetrating though it may at first seem. It has already been said that all the writers in this book see the century as one of continuity as well as change, and this is nowhere more clear than in their treatment of the Interregnum and Restoration. In religion, science and philosophy, for example, we see the important origins of rationalism in the first half of the century, while millenarian faith, like the old science, lives on strongly in the second half. Even in the fine arts the picture of the Interregnum as a barren period followed by a flowering after 1660 is largely mistaken, with architects like Pratt and Webb and painters like Lely and Cooper working through the 1650s as well as the 1660s. Even in terms of constitutional history, where Cromwell's assertion that there was nothing in the hearts and minds of men but 'overturn, overturn, overturn' seems more likely to be true, Ivan Roots sees few important changes in the actual machinery of government, and the same mixture of change and continuity as in other areas of activity.

The best symbol of the century is the Roman god Janus bifrons, the god of beginnings, who is depicted with two heads, one looking backwards, the other forwards. He it is who best represents such major figures as the conservative revolutionary Oliver Cromwell, the credulous physicist Newton, the vatic poet and liberal reformer Milton. He stands for many of the other confusingly janiform characteristics of the period also: for the essentially conservative impulses of Puritanism, for example, which yet has much to do with the challenge to authority involved in the great movements towards social, political and scientific change, or, in poetry, for the way in which we can see such poets as Marvell and Vaughan simultaneously looking forward in their treatment of nature to the great Romantics, and back to the Hermetic, Neoplatonic traditions of the Renaissance.

Looking backwards and forwards in a different sense are the participants in the debate between the Ancients and Moderns. Though this debate is usually located almost exclusively in the latter part of the century, it too has its roots in the earlier. Essentially it is an argument about whether the modern world can build, and thus improve, on the achievements of the classical world, or whether it is inevitably weaker, in the later stages of a terminal decline. Two factors weighed especially heavily for those who argued that, as Owen Felltham put it in 1623, 'surely in reason and nature, the end cannot be mightily distant. We have seen the infancy, the youth, the virility all past' (*Resolves*, 49). One was the emphasis placed by the Protestant reformers on Augustine's linear version of human history as a decline from paradisal bliss through sin to the terrible retribution of the apocalypse. The other was the verifiable superiority of most aspects of ancient Greek and Roman civilization over that of contemporary Europe. A Protestant Englishman with a classical education did not have to be of a particularly gloomy disposition to agree with Felltham, or the main spokesman for the party of doom, Godfrey Goodman, whose *Fall of Man* (1616) is a massive and tedious elaboration of the theme. The surprise is that more did not agree: most of Goodman's readers ought to have been pre-programmed by their education to believe humankind and nature were indeed in a parlous state, and that the end was near, but a large number took a more optimistic view. In 1605, Francis Bacon's *Advancement of Learning* put forward the argument for progress in human knowledge, and analysed the various impediments to its accelerating advance, with a cogency and eloquence that were never to be surpassed. On the specific subject of decline, George Hakewill answered Goodman with his Baconian *Apology or Declaration of the Power and Providence of God in the Government of the World* (1627), a book which deservedly caused much stir at the time. It brought the young Milton to Hakewill's defence in a Latin poem. 'Naturam non pati senium', in which God is said to have set the whole of His creation in motion with a strength and foresight that left no scope for decay: nature would retain all its original freshness, awaiting the promised end unaffected by age. Donne took a markedly different view: for him, corruption had entered at the very beginning with the Fall of Satan, and his 'First Anniversary' is the *locus* for his deep pessimism about the predicament of humanity in a universe which has by the early 1600s declined to the point where "tis all in pieces, all coherence gone'. Whereas for Bacon, science had opened up avenues of progress which were blocked only by prejudice and ignorance, for Donne the 'new philosophy' merely confirmed confusion and decay: to find that planets did not move in regular circles in a pattern of perfect harmony, that the earth might revolve around the sun and not vice versa, was evidence that the universe was in sharp accelerating decline:

> So did the world from the first hour decay,
> That evening was beginning of the day,
> And now the springs and summers which we see,
> Like sons of women after fifty be.
> And new philosophy calls all in doubt,
> The element of fire is quite put out,
> The sun is lost, and the earth, and no man's wit
> Can well direct him where to look for it.
> And freely men confess that this world's spent,
> When in the planets and the firmament
> They seek so many new.
>
> (Donne, 'The First Anniversary', 201–11)

Donne is unusual in combining inwardness with contemporary scientific thought with such a strong sense of the world's 'decrepit wane' (*Satire III*). Most of those sympathetic to the new knowledge of the universe and the new experimental methods advocated by Bacon would have accepted that the end of the world might indeed be imminent (1656 was a favoured date, since the Flood had occurred 1,656 years after the Fall of Adam). On the whole, however, they naturally tended to be optimistic not only about the state of nature, but also about the time humankind had left to explore it. In this optimism, and in the crucial matter of willingness to challenge received authority, they had something in common with those who advocated a return to the values of the classical world, the 'Ancients' who in other respects are now seen as in conflict with the 'Moderns'. By far the most important among these champions of Greek and Roman civilization in the early part of the century was Ben Jonson. Jonson's temperament was not such as to allow him to share the belief of Donne, his friend and contemporary, that earlier generations had been intrinsically capable of greater things than his own. For him, the classical authors whom he imitated were 'guides, not commanders'. By writing drama and lyric which built on the models of the classical period Jonson aimed to raise the despised head of poetry again, and stripping her out of those rotten and base rags wherewith the times have adulterated her form, restore her to her primitive habit, feature and majesty, and render her worthy to be embraced and kissed of all the great and master spirits of our world.

(Jonson, *Volpone*, Dedication)

This humanist cleansing of the Augean Stables was not a backward-looking affair. It looked forward to the creation of a truly civilized, sophisticated society, one in which literature was central – for was not the purpose of 'poesy, to inform men in the best reason of living'?

The 'Augustanism' which Jonson's programme of classical *imitatio* produced is, like the Ancients and Moderns debate, usually seen as belonging to the post-Restoration period. In fact Jonson's use of his classical models, like that of his poetical 'son' Robert Herrick, is as subtle and creative as anything belonging to the years after 1660. Because Jonson conceived of his art as a development in English of the classical tradition, rather than as an inevitably weaker imitation, he attracted younger poets and dramatists who saw in his example a way of writing which would allow them, too, entry to that tradition which stretched back to Homer. For 'Sons of Ben' like Herrick, Jonson had achieved, uniquely among English writers, his place in the classical pantheon. Looking back in the 1670s, John Oldham still recognized the magnitude of Jonson's achievement in annexing the classical tradition to the English:

> like some mighty Conqueror in Poetry
>   Design'd by Fate of choice to be
> Founder of its new universal Monarchy,
>   Boldly thou didst the learned World invade
> Whilst all around thy pow'rful genius sway'd,
>   Soon vanquish'd *Rome*, and *Greece* were made submit,
>   Both were thy humble Tributaries made,
> And thou return'dst in Triumph with her captive Wit.
> (Oldham, *Upon the Works of Ben. Johnson*)

Thus it is Jonson, rather than Dryden, who stands at the beginning of the Augustan tradition in English poetry. The young Dryden, beginning to write in the 1640s in a witty, conceited style, soon showed that he was heir to the neo-classicizing impulse of Jonson and his followers. He also inherited the heroic couplet which was to become the staple metre for English Augustanism not only from immediate predecessors like Denham, but also from pioneers of the form like Sir John Beaumont, who had died in 1627, four years before Dryden was born. Donne stood in a very different relationship to the classical poets from Jonson: his relative lack of interest in classical imitation did not indicate a lack of respect for classical writers, but rather his pessimistic sense of the decline of the modern world. Classical imitation implied for most practitioners a faith in the potential for improvement of the poet's society that Donne simply did not have: Jonson's enormous confidence and optimism allowed him to believe that he could recreate the values of Augustan Rome in an English setting.

In architecture, Jonson's collaborator in the court masques, Inigo Jones, provides a parallel case. Just as Dryden's neo-classicism grows out of Jonson's, so Wren's grows from that of Jones. Jones's confidence and commitment to a wholehearted but highly intellectualized programme of imitation which would enable him to create buildings based on the principles of classical architecture is, indeed, so close to Jonson's ambition for literature that it is not unreasonable to surmise, in the early years of their acquaintanceship, that there may have been a shared programme: certainly they moved in the shadowy early periods of their careers in the same circle, that associated with Lionel Cranfield, Donne, Richard Martin and others. Later, as Jones's influence grew at court and Jonson felt himself to be undervalued, they became enemies. Even this, though, was in part a product of their neo-classicism: it was an ideal of Jonson's that the poet should have the ear of kings, as he believed, or purported to believe, Virgil and Horace had had the ear of Augustus. To see the visual artist raised to precisely the position of influence that he believed belonged to the poet was a bitter blow, prompting satires on 'Inigo, Marquis Would-Be'. By the same token, it may well have been Jones's belief in the high status of the classical architect and designer that gained him the ear of kings. Predecessors of similar genius – Hilliard, the Smythsons – had been artisans, picture-makers or surveyors whom one employed as one might employ a tailor or a carpenter.

A growing grasp of the nature of the classical inheritance, then, went side by side, and not always in conflict, with an increasing consciousness of the modernness of modernity. If Jonson and Jones are presiding figures in the neo-classical movement, Bacon is the leading modernizer, particularly in scientific thought. Both movements proceeded by questioning received authority, and hence by discoveries: discoveries (on the one hand) of the properties of the magnet, of the circulation of the blood, of analytical geometry (in France) and differential calculus (in England and Germany); and such discoveries (on the other) as the true origin and meaning of the term 'satire', the criticism of Longinus, the thought of the *De Rerum Natura*, or the spirit of the Platonic dialogue. Modernizing thought looked back for its inspiration to the post-classical inventions of the mariner's compass, the telescope, the printing press and even (though with mixed feelings) gunpowder; by means of an increasing stream of editions, translations, and transmissions through the classroom, classicists extended both the circulation and the understanding of such ancient authors as – to name only the chief – Virgil, Homer, Plato, Horace, Cicero, Seneca and Ovid.

Later in the century, such developments as the creation of modern English prose and of modern stage comedy owed something to both movements: prose both to the tradition of ancient prose transmitted direct, and through the French from Montaigne and others, as well as to modern scientific or mathematical desires for clarity and simplicity; and comedy to the scepticism of experimental proto-scientists as well as to the Aristophanic or Roman traditions transmitted domestically through Jonson and continentally through Molière. Later heroic or tragic drama – simplified if not attenuated compared with Elizabethan – reflected traditions derived by France from ancient Athens. But there is no better example of the marriage of the drives represented by the Ancients and the Moderns than the species of translation known as *imitation* which flourished in the later seventeenth century. The poet might translate Horace, Juvenal or Persius, but he did so in a thoroughly modern accent, as if the classical poet were living and writing in seventeenth-century England. Although education, both in practice and in such theoretical works as Milton's *Tractate*, remained heavily classical in nearly every area of study, and although it was as true in Dryden's day as in Shakespeare's that an educated man would have known that upper-class Romans lived in more comfortable houses than he could hope to have, and had higher standards of medicine, hygiene and engineering, nevertheless as the century proceeded hopes increased of drawing level with and eventually even surpassing the Ancients in architecture, in geographical expertise, in medicine, in astronomy, in literature and even in designing (as in Harrington's *Oceana* or Milton's *Ready and Easy Way to Establish a Free Commonwealth*) viable political entities that might harmonize, as Renaissance Venice was thought to have done, the executive, legislative and judicial functions of government better than ever before. Jones had set the example in architecture, Jonson in lyric and comedy; with Milton and Dryden, epic, classical tragedy, and satire began to fulfil, it would soon be felt, such high hopes.

Chapter 2

English politics 1625–1700

Ivan Roots

The accession of Charles I was greeted with some enthusiasm. Monarchy was universally regarded as natural and justified by the laws of God and man, and in 1625 was more immediately appealing in the person of the young king than in his father's. James I had, however, done a better job of ruling England than might be supposed. (Few have disputed his quality as James VI of Scotland.) He had cannily faced many problems, including sordid court scandals. True, he failed to unite England and Scotland other than in his own person, but the consequences of that had yet to be seen. Much too much has been made of religious controversy under him. In fact only a few 'puritan' Englishmen were 'perplexed and troubled' enough to exile themselves. Dissidents were mostly content to stay and mutter, hardly threatening the stability of church or state. As always finance had produced strains, but though an extravagant king might still complain about an 'eating canker of want', parliament never denied him subsidies. Moreover, he went for a decade (1611–21) without any grants, and without arousing suspicions of the demise of parliamentary government, largely because there was no such thing, anyway.

The historiography of early Stuart politics is in flux. Two broad schools confront one another – an 'orthodox', stressing an age of deepening conflict, and a 'revisionist', finding consensus everywhere, with 1640–60 as an aberration with few permanent effects. Neither school is as monolithic as the other would have it. Generally the orthodox discern deep-seated issues making for troubles; but the Civil Wars are by no means inevitable for them all. Individual revisionists place different stresses on the extent of consensus, and on the chronology and content of often seemingly trivial issues. Obviously a synthesis is a long way off. In the meantime some light does accompany the heat. Significantly, revisionism is by no means peculiar to this period. In the Tudor age religion and parliamentary history are under sharp review, coming together, for example in the Elizabethan church settlement. In the eighteenth century a Walpoleian age of sleepy stability is being stirred. Each has implications for the pivotal seventeenth, and for the reign of Charles I in particular.

Between 1625 and 1629 Charles called three parliaments, none addled, but all disappointing, the third breaking up in disorder. The history of parliaments may not be the history of England, but in this period it made up a good part of it, concentrating the major issues of politics. Most of these centred on the king's inherited favourite, the Duke of Buckingham, portrayed as 'the grievance of grievances'. Certainly many strains derived from Buckingham's idiosyncratic and expensive foreign policies, which involved wars with two enemies themselves at odds with one another, Spain and France, and which met with recurrent disasters. Raised in parliament, these misfortunes turned consensus towards conflict, forcing Charles (as he felt) into abrupt dissolutions. Clarendon, looking back at the origins of 'the Rebellion', was to see them as a prime source of later evils. Charles may be blamed for mismanagement, and for listening too readily not only to the Duke, but also to counsellors like William Laud, Bishop of London, who, impatient with parliament's unwillingness to work for 'unity in Jerusalem', dismissed it as 'that noise'. That was foolish: yet the parliamentary leaders themselves showed ineptitude. If as they claimed parliament was 'the great eye' of the nation, they ought to have worked harder to keep it open by gestures which would have made the king at least half in love with them. In fact they overplayed their hand. Having secured his reluctant acceptance of the Petition of Right (1628), whereby he promised that right should be done in redress of egregious financial and judicial complaints, they pressed on too far too fast, turning what could have been a realistic eye-to-eye negotiation, given tact and forbearance on both sides, into an eyeball-to-eyeball confrontation. Chance – the assassination of Buckingham in 1628 – worked to Charles's favour, letting him contemplate retrenchment in foreign affairs to relieve the pressures that stemmed from financing the wars. Parliament broke up amid disorder in the Commons in March 1629, and expectation of another one soon was disappointed. Charles may not have decided to do without parliaments altogether, but he was determined to avoid one for a long time: that turned out to be eleven years.

The 1630s were a testing time for Charles's kingship, but not an impossible one. For most of the period there was no demand from below for a parliament nor, given his pacific foreign policy, any need on his part for one. Opposition – there was some, sporadically, but not enough to produce *the* Opposition – was denied its Westminster platform. Press and pulpit were censored. Legal actions went mostly in the king's favour, not because the judges were venal, though one or two were, but because the law itself generally pointed that way. Prerogative courts, implementing policy as much as equity, were busy. Financial expedients, some obsolescent if not obsolete, met little resistance. Ship money, the most notorious charge, extended in the mid-1630s from maritime areas to the whole country, was raised pretty effectively until the end of the decade. Difficulties with it stemmed more from traditional local complaints of an inability to pay than from constitutional niceties. The divided verdict (a bare majority for the king) in the case of John Hampden, who refused to pay, has had more significance for historians than it did in 1638. These were in fact halcyon years, pleasant enough to conventional and conservative men, which most of the political nation were. Their complacency was fed by reports in the new-fangled news-sheets of the horrors of what would become the Thirty Years' War on the continent, while

> Only the island which we sow [is]
> (A world without the world) so far
> From present worlds it cannot show
> An ancient scar.
>
> White Peace (the beautiful'st of things)
> Seems here her everlasting rest
> To fix and spread her downy wings
> Over the nest.
>
> (Sir Richard Fanshawe, 'Ode upon Occasion of His Majesty's Proclamation')

While 'everywhere Erynnis [a Fury] reigned', Charles and his queen attended, even performed in, elaborate, expensive masques in which monarchy was praised and raised almost literally to the skies. Comfortable, happy in his marriage, the king added lavishly to his already superb art collection and had himself, his family and half his court painted by Van Dyck, who gave to the diminutive, stammering, reserved, even withdrawn monarch a unique – if at bottom rather spurious – regality (see pp. 136–7).

Charles's tastes inclined him to the ceremonial and liturgy of a Church under bishops chosen by *congé d'élire* ready to enforce decency of observance and generally to preach up obedience to kingly authority. He abhorred controversy of the sort precipitated by Puritans keen to pull the rotting rags of popery from out of the dark and not-so-dark corners of the Church of England. For his part, he would let in Arminianism, that new doctrine which predicated a God who had given men – perhaps women, too – free will to partake or not of his grace. Arminian divines, among them William Laud, raised to Canterbury in 1633, seen by Puritans (and others) as 'the spawn of popery', were bound to generate discord, political, social and constitutional. Laud assailed lay (other than royal) influences over the Church, while extending clerical interference into secular matters. He himself sat, tireless and fussy, on the Admiralty Board, in Star Chamber and so on. He even secured the Lord Treasurership for his successor in the London see, William Juxon, arguing that doing the state such service was preaching the gospel to 'far greater edification than a formal going up into the pulpit' (not that mere formality was the way pursued by the prime practitioners of sermons and prophesying in their efforts to steer the hearts of the people. They put their own hearts, heads and energies passionately into expounding the Word.) Laud's concern with getting and spending looked like the worship of both God and Mammon. Unable at a blow to fill sees and parishes with little Lauds, he created what he professed to hate most – disunity – while making martyrs out of scribacious religious dissidents like William Prynne and the future Leveller, John Lilburne. Laud's stress on 'the beauty of holiness' in altars and vestments seemed idolatrous. Stained glass came to epitomize two contrasting philosophies about this world and the next, put succinctly by George Herbert:

> A man that looks on glass
> On it my stay his eye
> Or if he pleaseth through it pass
> And then the heaven espy.

The state of England, indeed of the whole British Isles, was becoming unfit for a campaigner like Laud or for his unlikely friend, Thomas Wentworth, Lord President of the Council of the North and Lord Deputy of Ireland, regarded by many as an apostate from whatever cause it was the Commons had in mind in the 1620s. Wentworth was busy 'Englishing' Ireland, partially at least through Laudian Anglicanism, and arousing fears and animosities on both sides of the Celtic Sea. Wentworth, belatedly accorded the earldom of Strafford in 1639, had set out to govern his king's territories as thoroughly as he administered his private estates. He saw the interests of kingship and of citizenship ravelled up inextricably together. In another metaphor he portrayed 'love and protection descending . . . loyalty ascending . . . each without diminishing or enlarging either' – or again, 'running in the worn wonted channels'. Though eloquently expressed here, these sentiments were commonplace. How far such ideals were or could be realized in Charles's England, even in those golden days of the so-called 'personal government', remains a question. No one, not even Strafford or Laud, could live up to them. Ready to condemn private interest, they were not without their own, though they could argue with some justice they gave a higher priority to the public, at least as embodied in the crown. As for Charles himself, he lacked (as they privately admitted) a largeness of application, giving only fitful attention to government, more obstinate than determined, more convinced than confident, and devious – when pushed, as he would be – to the point of shiftiness.

Between 1637 and 1640 the not-so-personal government petered out, the rot starting not in England but with a rising in Scotland against a religious policy which for over a decade had upset nobility and Kirk, ministers, townsmen and landowners alike. By acts of revocation Charles took back alienated Church lands and tiends (tithes), robbing the magnates of territorial power and wealth, and, by bringing bishops into the Privy

Council, of political influence at the centre. The Scottish coronation (1633) was deplored for its 'popish rites' and for the conspicuous role of the foreign Archbishop of Canterbury. Crisis came with the issue solely on royal authority of a new code of canons (1637) and a prayer-book, both denounced as papist. Resistance peaked in a 'National Covenant' widely subscribed 'in defence of our religion, liberties, laws and estates' – an amalgam of grievances. Soon most of the Lowlands – popery endured in the Highlands – were up in arms. Charles, concerned for the stability of England, hit back, meaning 'to be obeyed'. In two 'Bishops' Wars', he failed. English support against the rebels was meagre. Evidently Scotophobia had its limits.

An English parliament (The Short) called in April 1640 ignored the case against the Covenanters, preferring to list English discontents, religious, financial and constitutional which had begun to grow over the last two or three years, exemplified in the difficulties sheriffs were now finding in raising ship money, and the unwillingness of Justices of the Peace (JPs) to implement social policies that seemed to run counter to their own interests. Dissolution worsened the situation. Once again war had exposed deficiencies in the English state, precipitating a 'general crisis of the British Isles'. Promising to pay a Scots army £850 a day for its trouble in sitting down in the North, Charles was in effect 'brought to his knees' to another parliament. That met, after elections more fiercely contested over wider issues than usual, in circumstances that ensured its continuance while it sought and found reforms and remedies. Winning for immediate purposes the right to determine its own duration, the Long Parliament would survive twenty years of defections, exclusions, recruitments, purges, long interruptions and the abolition of its Upper House – a vivid example of history as the unintended consequence.

There was plenty to be done and initially at least a disposition to do some of it by consensus, both between and within the Houses. Under the leadership of John Pym, who had served his parliamentary apprenticeship in the 1620s, the Commons moved fast. Strafford, seen as likely to lead a coup, was executed by one medieval device – an Act of Attainder – after impeachment (another) had failed in the Lords. Charles made it plain he assented under duress: Strafford's fate remained on his conscience, and on the brink of his own execution he would refer sadly to it. Laud, too, was imprisoned, but his quietus came later (1645): unlike Strafford's Irish army, his forces were spiritual not martial. But in 1641 his command of the Church, such as it was, collapsed, impugned generally as innovative, decidedly not a good thing to be. (There would be, however, little accord on what should follow.) Other leading personnel of 1629–40 were removed or fled, while victims of 'the eleven years' tyranny' went free, among them Prynne, whose tedious attack on stage-plays, *Histriomastix*, had been held to insult Queen Henrietta. (Prynne, a tireless raker of records and scribbler of marginalia, would go on to offend other regimes until in 1660 he came back into the restored Long Parliament, now as a staunch advocate of the monarchy that had cropped his ears.)

Regular parliaments were to be catered for by a Triennial Act (1641) delineating machinery to operate when royal writs were withheld. (It was never used.) Prerogative courts, tarnished of late, were incontinently swept away. Common lawyers were happy at the demise of rivals dispensing quicker, cheaper, simpler justice, but something valuable was lost, too, and soon felt to be lost by litigants. Late financial expedients – revivals and experiments – were ended or modified. Ship money went and tonnage-and-poundage, claimed by Charles 'for life', was cruelly limited to two-monthly parliamentary grants. Industrial monopolies, unpopular as far back as the Tudors, were restricted to genuine inventors.

The collapse of censorship accompanying all this activity was devastating, and though successive administrations, unimpressed by Milton's assault on 'cloistered virtue' in *Areopagitica* (1644), tried to reimpose it, success was patchy. Through the next two decades the press gave individuals and groups (who proliferated) opportunity to push particular concerns or to anathematize practices and notions they resented. In such a heady atmosphere speculation flourished, casting all in doubt. A London bookseller, George Thomason, resonant to the times, gathered in all that he could of the pamphlets, broadsheets, and whatever pouring out. By 1660 he had some 20,000 items, even so, missing some. His collection has been a boon to historians, but a danger too, tempting them to attach undue significance and influence to often ephemeral, often cranky works disregarded by contemporaries, distorting our view of intellectual and cultural history. Nevertheless, the Thomason Tracts provide a rich context for English literature, particularly as some – Milton's, Winstanley's, Walwyn's, and Needham's are examples – were written in vigorous prose, overflowing with ideas. During the 1640s, too, English newspapers were born, with such titles as *Mercurius Aulicus* (royalist) and *Mercurius Pragmaticus* (parliamentarian).

Agreed reformative work went on through the summer of 1641 in a parliament which the king agreed could be dissolved only by its own consent – hence the Long Parliament. Charles seemed powerless. An attempt to buy off some critics by office collapsed. In Scotland even more drastic inhibitions met royal actions. Yet all was not lost. Under the glaze of harmony in parliament fine cracks appeared. The Peers' unfriendly reaction – shared by some MPs – to Strafford's impeachment is an example. Even more striking is the failure of well-orchestrated advocacy of root-and-branch extirpation of episcopacy to find general favour. Laudianism went condemned, but the traditional order it had overlain was still very acceptable to men who extended 'no bishop, no king' to fears of 'no peers, no gentry, no order'. If they came to 'a parity' in the Church, would it not come to state and society? They would have an eye to property. No one wanted to dislodge monarchy or Charles himself. Evil counsellors alone were held responsible for past and present discontents. The crown remained the keystone to the arch of government and the social structure, held up by and holding up the twin pillars of Church and state. Disturb any of the three, the others must tumble down. But stripped of parasitic Laudianism the church-pillar would stand clean and erect again. That perception gave the makings of a party to a king who advertised his loyalty to the Church of England as the first English ruler actually brought up in it. His sincerity was readily believed by those who felt already that reformation and perhaps reform, too, had gone far enough.

Others were not so sanguine. Not all radical 'root-and-branchers', they still felt insecure politically and personally. Fears of a royal rally, fed by rumours of army plots and by Charles's evident intention to buy off the Scots to ease the pressure on him in England led a declining majority to demand more say for parliament in running Church and state. Distrusting the queen and many courtiers, and doubting the strength of will, if not the will itself, of a king who had met a papal envoy to hold out against the lure of popery, they convinced themselves that there was not only a permanent latent urge of papists to take over, but also the imminence of a specific plot to let in Antichrist and, in tandem, absolutism. There is, indeed, some evidence that, however unrealistic it was, a plot of sorts was in the framing.

In the autumn of 1641 a Catholic rebellion flared up in Ulster, now heavily colonized by English and Scots Protestants, reported in England as a horror story of the slaughter of the innocents. Remembering Strafford's Irish army and hints that Charles was soliciting Spain and even Rome for men and money, Pym and his cohorts visualized Ireland as a base for popish onslaught upon the homeland. It was also, though less was said of that, of material interest as the first English colony. 'Lacking all civility', native Irish were more despised than north American Indians. Those whom we intend to exploit, we must first make contemptible. Pym has been characterized as either paranoid about popery or as brilliantly perceptive of the possibilities of 'no popery' as a slogan. Perhaps he was a little of both. Anyway, he concluded that Charles could never be trusted with an army to reduce the rebellion. In December 1641 he brought forward the Grand Remonstrance which, after a long partisan account of what had been done already, made fresh reformatory demands on Church and state, and, passing the Commons by only eleven votes, underlining the attenuation of consensus, was published before Charles I had had time to take it in. Such blatant 'talking down to the people' confirmed the views of wary constitutionalists like Edward Hyde and Sir John Culpepper that a halt must now be called. (Hyde had introduced the Bill for abolition of the

Council of the North.) They moved towards the king, full of advice, some of which would be taken. As for the militants they went on to demand control of the armed forces, such as they were, or would become.

The year 1642 opened with Charles's futile show of force in attempting to arrest in person five MPs (and one peer) for treason. Thwarted, he soon left London, perhaps already bent on war. Spring and summer he spent moving around the provinces, chiefly west and north – ignoring the south-east as being too obviously under parliamentary surveillance. That may have been an error on his part. Time would show he might have stiffened support there, too, by his presence. A war of manifestos was being fought outside the chamber and committee rooms of Westminster. Henry Parker, for example, argued that government depended upon consent of the governed – he meant 'men of substance' embodied in the political nation as represented in parliament, not 'the people' in any wider sense. The Houses continued to be winnowed by defections direct to the king or into a neutralism which would irritate convinced activists over the coming years. A Bill for parliamentary control of 'the militia', rejected with contempt by the king, became an ordinance of both Houses claiming the full force of law. This initiated a spate of legislation based on arguments that parliament was

> a council to provide for the necessities, prevent the imminent dangers, and preserve the public peace and safety of the kingdom and to declare the king's pleasure as requisite thereunto; and what they do herein hath the stamp of royal authority, although His Majesty, seduced by evil counsel, do in his own person, oppose or interrupt the same, for the King's supreme and royal pleasure is exercised and declared in the High Court of Law and Council, after a more eminent and obligatory manner than it can be by any personal act or resolution of his own.

Such claims were dredged up by MPs who 'troubled themselves in relics and records' – it was an age which favoured medieval research. Charles replied in like manner by commissions of array naming his own lords-lieutenant to command the militia. Things were going beyond legality. Men would obey either claimant – or ignore both – according to their principles and assessment of their own interests. In June, Nineteen Propositions – there could just as easily have been eighteen or twenty – were offered to Charles requiring relinquishment of his control of most major public business, including foreign policy, deepest of mysteries of state. Charles was certainly correct to see that acceptance would leave him 'but the picture, but the shadow of a king'. 'A handsome denying answer' was devised for him by constitutionalists like Culpepper rather than by increasingly out-and-out royalists like George Digby. Charles would abandon it by implication at his trial. The answer conceded that England was

> a limited and mixed monarchy, there being three kinds of government . . . absolute monarchy, aristocracy and democracy . . . all . . . having their particular conveniences and inconveniences. . . . The ill of absolute monarchy is tyranny, the ill of aristocracy . . . faction and division, the ills of democracy . . . tumults, violence and licentiousness. The good of monarchy is the uniting of a nation under one leader to resist invasion from abroad and insurrection at home; . . . of aristocracy . . . the conjunction of counsel in the ablest persons . . . for the public benefit; of democracy . . . liberty and the courage and industry which liberty begets.

England had the 'goods' of all three. It was a view repudiated by royalists almost as soon as it was penned. For one of the most eloquent and influential it was 'an opinion but of yesterday and of no antiquity, a mere innovation in policy, not so old as New England though calculated for that meridian'. History was very much on the side of that opinion which reflected what lay behind seventeenth-century political theory generally more accurately than anything of Hobbes's or Locke's.

As for Pym and company they heard the 'no' and ignored the gloss upon it. They limbered up for a war which was now becoming almost but not quite – nothing ever is – inevitable. A determined positive stand across the political nation could have headed it off. There was little enthusiasm anywhere. Petitions for king and parliament to return to traditional co-operation were met by both sides, however, with disdain. The Kentish Petition of March 1642 was denounced in parliament and its proponents, some of whom had favoured much of what had been done a year or so before, were brusquely handled, like Richard Lovelace the poet, as at least embryonic traitors. Some counties went into pacts of neutrality among gentry worried at the brink of the unknown and expressing the powerful localism that pervaded even national politics. But under the pressure of events they broke down. On 22 August Charles went to war, raising his standard at Nottingham. Parliament had already put itself in 'a posture of defence'.

PROLOGUE TO THE CIVIL WAR

A few loose generalizations can be made about the line-up for the war. Topographically, the north and west were broadly for the king, the south and east for parliament. This meant that parliament controlled finance and trading, an immense advantage in the long term over the king's initial military superiority. Charles's ambitions were always centred on London, where during subsequent negotiations he would have liked to come for 'a personal treaty'. Socially, lines of division were less clear. There were peers on both sides, gentry too. Attempts to sort them into improving landlords, 'feudal' magnates, rising, declining, stagnating gentry have not met with much conviction. In religion, Puritans 'naturally' gravitated towards parliament, but not all did, and the confident characterizing of the times as 'England's wars of religion' may yet turn out to be as misleading as it is helpful. Moreover, analysis must take account of both sides as shifting coalitions with friable edges, while in between throughout the war there were 'neuters', some through apathy, some positively inimical to both sides, the whole augmented from time to time by defections from activity. Below the political nation, identification of defined groups is as difficult if not more so. What is certain is that it will not do to confine attention to the war as one solely of cleavages limited to the 'natural' ruling class.

THE CIVIL WAR

What was at stake in the Civil War? The issues fluctuated. In war as in politics a week is a long time. Although Charles I kept alive throughout the image of one ready to negotiate reasonably, his goal was the full restoration back at least to 1641 of his authority and the maintenance of proper relationships with institutions such as the Church, his Privy Council and the militia. Parliament might not expire but it certainly would be disciplined. His Cavaliers were a heterogeneous lot, some happy with the view of mixed government put forward in the Answer to the Nineteen Propositions, others ready to go a long way along the road to absolutism. Ranged against them was a similar uneasy coalition held together by John Pym until his untimely death in December 1643. His objective was to preserve reform so far achieved in face of what was seen as a popish plot which threatened not only measures but also men, mindful of the fate they had meted out to Strafford. Beyond that the Nineteen Propositions, give or take a few, would have satisfied him and, no doubt, most Parliamentarians. These men were not revolutionaries, nor republicans, but rather conservatives, striving to preserve for posterity an 'ancient constitution' with fundamental laws, often mentioned, rarely defined. Monarchy and parliaments were of the essence here and they saw no irony in fighting for 'King and Parliament'. Where they differed among themselves in 1642 was in readiness to make actual war. Three broad, hardly discrete, groups emerged, with some individuals straddling all three. A war party would fight hard to win and to dictate a settlement. A peace party *per contra* would negotiate and seek a speedy end to the conflict, not least to check the drift towards radicalism in Church, state and society, which, even before the war broke out, was becoming apparent. A middle group, epitomized by Pym, would combine war with treating tactically.

As 'director of the whole machine', Pym pushed through ordinances giving parliament what it had never had before, the executive and administrative wherewithal to raise money and deploy men centrally and locally, thereby effectively controlling London and the south-east, then as now the richest and most developed part of the realm. The king, the legitimate exponent of the 'mysteries of state', could not, cut off as he was from the normal seats of government, match parliament's system, which through the excise (still with us), and by weekly and monthly assessments raised taxation far in excess of anything Charles had ever contemplated. Though successive regimes of the Interregnum to come met almost intractable financial obstacles, Pym's measures provided a base for military victory. That was reinforced by his last great contribution: an alliance with Covenanters which brought Scots forces into northern England to help reduce the royalist ascendancy there. Enthusiasm for this course was diluted by fears of Scots interference in English affairs, notably religion, and of getting England bogged down in the Byzantine politics of Scotland. The English Commissioners had to move towards Presbyterianism but they worked for an agreed form as 'according to the example of the best reformed churches', not exclusively the Kirk, which the Scots claimed was best of all. A Committee of Both Kingdoms co-ordinated activity. The Assembly of Divines at Westminster, convened in 1643 to make a Church settlement, came out in 1645 with a loose Presbyterianism, seen by full-blooded Scots as milk-and-water, replacing royal supremacy with parliamentary supervision. The allies drifted apart, though co-operation lasted long enough to achieve victory at Naseby (1645)

Pym's death shook but did not shatter the coalition. No one dominant individual took his place. Revisionist historians put consensus foremost in parliamentary politics (including religion) during these years, deferring until 1647 the onset of really adversary positions. That seems too facile. The three broad groupings survived, fraying at the edges, but even less understanding of one another. The 'backwardness to all action' of some commanders, mostly peers like Essex and Manchester was frustrating to war men at Westminster and in the field. Their impatience was stepped up by the prevailing provincialism which impeded swift movement of forces across the country for co-ordinated campaigns. They moved for the creation of an army at once professional and national, under dynamic and successful commanders like Sir Thomas Fairfax and the up-and-coming East Anglian squire, Oliver Cromwell. A Self-Denying Ordinance removed all peers, MPs and office-holders from command. Fairfax took on the New Model Army with Cromwell (still an MP by a special dispensation) as second in command. Of Cromwell's dedication to the cause there was no question. For him it was being directed by Providence, though a Providence demanding human co-operation. In Oliver's dictum 'trust in God and keep your powder dry' the key word is 'and'. The essence is initiative and activity. He encouraged his troops, too, to know what they fought for and to love what they knew. The upshot was victory at Naseby.

With Charles soon surrendering to the Scots and variously in the possession of parliament and the army over the next three years or so, the search for a settlement showed that the problems of peace could be as intractable as those of war. There was scope for deeper rifts in the parliamentary coalition. Kaleidoscopically, fragments of war, peace and middle groups made fresh unstable patterns. Two groups stand out: 'Presbyterians' and 'Independents', labels which conceal as much as they reveal of attitudes unconfinable within the narrow religious contexts they imply. But historians have been unable to come up with anything better, except to discover 'Independent Presbyterians' and 'Presbyterian-Independents'. Broadly, Presbyterians stood for the 'classical' Church structure laid down by the Westminster Assembly under a parliament in no way politically reformed, still dominated in both houses by 'men of substance'. Independents could visualize a national confession of faith but would like individual congregations to establish their own priorities, allowing a little liberty to 'tender consciences'. Their parliament would be moderately reformed in franchise and distribution of seats, according to population and contributors to national rates. Both monarchy and parliament would be subject to limitations. The in-between groups havered according to circumstances.

Charles I, determined to be 'king again', set himself to exploit these differences, and others, such as that between Scots and English, and within Scotland itself, where covenanting was by no means 'national'. Even without Charles's intervention in both countries, war had allowed novel forces to press home particular interests. One was the army itself, soon to become a sort of fourth estate, though one no more homogeneous than any of the others. The depth and extent of its politicalization and its radicalism have certainly been antedated and exaggerated but Charles was correct to see even in 1646 possibilities in it for his inveterate divide-and-rule tactics, even to the point of embroiling the army in another civil war. He had not shrunk from precipitating armed conflict in 1642. Why not, then, in 1646-9? The army's professional grievances, notably arrears of pay, by going unredressed by parliament, which tended to see it as a 'mere mercenary' force, argued a lack of appreciation of its contribution by sedentary politicians. The army's sense of honour and integrity was offended and its demands for 'soldiers' pay' slid into calls for 'soldiers' rights', particularly when parliament decided on a newer model army, reduced in size, and sent much of it, divorced from English politics, to Ireland to reduce the continuing rebellion there.

The consequences of all this included election by the regiments of 'agitators' – agents to get things done – to sit alongside officers on a General Council of the army. Some of these were, like some present-day shop stewards, more political than their constituents. By summer 1647 circumstances favoured their approach. One was a growth of civilian radicalism which could not be quarantined from an army no longer on field duties. Idleness gave opportunity for meditation and meditation for action. The prediction before the Civil War that 'talking down to the people' would bear strange fruit was being realized. Definition of 'the people' had widened, largely by spontaneous movement among groups normally excluded from direct politics. Radical notions – political, religious, social – were disseminated from press and pulpit, and discussed with loose tongues in alehouses and ordinaries. Heterodox opinions ejaculated in one environment spawned in another. The situation was vividly delineated by a Presbyterian publicist, Thomas Edwards, whose appalled *Gangraena* (1646) is a vast circumstantial catalogue of dangerous factions and individuals. Over-anxiety may have coloured some of Edwards's presentations. *Gangraena* is certainly not objective but it is plausible. Its characterization of William Walwyn as 'a wolf head by the ears' and 'in sheep's clothing' was shared by many who saw a threat in his awkward questionings and writings under such insidious titles as *A Still Soft Voice* and *A Whisper in the ear of Mr Thomas Edwards* advocating religious toleration and extensive social and political reforms. Walwyn was, in fact, part of an emergent radical movement soon derogatorily called 'the Levellers', who expected to share in the benefits of victory over Charles I.

The Levellers were always a heterogeneous lot, from leaders like John Lilburne ('Freeborn John'), their loudest voice, and Richard Overton, theoretician, down to obscure civilians and, soon, rank-and-file military men. Most were small property-holders, mainly metropolitan. Some had gentry backgrounds, like Lilburne (a Northerner) and Walwyn (from the Marches of Wales), often younger sons who had turned to trade and industry. The reforms they wanted would give to small men opportunities denied to them by the big men who were dominant if not monopolistic in parliament, trading companies, the City, and usurpers of the native rights of freeborn Englishmen. These included freedom of religion in faith, organization and practice. Levellers backed Parliament in the Civil War because they expected it would take off 'the Norman Yoke' of king and peers, the direct heirs of William the Conqueror and his colonels who had suppressed a free Anglo-Saxon England. History was read as the record of a sporadic restoration of ancient liberties. (An interest in history was common to most seventeenth-century movements, conservative as well as radical, reactionary and revolutionary, all finding support in an 'ancient constitution', some of it documentary, some quite mythological.) Lilburne put Coke's legalistic *Institutes* and Magna Carta alongside the Bible. Beginning as a martyred sectarian in the 1630s he found a remarkable flair for publicity and a capacity to equate his wrongs with those of all Englishmen. Cromwell spoke up for him in the Commons in 1641, but their friendship turned sour, and as a Leveller Lilburne would denounce Oliver as 'the dissemblingest perjured villain alive'. Walwyn was less legalistic. For him Magna Carta was a 'mess of pottage'. Admitting that the abolition of private property was unlikely, he nevertheless thought we ought to 'endeavour it'. This brought him close to another radical tendency – the Diggers or True Levellers – who appeared in 1649, led by a failed clothier, Gerrard Winstanley, to attempt communistic settlements in Surrey and thereabouts. Winstanley, set off by a vision, but also very practical, like Lilburne and Walwyn wrote compelling prose which has appealed both in form and content to many modern historians. He saw 'the times going up like parchment in the fire', 'freedom [as] the man that will turn the world upside down'. That did not come about, but Diggers, Levellers, and, later, Quakers and Ranters, optimists and radicals flung up in the Interregnum, offer us, though they were always minorities, insights into the extraordinary dispensations of an age when God, as was (according to Milton) his wont, revealed himself first to his Englishmen.

Levellers in 1647 stood for a sort of property-owning democracy through a reformed parliament elected on an extended franchise (variously defined) and denied certain powers inalienable by 'the people'. It all came together in a draft constitution – 'The Agreement of the People' – embracing proposals set out in a spate of petitions and pamphlets. Some of these notions seeped into the army. Many soldiers came from similar backgrounds to civilian Levellers. Literate and articulate, they could make a connection between their professional and their human rights. Though the army was never 'one Lilburne throughout', Levellerism was certainly in 1647 a thick strand in army politics. Its place in the pattern was brought out in discussions in October and November associated with the Army Council, and known today as the Putney Debates. (The army was now based largely around London, to the alarm of Westminster and the City.) The debates have been conspicuous in the history of the 1640s because we have a more or less verbatim account of what was said in them not only by Grandees like Cromwell but also by obscure rankers like Buff-Coat. With some co-opted civilians there too, they contemplated under Cromwell's chairmanship the immediate and long-term implications of the content of the Agreement, notably the franchise. Cromwell and his sharp son-in-law, Henry Ireton (chief author of the Grandees' own plan for a settlement, 'The Heads of the Proposals' of August 1647), took it that manhood suffrage was aimed at. Certainly some Levellers gave that impression, remarking that 'the poorest he that is in England' had 'a right to live as the richest'. Cromwell saw anarchy looming up when men who had 'but the interest of breaking' gained a voice in government. For Ireton 'no person hath a right to a . . . share in the disposing of the affairs of the kingdom . . . that hath no permanent fixed interest'. Government was solely for 'those persons in whom all land lies and those in corporations in whom all trading lies'. Ireton's position is crystal clear, the Levellers' ambiguous. Some of these would exclude from the vote men who were dependent by employment (servants) or tenancy on richer men, who, given current electoral practice without secret ballots, could unduly influence, even determine, decisions. There is a considerable discrepancy in the estimates of the difference implementation of the Agreement might have made in the size of the electorate, from not much to more than doubling.

The debates were inconclusive. A possibility of a direct follow-up within the regiments themselves was headed off by Cromwell in the name of military discipline. The need for that was underlined in 1648 by a second Civil War, fiercely fought, brought about in part – though it was actually a very complex affair – by Charles I's divide-and-rule manoeuvres among the various English and Scots factions.

THE COMMONWEALTH

The execution of Charles I (30 January 1649) was, *pace* Marvell's *Horatian Ode*, not the effect of a subtle Cromwellian plot. Charles was his own executioner. Exasperation rather than malice led an *ad hoc* group of politicians and officers to conclude that no settlement could be had with someone who thought and persuaded parliament that no settlement could be had without him. Pride's Purge (12 December 1648) of likely negotiators in the Commons led on to a formal trial of 'that man of blood' for making war on his own people, a unique but lethal charge. Cromwell acquiesced but was slow to come around to 'stone dead hath no fellow'. Once he did, however, he was as usual devastating in action. Charles rejected the court's jurisdiction. Sovereignty (himself) and subjection (his people) were 'clean different things', his responsibility to govern not subject to their scrutiny. The court – not all those nominated attended – found him guilty. The warrant – not all attenders signed – meant a speedy execution at Whitehall, a great set piece of English history epitomized in Marvell's metaphor of 'the royal actor' giving, his stammer gone, the performance of his life.

Though deplored throughout Europe, Charles's fate did not, in fact precipitate a foreign intervention. France and Spain, still locked in conflict (until 1659), looked rather for support from the well-armed regicide republic against each other. Monarchy was abolished, so was the Lords (as 'useless and dangerous', having refused to have any part in the trial). But what was set up as the Commonwealth was really an expedient: there were ideological republicans but they were only a minority in the Rump which was in fact reinforced in moderation by the re-admission of MPs who were not required to look back with approval on Charles's execution. The prime characteristic was middling conservatism. Bulstrode Whitelocke, legalistic, placid, unsinkable, is more typical than Sir Arthur Hesilrige, who had been with the war party since 1642 and was becoming the most voluble of the Commonwealthsmen (republicans). But the Rump's situation elicited a major controversy in political thought, which produced a masterpiece in Thomas Hobbes's *Leviathan* (1651). In 1650 the new state demanded an 'engagement' to itself from all men over the age of 18. No commitment to the past was called for, only to government as at present constituted without king and Lords. Backed by Cromwell and the army (purged of Levellerism) the Rump was clearly *de facto* in power. The royalists at home and abroad were in disarray. Ireland and Scotland were being mopped up. But the regime felt it necessary to seek legitimacy.

A pamphlet campaign ensued, centred on Romans 13, 'the powers that be are ordained of God'. Providence, it was claimed, had set up the Commonwealth. To resist it was a sort of blasphemy. *Per contra*, it was argued that nothing could relieve the obligation imposed by oaths to the former government which had had history and 'that divinity that doth hedge a king' on its side. There were, however, 'loyalists' ready to serve any regime that provided stability (and could pay their wages). Civil servants and professionals among them, they covered a wide spectrum. The court painters, Lely and Cooper, are dealt with in Chapter 5; along with them went Thomas Simon, who had designed medals and seals for Charles I and the Long Parliament, and would do so for the Protectorate of Oliver Cromwell and for Charles II. On a different tack, Gerrard Winstanley rather unrealistically advocated taking the engagement as a means of encouraging 'the keepers of the liberties of England' to bring in his drastic sort of reforms. *Leviathan* is of a different order, at once vast and deep, the expression of a bleak view of human psychology and of relations between individuals and groups and with their maker. Starting from a state of nature in which all were equal, competitive but fearful, uncertain, lacking co-operation, arts and commerce, Hobbes concluded that men would at length face facts and by limiting their absolute freedom put themselves into the hands of a protector – Leviathan – giving the stability out of which security would emerge. The protector to be effective must have undivided sovereignty. It seemed to Hobbes and his twin brother, fear, that in 1651 England had such a protector in the Rump or, it might be, in Cromwell: Leviathan could be an individual or an institution. *Leviathan* transcended the specific circumstances of 1651. It is patient of interpretation and has needed to be ever since outraged royalists like Edward Hyde condemned it for offering legitimacy to king-killers.

In practice reactions to the engagement were as pragmatic as the motives that imposed it. The Commonwealth survived only until another power decided otherwise. That power was Oliver Cromwell and the army, who, having served the Rump well at home, in Ireland and in Scotland, grew impatient with its tardiness in reform and (for Oliver in particular) in 'healing and settling'. In another of his abrupt interventions Cromwell would throw them out. Yet it would be unjust to say the Rump had done nothing. Its Navigation Act (1651) confining colonial trade to 'English bottoms' was to be basic to English commercial policy for more than a century. There was a great concern – if not always an agreement on how to achieve it – for the economic health of the nation. Additional revenues were raised by the sale of alienated lay and ecclesiastical lands, to the point that a survey of crown lands was carried out which amounted to a sort of neo-Domesday Book. Moral and legal reforms were contemplated, many getting as far as a Bill, some even enacted. There is no doubt that some Rumpers were hard working and in spite of such savage denunciations as Walker's *History of Independency* honest and public spirited, certainly as much as any normal seventeenth-century administration.

But it was not enough. The extraordinary events stemming particularly from Parliament's victory in 1646 seemed to many to provide under the benign dispensation of Providence for changes which if carried out would have been revolutionary in the modern sense rather than the more circumscribed contemporary term's. That revolution need not have been 'progressive'. Many aspirations would in fact have turned back the clock of social, economic and religious development, and back a very long way at that. Religious toleration may serve as an example. The voices of those that called for it were deafened by those of others who knew themselves to be right about God and man and would not respond to Cromwell's appeal to think it possible they might be mistaken. These included the Fifth Monarchists, millenarians sure that the English were an elect nation or rather that the saints (themselves) within it were. They intended to put England into such a state that it was fit to face the imminent coming of Christ. Strong in London and exhorted by fiery preachers and Bible-thumpers they were impatient with the Rump's pusillanimity. That impatience coincided with the army's, though hopes there were mostly different. In the spring of 1653 the crunch came.

On 20 April, Oliver Cromwell strode abruptly into the House of Commons, interrupted the debate, upbraided individual MPs, denounced the whole house as 'no-parliament' and had the chamber cleared by soldiers. The circumstances of that act of force are controversial. Certainly the immediate issue was a Bill for a 'new Representative', something the army had wanted since 1647. After the ejection Oliver claimed that the Rump was intending to perpetuate itself, but there is some cogency in the argument that what was intended was really a new assembly, genuinely 'freely' elected, and therefore likely to be *inter alia* inimical to the army. The Bill disappeared, by accident or because it was in someone's (whose?) interest that it should. Be that as it may, the Rump was gone and Lord General Cromwell and his Council of Officers, as they at once modestly and emphatically asserted, were the only constituted authority left. They set about divesting themselves of the appearance if not the reality of naked sword-power. It seemed a time to listen to the Fifth Monarchists who took the dissolution as a signal that the reign of King Jesus was at hand so that England (at least) could go to heaven.

Cromwell, a restless blend of the mundane and the messianic, was prepared to accept that the rule of the saints was feasible. The Council of Officers met, drew up lists of likely men and called (by writ) a nominated assembly, known to popular history as Barebone's Parliament after one of its (rather few) fanatical members, Praise-God Barebone. The members nominated were by no means all saints in a technical or even in a loose sense, nor were they all inexperienced or unrealistic, though some, more voluble than numerous, certainly were. Cromwell handed on power to the assembly, which, meeting at Westminster, transformed itself immediately into a single-chamber parliament with a Speaker. It was, said Cromwell on 4 July 1653, '*the* day' – or was it merely '*a* day'? – 'of the Lord'? The Assembly took itself seriously, too seriously. It enacted some measures initiated in the Rump and brought in some of its own, by no means impractical or irrelevant. But the minority's interest in abolishing tithes and pruning back other vested interests aroused the fears of its moderate majority, who voted themselves dissolved while the others were at a prayer meeting, and handed supreme authority back to Cromwell in December 1653.

That gesture he may not have expected, but others certainly did, and no sooner was the move towards a new Jerusalem halted than he was presented with a very different plan for divesting himself of sovereignty. It was a written constitution, the Instrument (or document) of Government, formulated by Major-General John Lambert, who had in 1647 had a hand in the framing of the Grandees' Heads of the Proposals for a settlement. The Instrument, the first thing of its kind to be implemented in England, provided for a legislative (a single-chamber parliament elected on moderately refined franchises by revised constituencies), and an executive shared between 'a single person', the Lord Protector, holding an office with somewhat of monarchical in it, and a Council of State, nominated in the first instance, of civilians and swordsmen. The Council, with powers that could check both Protector and Parliament, was the key to the constitution. It was an imperfect constitution, with the drafting deficiencies of a prototype, and its general acceptability inhibited by its provenance – 'a work of darkness' – but it did meet some of the facts of the situation. Cromwell accepted it and was rapidly installed as Protector – at the time there could have been no other candidate – exchanging his military for a civil sword. The symbolism was clear. From now on it was his major objective to bring it to reality.

The first (triennial) parliament was to meet on 3 September 1654 (a symbolic date, anniversary of Cromwell's great victories at Dunbar in 1650 and Worcester in 1651) with Scots and Irish representatives. Before then Protector and Council were empowered to issue ordinances with force of law for the security and welfare of the Commonwealth. A hundred or more were put out, some substantial, some trivial, some formative, others more routine. (It is a characteristic of the administrations of the Interregnum that they had to cope with the problems of both an insecure illicit regime and those of any, even long stabilized, government.) Of prime significance were arrangements for a loose national Church on Independent lines with commissioners of Triers and Ejectors to supply and oversee the personnel of livings. (Tithes were not abolished.) Outside the Church there was considerable toleration laid down in a controversial clause of the Instrument. Chancery was reformed, lightly but too radically for legal professionals like Bulstrode Whitelock. (Cromwell had a very able legal adviser in William Shepherd and there is no doubt of the sincerity of his personal strictures upon the law's delays and other defects.) Scotland was united to England by ordinance, Ireland by mere assumption (symptoms of the contrasting attitudes of the English to the inhabitants of the other constituents of the British Isles).

When Cromwell addressed the MPs – there had been no want of contestants at the elections – in the Painted Chamber at Westminster on 4 September 1654 he was optimistic, taking it for granted that the Instrument was accepted – they were there under its terms, weren't they? – and putting before them a programme for a return to something like normalcy. But ignoring all that, the House tore into the Instrument, intending at the least to enhance its own constitutional role within it. A few days later, less friendly, Oliver was back, to tell them that though there might be some provisions which could be altered (circumstantials) there were some others (fundamentals) which could not. The latter included rule by a single person and a parliament, control of the militia and some liberty to tender consciences. Those who could not accept these were to be excluded – or to exclude themselves. So soon winnowed, the parliament went on to prepare clause by clause a constitutional Bill still dangerously close to emasculating the Instrument and neglecting to complete any other legislative work. Exasperated, the Protector dismissed it as soon as it had reached the laid-down minimum of five months – interpreted as twenty-eight-day lunar months – charging MPs *inter alia* with encouraging disaffection and disorder (22 January 1655).

That there was disaffection was quickly demonstrated by a royalist rising (Penruddock's) in the south-west, intended to be a co-ordinated national upheaval, but in the event coming off with only minuscule participation, and rapidly suppressed. The failure lay in the internal divisions of the royalists – exiles, for instance, could not grasp the difficulties confronting royalists at home – but also in the very competent intelligence and interception system established, along with the Post Office, by Cromwell's able secretary of state John Thurloe. The threat to orderly everyday life posed by the rising was exploited by the government to bring in a military supervision of the provinces, somewhat co-ordinated at the centre, known not entirely justly, as 'Cromwell's major-generals'. (There were many other motivations for this move, the nature of which has been much distorted by contemporaries and historians.) The instructions given to the major-generals, like the ordinances of 1654, were a fascinating blend of the routine and the peculiar to the mid-1650s. The major-generals themselves were an unmonolithic lot who showed surprising diversity in the priorities they gave to their duties. Interestingly, all of these hard-headed militarists wanted to be regularized as JPs. But whatever can be said for or against 'the system' it was unpopular among the bulk of the normal rulers of the countryside, resentful as always of outside interference.

Cromwell had long visualized a European if not a world role for his England – in the interests of Protestantism or economic advance or imperialism? Most likely all three. In 1656 he entered into the war with papist Spain, 'naturally' England's enemy, and in alliance with a presumably not so popish France. As usual war meant increased financial strains. How could they be met? Some councillors suggested by arbitrary levies raised by soldiers at their 'sword's point'. That was risky as well as unappealing. The solution was parliamentary taxation. Writs went out for an extraordinary (not triennial) parliament to meet in September 1656. The elections were hard fought. The campaign by the major-generals to determine their outcome was largely unsuccessful though they themselves got in, in spite of the slogan 'No swordsmen, no decimators', a reference to the decimation tax imposed upon royalists. The Council, exercising power given it in the Instrument, excluded a hundred or so members, among them Commonwealthsmen obviously unreconciled to Protector or Protectorate. Their exclusion produced a parliament more amenable – though certainly not supine – to the regime.

As usual Cromwell met MPs in a positive spirit, with one of his long unstructured extempore harangues, mingling history with spiritual exhortation, self-justification with readiness to serve the community, clarity of phraseology and vision with opacity and obscurity. Recognizing at last the value of keeping the House in being, the members responded by appropriate gestures. Traditionally, parliaments were called to legislate for matters great and small, local and national. All right, they would bring in, even pass, Bills public and private. Parliaments should debate and exchange opinions with a view to consensus. They would do, and did, just that. Some things they did were very acceptable to the government, notably taking into serious consideration the funding of the war and contemplating legitimizing the legislation by ordinance of 1654. They would throw out the Decimation Bill unwisely brought in by the major-generals but Oliver, who had been somewhat lukewarm anyway in their defence, was not averse to that. They congratulated him on escaping an assassination attempt. They went on to revise the constitution, this time with more tact and circumspection than their predecessors of 1654–5. The origins of that endeavour were to be found in a seemingly ephemeral incident far away down in the West Country.

In October 1656 a leading 'fanatic', the Quaker James Nayler, rode into Bristol parodying Christ's entry into Jerusalem. Getting wind of it the Commons ordered him up for examination for 'horrid blasphemy'. Debates on a committee's hostile report showed how critical of toleration were many MPs, including some otherwise firm supporters of the Protectorate. No obvious lines of social or political outlook differentiated hard-liners and 'the merciful men'. The uncertainties of interpretation of the Instrument of Government were starkly exposed. How could Nayler's case be defined under it? How punished? By whom? It was argued that with abolition of the House of Lords its judicial authority and function had devolved *de facto* upon the Commons as the High Court of Parliament. But some MPs were disturbed about the precedent of condemning Nayler by a sovereign chamber acting as prosecutors, trial managers, judge and jury. 'Vile wretch' though he was 'the case of James Nayler might happen to be your own case'. Who could be safe? A nine-days' wonder was widening out into a major constitutional issue, especially when Oliver enquired mildly about the grounds of proceedings taken 'wholly without us'. Protector and parliament confronted one another without an arbiter. Surely someone or something must take on that role, to act as 'a screen' or 'a balance'. Soon 'a paper' was presented (February 1657) advocating the offer by parliament to the Protector of a crown with a second chamber to come between king and Commons. Such were the origins of a new constitution – The Humble Petition and Advice – pushed by 'kinglings' (civilian Cromwellians and constitutional conservatives, some no doubt covert Stuart royalists seeing the revival of monarchy as 'a ladder of stairs' up which Charles II might clamber back).

Transformed into a detailed document, The Humble Petition was presented to Oliver with acceptance of the crown as a *sine qua non;* there followed weeks of negotiations between Protector and a Commons committee big with lawyers. Cromwell's speeches while he sounded out opinion providential and mundane show his mastery of verbal opacity. He liked almost everything in the Petition but eventually turned down the crown. Providence in this instance had taken on the shape of the army. A startling turnabout ensued with defections from original supporters while erstwhile opponents found themselves ready for a second protectorate with 'somewhat' more of 'monarchical in it'.

Along with constitution-making went a continued legislative programme and attention to the state's financial needs. This was, indeed, no addled parliament, but one for all its novelty providing what parliaments were supposed to – the daily diet as well as remedial dosages for the constitution. The second protectoral installation (June 1657) was more royal and civilian than the first. The Commons went into recess, to come back in January 1658 a very different institution. Parliament was now bicameral, though the relationship of the two Houses had yet to be worked out. Was one upper, the other lower? Was the Lords reborn? Was authority co-ordinated? Cromwell had been given the right to compose 'the Other House'. To be effective it had to have weight. To be useful to the government demanded a spectrum of political support. Writs went out to some old peers and peers' sons, substantial gentry, army officers, a fair number of sitting MPs. Not all accepted, but withdrawals from the Commons left there a political vacuum filled by 'the secluded MPs' who were formally allowed back under the new constitution. They showed no gratitude. Instead, ardent exponents of parliamentary tactics, they were, like Sir Arthur Hesilrige, all the more voluble and obstructive. Cromwell's optimism dissipated in face of their refusal to work with the Other House. He was provoked into another abrupt dissolution (9 February 1658), avowing his readiness to have God judge between them and him.

Within eight months, rapidly aged, Cromwell was dead on 3 September, still perhaps his lucky day. Overseas these were months of triumph for English arms, at home of oppression, halting progress towards acceptable stability. That there had been some of that is signified in the effortless transition to protectoral office of Oliver's eldest son Richard. Royalists were depressed. The big moment of their oppressor's long-desired demise meant nothing. Stuart restoration seemed utterly remote, especially when Richard showed himself a feasible Richard IV and no man's enemy. Yet within a few more months he was gone. Calling a parliament early in 1659, on old franchises and with no exclusions, he found himself up against the Commonwealthsmen, again refusing to recognize the regime, harking back to 'the golden days' of the Commonwealth, striving to set the army (where Richard lacked his father's base) at odds within itself – and dangerously succeeding. Forced by Grandees to dismiss the parliament, Richard very sensibly resigned: an action which would make him Voltaire's 'mon homme', a genuine hero who would not plunge his country again into bloodshed. The Grandees, increasingly divided, rather despairingly recalled the Rump. Like the Nominated Assembly it took itself seriously, treating the army as its servant. In the autumn of 1659 a premature crypto-royalist rising in Cheshire (Booth's), gaining little local support, was put quickly down. There seemed more expectation of a slide into anarchy, welcome, it was feared, to Quakers and other radicals, than of a steady march towards a return of the Stuarts. The Good Old Cause was fast becoming a rag-bag of high-sounding nothings, in spite of earnest discussions of intellectuals like James Harrington, author of the Utopian *Oceana* (1656) and William Walwyn at The Rota and of pamphlets with comfortable titles like Milton's *A ready and easy way to a Commonwealth*. There was none.

In October 1659 soldiers locked out the Rump. Civil war shuffled nearer. Talk of Charles II became open. By December the Rump was back with the Commonwealthsmen, forgetting nothing, learning nothing, at it again.

The army disintegrated; unpaid soldiers talked of forming a ring for their officers to fight in. At this point General George Monck decided to move – to what end was uncertain, perhaps even to himself. The result, taking even soothsayers by surprise, was the Restoration in May 1660.

The Restoration was one of many demonstrations that the Great Rebellion was not a purely English phenomenon. Monck's Scottish connection was crucial. The ex-royalist from Devon had stabilized Scotland during the Protectorate while keeping his army, paid and disciplined, purged of malcontents and isolated from politics, especially English politics. More and more eyes turned to him as a possible *deus ex machina*, who could if he would intervene to some purpose. Royalists tried to get him committed through his kinsmen, but he remained 'so dark a man no perspective [could] see through him'. But he quietly secured from leading Scots guarantees that if he went south there would be no rising behind him for Charles or anyone else. At the end of December 1659 he crossed the border at Coldstream on a slow march to London. Meeting delegations for a 'free and full parliament', even for the Stuarts, he said nothing. After the Restoration it was claimed that he was then already committed to it. If so his decision was still locked in his bosom. Once in London, he was the one man who could head off the social and economic breakdown which the citizenry feared. He did so in his own way. The Rump was persuaded to let in the secluded MPs of December 1648, among them the scribacious William Prynne, now a convinced royalist. The augmented Long Parliament at last voted its own dissolution, having arranged for a Convention freely elected to meet in April. Monck meanwhile kept his 'dear friends and fellow-soldiers' in the English armies quiet by promising that 'nothing was intended for the alteration of government, but that it should continue as a free state and commonwealth' and by 'encouragement of supplies of money'. At about the same time he was in fact directly in touch with Charles Stuart urging him to be patient, to 'let George do it', and take the advice which led to the conciliatory Declaration of Breda (April 1660). The Convention met on 25 April, with the old, not the Oliverian, Lords. On 1 May the Declaration was accepted by both houses, followed by a resolution that by the fundamental laws 'the government is and ought to be by King, Lords and Commons'. On the 8th Charles II was proclaimed as king since January 1649. The 25th found him at Dover, the 29th in his capital, wondering amid the cheers, the bells and the bonfires why he had stayed away so long. Many of those present could have told him.

REIGN OF CHARLES II

The Convention Parliament, legitimized, lasted until December 1660, when members went home to celebrate a no-longer-banned Christmas. It enacted important measures, dragging its heels over some of them, irritating the king who wanted a firm quick-set hedge against instability, in particular (wisely) a swift, generous Act of Oblivion and Indemnity, ending the war period. Basically only the regicides were faced with death and some other 'detestable' individuals were imprisoned or excluded from politics for life. Many others went voluntarily into obscurity or exile. Charles also chased up parliament to provide the wherewithal to pay off the army, lest, unsatisfied, it became politicized again. A few regiments were kept on – among them what became the Coldstream Guards – to provide the nucleus for a standing army, an institution more appealing to the crown than to the bulk of the body politic, mindful of the 1640s and 1650s and of continental absolutisms. 'No standing armies' became a popular slogan for the rest of the century. (The navy, understandably in an island state, met with no such hostility.) But command of the forces – that prime occasion of the Civil War – was conceded to the king *solus*, though within a few decades in practice his freedom of action was checked by sheer costs. The Convention did produce a revenue settlement which, with a few supplements like the imaginative hearth tax, gave the crown adequate peace-time finances, based largely on indirect taxes like the excise, one of the easiest identified permanent consequences of the Interregnum. The difficult problem of settling the late land upheaval – confiscation and other disposals of crown, Church and royalist lands – promised in the Declaration of Breda was resolved by the Convention, not to everyone's satisfaction perhaps, but not to be undone. What was not achieved was an ecclesiastical settlement including the toleration of 'tender consciences' promised at Breda. This failure to overcome prejudices and partisan interests accounts for a good deal of the difficult and depressing religious history of the next half-century or more.

The Convention had hardly repaired 'within a year' all that had been 'decaying in twenty', but it had made a good start on a Restoration settlement that would take more than twenty years to complete, encouraging Chancellor Hyde to claim that the malignity of an evil star which had prevailed for so many years had expired and that 'the good genius of this kingdom is become superior . . . and our own good old stars govern us again'. The next stage came with the Cavalier parliament, which met in 1661 and as another (though very different) Long Parliament lasted until 1678. Dominated by Anglicans (the Presbyterians of the Convention sent into eclipse) it gave some priority to religion and produced a harsh and restrictive (misnamed Clarendon) code. Persecution and the threat of ejection and second-class citizenship forced many back into the Established Church where they evolved the Low Church tradition. But nonconformity could not be totally expunged even by the tight alliance of high-flying squires and parsons. Religious pluralism was another enduring effect of the Interregnum, though it would be a long time before the gut-reaction of 'the Church in danger' not just from papists but from Protestant dissenters, all potential rebels, would fade away.

The reign began with a broad-bottomed ministry – 'old' royalists, and neo-royalists, some very late converts indeed. Among them George Monck got a dukedom and major military and naval commands, but unlike many king-makers he was content for others from now on to make the political running – Charles II himself and Edward Hyde (now Earl of Clarendon). Anthony Ashley Cooper (Earl of Shaftesbury) was Chancellor of the Exchequer. Brilliant but wayward, Dryden's Achitophel, Shaftesbury would overreach himself with the Popish Plot and Exclusion Crisis (1678–81). So, much earlier and less flamboyantly, would Clarendon whom Charles, bored, would not defend against enemies who were moved less by principle than by envy. Into exile he went, brushing up his French in Rouen but penning, too, in superb, if slightly old-fashioned English prose, his *History of the Rebellion* which would not be published (and then only for immediate party political purposes) until the reign of Anne.

After Hyde, leading ministers came and went as politics gradually fell to younger generations, with the youths or children of 'the late troubles' looking to the future, mingling at Whitehall and Westminster, in local administration, diplomacy, with others who looked back, some with nostalgia, most with anxiety to 1641 and 1649. They made the Restoration settlement an uneasy mix of change and continuity as the euphoria of Charles's miraculous return wore off. While it endured it helped outweigh the monarchy's losses since 1640, particularly the measures to which Charles I had assented, even if under duress, before 1642. Bishops came back to the Lords, the Triennial Act lost its enforcing machinery. Dropped were demands for direct ministerial responsibility, but practicalities could limit royal freedom of action. Efficiency demanded that administrators, diplomats and judges had to have talent as well as loyalty. Ability to influence MPs and peers was also requisite. Sometimes politicians could force their way into office, like Sir Edward Seymour, by being awkward. Some offices, too, were held by reversion and tenures amounting almost to freeholds, though not enough of them to produce a genuine *noblesse de la robe*. On the other hand royal patronage, imaginatively deployed, could influence opinion and win electoral support. Office brought men royal bounty, less in salaries than in access to fees and perquisites and influence. Studies of patronage throughout the century (including the 1650s) show much continuity in the use of this lubricating oil of politics. Time would bring some changes but there was no Stuart (if ever there had been a Tudor) revolution in government.

As parliament in time became a permanent instead of an occasional feature of political life, patronage if anything increased in significance. Ministers like the Earl of Danby in the 1670s could deploy patronage to command clientage among politicians, though venality need not preclude conviction or vice versa. Inside or outside parliament, the royal prerogative was rarely impugned. Rather with a growing emphasis on king-in-parliament, it would be valued more after the Revolution of 1688/9 as essential to that strong government which the British are still supposed to prefer. As political parties began to organize and monarchy (very much more slowly) to withdraw from its independent exercise, the politicians sought to capture it for ministries run by themselves. This served the interests of 'outs' as well as 'ins', for today's 'outs' might be tomorrow's 'ins' and need prerogative themselves. Hence it had and has an inbuilt protection.

Meanwhile, parliament reappeared in its historic form of king, lords and commons. The Scottish and Irish representation of the imperial parliaments of the 1650s ended, until 1707 and 1801 respectively, when the English saw something for themselves in union. The old franchises and constituencies of the Commons reappeared, given perhaps a longer lease of life by reactions against recent radicalism. Interference with borough charters under Charles II and James II and economic and demographic changes would modify and enlarge the effective electorate over coming decades, but how far that had an impact upon 'high' politics is as yet uncertain. The same sort of men got elected around 1700 as around 1600. Electoral arrangements – including electoral pacts to cut expenses – were much the same too, though as in 1640, in 1661, 1680–1, 1689 national issues might from time to time overlay somewhat the usual stuff of local politics.

Experience of civil war and its aftermath never quite expunged, argued against situations which might lead to their recrudescence. Even in the most divisive years of Charles's reign as in the Exclusion Crisis of 1678–81, when determined efforts were made to alter the succession to prevent James, Duke of York, brother of the (legitimately childless) king from eventually coming to the throne, something held back the ultimate gesture to turn the campaigns of tongue and pen, fiercely fought, into shooting wars. Nevertheless contrasting political attitudes – 'adversary politics' is the present vogue term – confronted one another in government, in parliament, in metropolitan coffee-houses and provincial ordinaries. Though never quite clear-cut, like those of the Interregnum, they went by various names, but chiefly 'Whigs' and 'Tories' or 'Court' and 'Country', sneering nicknames quickly adopted, like 'Leveller' before, as badges of honour. That Whigs were heirs to the Roundheads and Tories to Cavaliers has some plausibility but there was more to it than that. Like all such labels they conceal as much as they reveal. Old issues were interlarded with new ones. The composition of Court and Country – never unrelated to being 'in' or 'out' – fluctuated. Both principles and material interests informed views and actions. The Court could equate its own ambitions with the interests of the crown. Conflicts could and sometimes did express mere factions but there were the makings of political philosophies in facing up to the issues of the time – in religion, foreign policy and constitutional development. Embryonic programmes and organization can be discerned, even some internal discipline. Personalities, like Shaftesbury's or Danby's, could count for much. Party leadership required tact, flexibility and political *nous*, that indefinable but necessary something.

To make sense of the politics of party and faction calls for close attention to a spectrum of interests and issues, and, incidentally, contemporary literature, including particularly a very politicized drama, plays performed but not always published. The generalizations we can make – Tories landed, Whigs monied, Whigs pro-dissenters, Tories sky-high Anglicans – can be pushed very quickly too far. Attitudes to the crown similarly call for careful consideration, not least of the king himself, who, though certainly lazy and anxious not to have to travel again, was no *roi fainéant*. He was the object of all manner of influences, including those of mistresses who adopted with him political as well as other sorts of postures. 'The rule of the strumpets', if it existed at all, was, however, a very precarious one. If, again, Charles was very close to the Tories in the Exclusion Crisis and in his last few years when he did without a parliament it was very much for his own purposes and those of the house of Stuart, one of the few things to which he was fiercely loyal. He had no intention in the long run of being dependent in any way on anyone.

The political and constitutional record of the reign is tortuous. A few episodes must be mentioned. Clarendon gave way to a six-year ascendancy of the Cabal – Clifford, Arlington, Buckingham, Ashley (Shaftesbury), Lauderdale – an inner group of the Privy Council, diverse in age, background, outlook and ambitions, given a false homogeneity by the nickname and brought together for urgent confidential matters, notably in foreign policy, a field which always encourages intrigue and secrecy. Even all of those in this narrow group did not know all that was going on. Only Clifford and Arlington were aware of the dangerous secret clauses of the Treaty of Dover (1670) with Louis XIV of France, whereby Charles was to bring England back to Catholicism. What was open in the treaty was unpopular. Times were never ripe for Charles to contemplate implementing the treachery of the rest. The secrecy involved epitomizes pragmatic limitations upon the king's freedom of action and hints at more to come over the next century.

In 1678 amid intense party, or rather, factional political conflict, a venal refugee from Catholicism, Titus Oates, 'revealed' a 'damnable and hellish' plot to assassinate the king, to intrude a grossly papist ministry and – the thing developed wildly as Oates's imagination took hold – to massacre hordes of decent, loyal Protestants. The murder of the magistrate to whom Oates first deposed the plot thickened the atmosphere which Shaftesbury and his resentful out-of-office Whigs exploited against the Tories and the Duke of York, the obvious beneficiary of the plot, if plot there was. In the ensuing crisis Charles cynically played along with popular fears and prejudices, allowing the trial and condemnation of many certainly innocent 'conspirators' and assenting to an act to disable papists from either house (the Second Test Act).

Though it became increasingly obvious that the Popish Plot was a fabrication, the political situation remained overheated. It merged into the pivotal event of the reign, the Exclusion Crisis (already much mentioned) which was sustained by the anticipation of the succession of an openly Catholic sovereign. Exclusion Bills, promoted by Whigs in three short and rapid parliaments contrasting with the longevity of the Cavalier one, went beyond the Test Acts of 1673 and 1678 to the highest office of all, the throne. Playing for time to rally support, Charles found it at length in the Tories, by indicating to them willingness to consider some limitations to come into effect on a popish accession. Such palliatives were not enough for the Shaftesbury Whigs, who whipped up petitions for statutory Exclusion, while Tory petitioners countered by abhorring it (hence the nicknames 'petitioners' and 'abhorrers'). A red-hot press was facilitated by a lapse in the Licensing Act. James was well-supported by the theatre of which he had long been a patron, but some of Charles's own ministers, among them Halifax, delineator of *The Character of a Trimmer* and himself a prime embodiment of its pragmatic philosophy, began to talk of James having to be thrown over. Charles sent his brother into exile but otherwise refused to impugn his hereditary rights. The Whigs went too far when some of them contemplated Charles's romantic but trivial illegitimate son, the Duke of Monmouth, for king. This prompted the most accessible propaganda piece of the crisis – John Dryden's *Absalom and Achitophel*, astonishingly apt in its biblical reference and effective in its flowing couplets, which focused on Shaftesbury's (Achitophel's) 'close designs' upon and 'crooked counsel' to Monmouth (Absalom). The Tories rallied round the crown, Shaftesbury fled into exile, and the crisis blew over – a triumph it seemed for the monarchy, though within less than a decade it looked more like one for the Tories. It was a many-layered episode, providing a particularly dense context for literature. The publication of Robert Filmer's long-ago written *Patriarcha* as Tory propaganda would occasion the writing of *The Two Treatises of Government* by the friend and adviser of Shaftesbury, John Locke, who sagely would not put his own book into the press until more propitious times at the Revolution.

Meanwhile Charles II went, quite legally, without a parliament for nearly four years, sustained chiefly by unexpectedly high revenues from customs dues and by the avoidance of war. Much of the time was spent in eliminating potential opposition and in making electoral arrangements by purging corporations and JPs to ensure that when parliament next assembled it would be emphatically amenable. It would not come under Charles. He died peaceably, a papist (it seems) at last on 6 February 1685, and in his own bed. His stiff brother succeeded automatically, exclusion forgotten.

Speaking off the cuff to the Privy Council he vowed to respect the Church as by law established and assured them that though he was given out to be a man for arbitrary government that was not 'the only story' that could be made of him. His initial ministry was clearly intended to appear to reinforce these promises, including as it did his High Tory brothers in law, Clarendon (the second earl) and Rochester (not the rake and the poet). The swift coronation (23 April) was spectacular, traditional and Anglican, to impress everybody with the uniqueness of regality. Parliament was called for May to vote revenues which should have died with Charles II but which James unhesitatingly went on collecting. It was, thanks to Charles II, a compliant bloc of Tories, glad to be a 'king's parliament'.

THE REVOLUTION 1685–1702

Two risings ('King' Monmouth's in the south-west and Argyll's in Scotland) spurred the Commons to be very generous. Remote from each other and from London the rebellions failed. Both leaders – abject failures – were swiftly executed. Their followers, victims of the greater men's vanity, met a fierce judicial revenge, notably in Judge George Jeffrey's 'campaign in the West', which went on, though with no great outcry at the time, to become, after the Revolution of 1688–9, the legendary 'Bloody Assizes'. James took advantage of the lack-lustre performance of the local militia against their own fellow-countrymen in Somerset to demand a parliamentary recognition of a well-paid standing army in which papist officers could serve. This was to ask too much even of high-principled non-resistance Tories. Parliament was dismissed in November 1685 with no immediate prospect of another. Everyone expected that James would as a matter of course do something for his co-religionaries and a little quiet relief might have been unexceptionable. But he embarked upon an accelerating policy of removing penalties by the use of prerogative, suspending and dispensing powers, by edicts of toleration which wooed Protestant dissenters too – whether genuinely or hypocritically is still arguable – and by measures which offered active political citizenship locally and centrally. As his heir was his staunchly Protestant daughter, Mary, married to the Calvinistic Dutch stadtholder, William of Orange, James felt that he must get on to improve the lot of Catholics in such a way that it would not be politic for his successor to undo it. The birth of a Prince of Wales in June 1688 would widen his horizons. A Catholic son could build upon whatever his father had achieved. Not surprisingly fears for the Established Church grew.

Determined to take off the inhibiting Test Acts, James reversed his brother's policy of purging corporations. Charles's object had been to put Tories in, James's was to get them out, in favour of papists, co-operative Protestant dissenters and even pliant Whigs: there were by now some of these, impatient of being kept out of office by their principles. This political onslaught – intended to ensure a supine parliament – hinted at a social revolution. Lord-Lieutenancies, for instance, were going to individuals who lacked the normal regional and social standing considered appropriate for an office which was by no means merely honorific. Moreover, every one of James's actions suggested an urge towards absolutism, whose connections with popery seemed almost axiomatic. James was suspected, almost certainly wrongly but plausibly, to be ready to be a client of the bigoted despot Louis XIV of France. So the king could be seen as combining threats to the constitution, the social order, the Established Church and English national interests generally. No institution seemed safe from interference – parliament, Church, universities. The trial of seven bishops (June 1688) for seditious libel in appealing in writing against having to order the reading in churches throughout the land of James's second Declaration of Indulgence, showed how far and fast he was going, in straining the traditional interrelationship of episcopacy and monarchy.

Protestant nonconformists might have been expected to welcome the sight of their chief persecutors under fire. Some did, but many more were embarrassed by what lay behind the declaration, aware as they were of the link between their religious liberty being offered and popery. They wanted toleration, certainly, but not on the whim or the stretched prerogative of a papist king. Ungratefully they hung back, comforting themselves by the prospect that a statutory, even if limited, relief would come their way if the political atmosphere changed as Providence, no doubt, would ensure it must.

The hugger-mugger circumstances of the birth of the Prince of Wales on 10 June 1688, which would ensure a papist successor to James himself, and the more or less coincident acquittal of the seven bishops clinched for some of the contacts in various factions with William of Orange the need for him to convert the watching brief he had long held into direct intervention. The time was apt. The prospect of European war against Louis XIV, with William well to the fore, enhanced his interest in English affairs and in prospective resources of men and money. An invitation was sent to William to come over; signed by a few Whigs and Tories and the Bishop of London (30 June 1688), it exaggerated the open expression, if not the potential, of national discontents. William was not offered the crown: indeed, just what he should do and what he might expect as his reward was left vague. It was clear, though, that much would depend on what James himself did in response. He might fight, so William must bring over the troops. James might negotiate, so William must push terms protective of his wife's and his own (more remote but not negligible) rights to the succession. A 'free and full' parliament should heal the wounded liberties of the political nation. William accepted. Everything from now on was risky. Even the weather – it was late autumn before William was ready – could not be relied upon. But William, a convinced predestinarian, was one who could take a calculated risk, believing like Gustavus Adolphus fifty years before, that he was in God's pocket, and that the ship could not sink that carried him over.

The expedition, blown by 'predestination' to land at Torbay (5 November 1685), was slow to receive support in a region where the harsh fate of Monmouth's rebellion counselled caution. Nor was there an immediate response elsewhere; but by dithering James fostered desertions among peers, army officers and gentry everywhere. Even James's younger daughter Princess Anne came over to William. Then at the end of the year James fled, twice – the second time, to William's intense relief, successfully. With him gone, the danger, much feared, of civil war receded. William held *de facto* power, reinforced by his wife's hereditary claim, his own Stuart blood, their joint religious suitability and his obvious capabilities as a ruler. He was indeed a *sine qua non*. No wonder John Locke in a Preface to his *Two Treatises of Government*, written during the Exclusion Crisis, but now brought out to defend what would come to be labelled the Glorious Revolution, called him 'our great deliverer'. The book itself was not a sheer propaganda necessity nor was it immediately influential. Political theory, however eloquent and convincing, stayed in the background. Expediency, pragmatism, even fudge, were the keynotes that the ears of the men of 1689 would listen to.

The great deliverer was no philanthropist. He wanted England badly but for his own purposes. His greatest asset was that like him, loathe him, the political nation, momentarily united, and mindful of past 'troubles' needed a quick end to the crisis. The regicide Edmund Ludlow, glimpsing an opportunity to revive his republican version of the Good Old Cause, came out of exile from Switzerland but soon grasped that time had passed him by. He quietly slipped away again (see pp. 161–2). If the Civil War and Interregnum were to be mentioned at all it was in admonition. Old hands like Colonel John Birch and Serjeant John Maynard, sharp-memoried and voluble, saw to that in the Convention Parliament which met in February 1689 to legitimize the coup. Beyond that, hugely taken with settlement, word and thing, it set itself to provide effective answers, never mind their logic, to immediate questions. What did James's flight mean? Had he abdicated or merely deserted the throne? Should there be a regency? Was Mary automatically a sovereign queen? Where did William come in? Lords and Commons, Whigs and Tories, argued profusely, but the situation forced everybody directly involved to turn in the same direction. William speeded things up by scotching any notion of a regency. He would not be his wife's 'gentleman usher' nor would Mary expect him to be. The throne was declared vacant and offered to William and Mary jointly, the survivor to continue *solus*. Next in line, failing a child of their bodies, was Mary's sister Anne, a sound Protestant, an Anglican – still bearing children by her amiable husband, George of Denmark, who certainly could be relied upon to be content to be *his* wife's gentleman usher. The vital 'no papist' succession seemed assured.

The offer was accompanied by a declaration of rights, made shortly with some amendments into a Bill, and then a statute. Devised by a broad-bottomed committee of both Houses, it was an eclectic, unsystematic catalogue of grievances to be remedied, some from the reigns of both Charles II and of James II, some put in by Tories, some by Whigs, some by both. There was little really innovative, far less revolutionary: rather it was restorative, or at least it could be made to seem so. It was not strikingly restrictive on the new monarchs. It was not comprehensive and would have to be thickened by piecemeal additions and revisions, some embodied in legislation, some by convention and usage. New laws included a mild Toleration Act (1689) for the relief of Protestant nonconformists, not a great step forward but firmly statutory. A Triennial Act defined the maximum duration of parliaments lest they become too pliant to a government with copious sources of patronage and influence. More all-embracing was the Act of Settlement of 1701, with provisions partly to anticipate and partly to coincide with the Hanoverian Succession which would meet the problems raised by the death of Anne's last surviving child, the 11-year-old Duke of Gloucester.

Even so, settlement was a long time coming and it is impossible to put a date to its completion. It was still going on well into the eighteenth century in, for instance, the Act of Union with Scotland, which underlined what has only been hinted at in this survey, that the history of England and Wales cannot be isolated from that of the whole British Isles. Scotland had its own revolutionary settlement, hard to call glorious. There was another, in Ireland, where James II attempted a comeback, to be defeated at the Battle of the Boyne, with consequences that unhappily have still not worked themselves out.

Nothing in the revolutionary settlement sapped the monarchy fundamentally. Rather in a sense it emerged strengthened. The dynastic change headed off a reduction of power which would certainly have been pushed if James had stayed on. Most of the legacy of Charles II came to William III as residuary legatee. What the revolution made for in the long term was the ascendancy of the king-in-parliament. That would take its time coming, but was assured by the fact that in no year since 1689 has there been no sitting of parliament. The longevity of monarchy and the two Houses was thereby assured. Meanwhile William ruled as well as reigned and he was not the last. But he had to cope with the existence of political parties led by men who could be called professional politicians. Historians argue over whether their politics should be labelled Whig and Tory or Court and Country. The evidence suggests that both pairs existed as shifting coalitions, with the Whigs and Tories gradually taking over as discrete entities. William for his part was less interested in labels than in contents. Under him there was opposition to aspects, particularly financial, of his policies domestic and foreign, but it would be wrong to speak of 'the Opposition'. Any notion of 'His Majesty's Loyal Opposition' was far too sophisticated for the age. William took adverse reactions into account, yielding a little, sometimes refusing to budge. An example came in 1697, following the Peace of Ryswick. William, by no means finished yet with Louis XIV, saw peace as an opportunity to recoup and regroup for war. He wanted to keep a large force in trained preparedness but got support for less than half of it. Over this frustration he may have contemplated abdication but did not go further. He died in a trivial accident in 1702, leaving Anne to cope with a mixed but not impossible inheritance.

The Act of Settlement (1701) was meant to provide for the prospect of rule by yet another foreigner by arrangements which would give priority to perceived English interests. It set out to avoid national entanglement through Hanover in the tortuous politics of the Holy Roman Empire. It embraced, too, elements of domestic reform such as the change of the tenure of judges from royal pleasure to good behaviour, bad behaviour to be determined in individual cases by a vote of both Houses of parliament. This, combined with high salaries, has ensured a more or less effective independent judiciary. Judicial behaviour ever since has had its oddities as judges have read the law, which by its nature thrives on ambiguities, sometimes too broadly, sometimes narrowly, occasionally a little too responsively to the promptings of the requirements of the executive. But partiality more often lies in the actual laws they are expected to implement.

Was England significantly different in 1700 in constitutional and political terms from the England of the 1620s? A single generalized answer would be misleading. (We are on firmer ground in asserting that it was different in style – in prose, poetry and the arts.) If pressed one could say, yes, but not perhaps as much as interpretations of the century as one of revolution would suggest. An analogy might be found in science. There was surely a scientific revolution. Isaac Newton was a prime contributor, but (as P.W. Thomas shows, p. 168) he was a man of two worlds, one looking forward to the Enlightenment, the other backward to the era of astrology and alchemy. Constitutionally England was still a monarchy based upon an amalgam of legitimacy, contractual theory, custom, consent, utility and a hint of divinity. (Anne still touched for the king's evil.) Reigning and ruling still went along together. The royal prerogative survived (and still does) though exercised under changed, and ever-changing auspices. Each reign and regime since 1625 had experienced strain, sometimes almost to breaking point, but the institution of monarchy had, like the Church of England, the Common Law, parliament and much else, survived though, as the 1650s had demonstrated, not inevitably. Much had depended, and still would, upon the personalities of the occupants of the throne. Here style comes into it again. The historical context of the literature of the seventeenth century shows all the characteristics of that literature. Together history and literature can inform students of both, provided they are not too hot for certainties.

FURTHER READING

Aylmer, G.E. (ed.), *The Interregnum* (London, 1972).
——*Rebellion or Revolution?* (Oxford, 1986).
Baxter, S.B., *William III* (London, 1965).
Browning, A., *English Historical Documents 1660–1714* (London, 1953).
Burton, Thomas, *The Diary of Thomas Burton M.P.*, ed. J.R. Rutt (1828; new edn New York, 1974, ed. I. Roots).
Carlyle, T. (ed.), *Letters and Speeches of Oliver Cromwell* (London, 1845).
Clarendon, Edward Hyde, Earl of, *The History of the Rebellion*, ed. W. Macray, 5 vols (Oxford, 1888).
Clark, J.C.D., *Revolution and Rebellion* (Cambridge, 1986).
Coward, B., *The Stuart Era* (London, 1980).
Cust, R., *The Forced Loan and English Politics 1626–28* (Oxford, 1987).
Edwards, T., *Gangraena* (1646; Exeter, 1977).
Filmer, Sir Robert, *Patriarcha*, ed. P. Laslett (Oxford, 1949).
Fletcher, A., *The Outbreak of the English Civil War* (London, 1981).
——*Reform in the Provinces: The Government of Stuart England* (New Haven, 1986).
Haley, K.H.D., *The First Earl of Shaftesbury* (Oxford, 1967).
Halifax, George Savile, Marquess of, *Complete Works*, ed. J.P. Kenyon (Harmondsworth, 1969).
Harrington, James, *The Political Works*, ed. J.G.A. Pocock (Cambridge, 1975).
Hill, C., *The Century of Revolution* (Edinburgh, 1961).
——*God's Englishman: Oliver Cromwell and the English Revolution* (London, 1970).
——*The World Turned Upside Down* (London, 1972).
——*Milton and the English Revolution* (New York, 1977).
——(ed.), *Gerrard Winstanley: The Law of Freedom* etc. (Harmondsworth, 1979).
Hirst, D., *Authority and Conflict 1603–58* (London, 1986).
Hobbes, Thomas, *Leviathan*, ed. C.B. Macpherson (Harmondsworth, 1968).
Holmes, G. (ed.), *Britain after the Glorious Revolution* (London, 1969).
Hughes, A., *The Causes of the English Civil War* (London, 1991).
Hutton, R., *The Restoration* (Oxford, 1935).
——*Charles II* (Oxford, 1989).
Jones, C., Newitt, M. and Roberts, S.K. (eds), *People and Politics in the English Revolution* (Oxford, 1986).
Jones, J.R., *The Revolution of 1688* (London, 1972).
——*Country and Court 1658–1714* (London, 1978).
——*Charles II: Royal Politician* (Oxford, 1987).
Kenyon, J.P., *Robert Spencer, Earl of Sunderland* (London, 1958).
——*Stuart England* (London, 1978).

——*The Stuart Constitution 1603–1688* (Cambridge, 1984).
——*The English Civil Wars* (London, 1988).
Kishlansky, M., *The Rise of the New Model Army* (Cambridge, 1990).
Knowler, W. (ed.), *Letters and Despatches of the Earl of Strafford*, 2 vols (London, 1741).
Locke, John, *Two Treatises of Government*, ed. P. Laslett (London, 1988).
McMichael, J.R. and Taft, B. (eds), *The Writings of William Walwyn* (Athens, Georgia, 1989).
Miller, J., *Popery and Politics 1660–1688* (Cambridge, 1973).
Morrill, J.S. (ed.), *Seventeenth-Century England 1603–1714* (Folkestone, 1980) (bibliography).
——*Reactions to the English Civil War* (London, 1982).
——(ed.), *Oliver Cromwell and the English Revolution* (London, 1990).
Ogg, O., *England in The Reigns of James II and William III* (Oxford, 1959).
Parry, J.R. (ed.), *The English Civil War and After* (London, 1970).
Pennington, D.H. and Thomas, K. (eds), *Puritans and Revolutionaries* (Oxford, 1978).
Richardson, R.C., *The Debates on the English Revolution Revisited* (London, 1988).
Roots, I., *The Great Rebellion 1642–1660* (London, 1966).
——*'Into Another Mould': Aspects of the Interregnum* (Exeter, 1981).
——(ed.), *Speeches of Oliver Cromwell* (London, 1989).
Russell, C. (ed.), *Origins of the English Civil War* (London, 1973).
——*Parliament and English Politics 1621–1629* (Oxford, 1979).
——*The Fall of the British Monarchies* (Oxford, 1991).
Sachse, W.L. (ed.), *Restoration England 1660–1689* (Cambridge, 1979) (bibliography).
Sharpe, K. (ed.), *Faction and Parliament* (Oxford, 1978).
——*Politics and Ideas in Early Stuart England* (London, 1989).
Speck, W.A., *Reluctant Revolutionaries* (Oxford, 1989).
Trevor-Roper, H.R., *Archbishop Laud* (London, 1938).
Tyzacke, N., *Anti-Calvinists: The Rise of English Arminianism* (Oxford, 1987).
Underdown, D., *Pride's Purge* (Oxford, 1971).
Wallace, J.M., *'Destiny His Choice': The Loyalism of Andrew Marvell* (Cambridge, 1968).
Wedgwood, C.V., *Strafford* (London, 1961).
Woodhouse, A.S.P. (ed.), *Puritanism and Liberty* (London, 1938, new edn, intro. by I. Roots, 1984).
Woolrych, A.H., *Commonwealth to Protectorate* (Oxford, 1982).
Worden, B., *The Rump Parliament 1649–1653* (Cambridge, 1973).

Chapter 3

From faith to faith in reason?
Religious thought in the seventeenth century

Margarita Stocker

I

While it is customary to view the seventeenth century as a watershed between medieval theocentricity and the rationalism of the Enlightenment, we should resist the tendency of hindsight to exaggerate the pace of change. Precisely because this is a period of significant transition, the pattern of continuity and change within it is remarkably complex. The age of scepticism did not arrive in 1660, nor did rationalism then forever banish the religious sense. In religion, as in other respects, the period between 1625 and 1700 is marked by shifting currents of thought in which 'faith' and 'reason' are not necessarily antagonists. In religious terms the watershed between pre-modern and modern thought must be dated much earlier, in the Tudor Reformation. The English revolution that occurs in the seventeenth century is, in that context, a signal consequence of the break with Rome. In that light we can best comprehend the history of belief in this period.

Even so, it is necessary to begin such a history with a caveat. Religious developments of this period have been much studied, especially in relation to its political upheaval, but the consequence of such researches has been to render the subject not less but more difficult to comprehend. Over and above the vicissitude and diversity of religious thought, and its entanglement in political alterations which may obscure purely theological arguments, are the current controversies among historians and literary critics. Inevitably, the convictions of modern commentators act upon their versions of the past, and the preoccupations of the present refight past battles in their own image. And religion, in a period as proud of its scepticism as our own, evokes or offends all manner of prejudices. By its very nature, this chapter must leave such prejudices to fend for themselves. My concern must be to interpret the evidence, and to attempt to convey something of the immediacy and significance of religion to its seventeenth-century adherents.

Even the most basic definitions of the two great antagonists in religion then – Anglicanism and Puritanism – are almost insuperably difficult: any such definition is necessarily an interpretation of a large and complex body of evidence. First, Anglicanism is essentially not a doctrinal position but an attitude to Christianity. Its fluidity was such that one might say it achieved self-definition only in contrast to its alternatives, Roman Catholicism and Puritanism. Anglicanism regarded itself as the true form of 'catholicism', of the Church as instituted in apostolic times, which Roman Catholicism was regarded as having corrupted by institutional and doctrinal accretions. Thus Anglicanism denied the Roman claim to primacy among churches, repudiated papal authority, and rejected such doctrines as those of purgatory and transubstantiation. It retained a prelatical church-government and a formal liturgy, yet these forms were to be recognized as forms, not essentials to salvation. In general, Anglicanism followed the Protestant way of emphasizing the spirit rather than the letter of devotion. So, however, did Puritanism, only more so. The very fluidity of early Anglicanism allowed for some diversity, while theologians struggled to give it form. Although modern commentators have frequently taken Richard Hooker's *Laws of Ecclesiastical Polity* (of which the first four books were issued in 1594) as representative of Anglicanism, its influence lay dormant till late in the century. In fact only once Anglicanism had taken shape in the crucible of seventeenth-century debate could its character as the *via media* between Roman Catholicism and Calvinism be confidently stated in modern terms. In many ways the essence of liberal Anglicanism is best represented by the writings of Jeremy Taylor, Bishop of Down and Connor after 1660, especially his *Ductor Dubitantium* (1660): a manual for temperate spirituality, ordered by a moderate regime of devotional behaviour. That approach to Anglicanism did not, however, prevent his violent hostility both to Catholicism and to Presbyterianism.

Late seventeenth-century Anglicanism depended for its identity upon a sense of Puritanism as its antagonistic 'Other', equally as the restored monarchy wished to demonize Puritanism as that which had overthrown monarchy. We, however, need to disentangle Puritanism from the propaganda of its opponents. Ultimately defeated and marginalized by the Restoration settlement, Puritanism has generally been conceived (and especially in literary circles) in forms inherited from its victorious antagonists. The majority of our modern labels for seventeenth-century religious groups were invented by their enemies, and 'Puritanism' is no exception. In 1641 John Ley, pastor of Budworth in Cheshire, vainly protested against this tendency in *A Discourse Concerning Puritans: A vindication of those, who unjustly suffer by the mistake, abuse, and misapplication of that NAME*. The term remains misleading, because recalcitrant to definition. In effect it is impossible to draw a strict line of distinction between Puritanism and Anglicanism, neither will any such distinction hold true for the whole period, since religious differences were themselves ineluctably involved with ecclesiastical and political change.

Both Puritanism and High Anglicanism were effects of the intrinsic problems of reformed religion in England. Its mediation between Roman Catholicism and the extremes of continental Protestantism was the attraction of 'The British Church' for George Herbert: 'Beautie in thee takes up her place . . . Neither too mean, nor yet too gay, / Shows who is best', as distinguished from both the 'painted' face of Catholicism and the 'undrest' radical form. Yet the ill-defined features of the unpainted church encouraged the submission of the 'Thirty-Nine Articles' of Anglican faith to varied interpretative emphases. Until the 1620s the most widespread interpretation of Anglicanism included Calvinist predestinarian doctrine (Article XVII), with its insistence that God's saving grace was limited to elect souls or 'saints', the rest being irredeemably damned. In these early years the term 'Puritan' designated those Protestants who did not conform to the ceremonies and rites of the Church of England, or those who as Presbyterians rejected church-government by bishops. In this sense Puritanism was an expression of an English anticlerical tradition which reached back to the Lollards, and the recurrent quarrel of the government and episcopacy with Puritanism was motivated more by the political implications of nonconformity than by hostility to Calvinism. During the 1620s, however, the rise of Arminianism in the English Church helped to destroy its consensus.

In this form, Arminian rejection of predestination had as its concomitant an emphasis upon the grace attainable by all through the sacraments, and hence reasserted the significance of liturgy and ritual. Both elements – doctrinal emphasis upon free will and ecclesiastical emphasis upon sacerdotalism and ceremony – effectively represented a revolution in the Anglican Church which, to traditionalists, smacked of counter-reformation. Under William Laud, Archbishop of Canterbury from 1633, and with the blessing of Charles I, the Arminian ascendancy effectively outlawed Calvinism, and in the Church the Calvinist stress upon 'ministerly' or advisory preaching was replaced by a sacramentalism which reinstituted the hieratic difference between the priest and those he 'instructed'. Laudian policy was in fact an attempt to redignify the Church against the Protestant tendency to indulge anticlericalism. In the early years of the century many church buildings had been treated with scant respect, as part-time barns or storerooms, and local clergy were often censured as theologically illiterate or ill-living. To re-educate the clergy and impose discipline were therefore complementary tasks of Laudian reform. That reform, in the very act of giving higher definition to the ecclesiastical character of Anglicanism, exacted a price from its capacity to comprehend a spectrum of views. Now 'Puritanism' was redefined by Arminian bishops to include adherence to Calvinist doctrine, despite the protests of such prominent 'Puritans' as John

Pym that the Arminians were the real revolutionaries. And once Calvinists generally were thus described, nonconformists perforce became radicals.

The essential point, therefore, to grasp about Puritans in the 1630s is that they were traditionalists. The Puritan gentry in parliament were as conservative in their religious attitudes as in their constitutional opposition to Charles I's 'personal rule'. The Church of England had been established with the monarch as head, and it was hard to break the habit of thought which inferred from the kingship of Christ that a monarch was his earthly counterpart. We must recognize that, given their traditionalist and generally monarchist bent, Puritan Parliamentarians were placed in a difficult position by an Arminian episcopacy and an absolutist and Arminian monarch. It became increasingly difficult for them to maintain their initial attempt to distinguish resistance to Laudianism and absolutism from loyalty to the king himself. Indeed, such a distinction became, as events unfolded, largely a fiction: MPs such as John Dutton were eventually forced to a choice which they had not wanted to make. Dutton chose loyalty, was expelled from the Long Parliament, and joined the 'royalist parliament' in Oxford.

As for the clergy, even ministers who counted themselves among the 'godly' and had supported parliament in its reforming task, were driven to protest in print against its intention to execute the king. In 1649 nineteen Puritan ministers of Banbury and Brackley signed a petition to General Fairfax which, while congratulating parliament upon its moves to restore 'our Religion in purity', yet insisted upon 'our utter dissent from all proceedings against his Majesties Crown and Life'. They urged an authority that any godly parliament must recognize, 'The sacred Scripture', which in no way 'doth warrant or countenance such actings of Subjects against their lawfull Soveraign'. Rather the Bible shows that 'when the ten Tribes forsook their King, they also forsook their God', and suffered his vengeance. If parliament will not listen to the warning which God has prompted them to pronounce, then 'we desire to wash our hands, as from the blood of all men, so especially of our dread Soveraign', for which the members of the General Council of War will answer at the Judgement. In this petition the protesting ministers were speaking the Council's own language, even as they rebuked it.

Similarly, the Calvinist notion of a spiritual aristocracy of the elect, preselected for salvation, far from inevitably fostering revolutionary attitudes through individualism, was capable of colluding with the ideology of an established social hierarchy. A preselected social classification could be viewed as analogous. And by the same token, the republicanism of such Parliamentarians as Sir Henry Vane the Younger achieved part of its appeal because of the oligarchic possibilities of the idea of spiritual election. This species of republicanism, shared to an extent by Milton, identified the Rule of the Saints with an educated governing cadre. At the heart of *Paradise Lost* is a vision of the perfectibility of humankind, growing up to the millennial state of being (VII: 155-61), of which the political counterpart here is the evolution of meritocracy into oligarchy. Although some modern commentators present the republicanism of a Parliamentarian minority as if it were contiguous with the democratic ideas emerging during the Civil War, it should be stressed that oligarchic republicanism – had it attained power – would have been set on a collision course with the more radical religio-democratic movements: a consequence readily inferred from Vane's own *A Healing Question* (1656).

Although religious reform proved to be inextricable from political action, parliament's mission to 'purify religion' had been inspired by basic premises of Reformation thought. In their resistance to what they regarded, with some reason, as a 'popish' takeover of the Church, Puritans were expressing traditional reformed anti-Catholicism and anticlericalism. Since the Anglo-Spanish conflicts of Elizabeth's reign England had been a virulently anti-Catholic nation, fearful of subversion whether by foreign nations or by recusants at home. Roman Catholics suffered from civil disabilities and fines. After 1605 the abortive Gunpowder Plot became a symbol both of recusant treachery and of God's special care for his chosen nation. Milton's 'In Quintum Novembris' evokes that mood of ritual purgation – at times becoming a mob hysteria – which imbued 'pope-burnings' on Guy Fawkes's Night, celebrated in this manner throughout the century. In the light of popular anti-Catholic sentiment we can comprehend also the animus of a political poem such as Marvell's 'Upon the Victory obtained by Blake', where the defeat in 1657 of a Spanish fleet is celebrated as a replay of the Armada's misfortunes in 1588: nationalism and Protestantism are identified.

Far from abating after 1660, fear of popery remained an automatic trigger for national hysteria, as when rumour attributed the Fire of London in 1666 to papist incendiaries. For the political opposition the 'Popish Plot' scare of 1678 provided an opportunity to force the Exclusion Crisis (see p. 45). A crypto-papist, Charles II did not dare convert until on his deathbed; the foreigner William III would not have gained the throne had he not been a celebrated Protestant military champion, and had James II not been a Catholic. But the most spectacular consequence of this abiding religious antipathy was the Civil War itself. Owing particularly to his Arminian patronage of the Church and his papist consort, it was the suspicion that Charles I was secretly popish that hardened his opponents' distrust of the king's promises of ecclesiastical and constitutional reform. For this reason fear of popery, apart from the underlying constitutional issues, was the 'efficient cause' of the Civil War.

This religious element was crucial among the intense forces necessary to provoke the Parliamentarians into taking arms against the king. For in order to understand the lines of opposition in the Civil War it is necessary to grasp the general prevalence of the religious ideology of monarchy.

The Stuart proponence of Divine Right had its basis in one strand of medieval political thought, reinforced by Reformation attitudes to the role of the monarch in England's divine mission to defend and promulgate Protestantism. There was a widespread belief among all classes and parties that this was the 'last age' of the world, when Protestantism would finally vanquish the Antichrist (usually identified with the Pope) and clear the way for Christ's second coming. Before the Civil War this ideology underpinned a messianic attitude to kingship, which Puritans shared. Indeed, Puritan opposition to episcopacy frequently expressed itself as a defence of the monarch's sovereignty against clerical incursion and episcopal claims to *iure divino* status. Reflecting Stuart ideology, the court masques endowed Charles with a supernatural power, just as (when heir to the throne) he had been portrayed as a Christ-like 'Prince of Peace' to the nation. Courtly poets like Sir Richard Fanshawe celebrated the peaceful opening years of his reign in a manner which linked Charles's irenic aegis to God's providential care of his elect nation. Similarly, the courtly clergyman Robert Herrick celebrates the birth of Charles's heir under 'a silver Star, / Bright as the Wise-mens Torch, which guided them / To Gods sweet Babe' ('A Pastorall upon the Birth of Prince Charles', 20–2). Recalling the traditional association between pastoral and Christianity in the character of the good shepherd, this birth song can say of the messianic heir that 'As he is Prince, he's Shepherd too' (44): for in due time he will be pastoral guardian of the Anglican Church, just as his destined kingship anticipates the future reign of Christ the king in the millennium. The same messianic and millenarian tendencies prompt the Puritan Marvell, eulogizing Cromwell's quasi-monarchical government, to portray the Lord Protector as 'Sun-like' because his rule prepares for that of 'the approaching . . . Son' (*The First Anniversary of the Government . . .*, 8, 106), Christ the Son of God and Sun of Righteousness (Malachi 4:2), whose second coming is imminent. Such apocalyptic hopes of the new regime were frustrated by its collapse in 1659, but in extolling Charles II's restoration Dryden sounds anew the explicitly monarchist note of messianic praise. In his 'Astraea Redux' (1660) Charles's homecoming is imitative of Christ's return to earth as 'Prince of Peace', sanctifying the notion that England has reverted to her true – monarchic – character. 'The Prince of Peace would like himself confer / A gift unhop'd without the price of war' (139–40); bloodless Restoration is a messianic miracle. 'Royalist' and 'Puritan' eulogies share a similar religious theme.

Given this context, and the traditionalist cast of Puritanism, it is inconceivable that the Puritan regicides could have brought themselves to execute Charles I without a religious ideology which could give colour to an unprecedented act – fundamentally different, because legalized and public, from guilty assassinations of monarchs in the medieval period. For Puritan reformers the Civil War represented a Latter-Day conflict between the Archangel Michael and the forces of Antichrist, in which inevitably the king became an antichristian agent. Initially at least he was usually regarded as a righteous man in error, but so generous an estimate naturally could not survive the bitterness of armed conflict; and, in any case, an antichristian tool was equally dangerous whether or not he himself was conscious of this role. Puritan reformers like Milton were as convinced as the royalist Fanshawe of God's especial care of England, although for propaganda purposes in the Civil War period that very notion was used to reinforce the reformers' sense that God had purified the nation by dislodging an unrighteous king and his episcopal allies. Despite propagandist rhetoric and the gradual hardening of attitudes, we should not lose sight of the fact that Puritans were *forced* to relinquish king-worship.

Once hostilities had begun, the exigencies of propaganda often obscured both the sincerity of some religious convictions and the similarities of 'royalist' and 'Puritan' ideologies. Nevertheless, it is in the propaganda war that one common assumption emerges most forcibly. On the one hand, Cromwell was accustomed to ascribe his military successes to 'the mercy of God' favouring a righteous cause, rather than to any 'reasonable design' of strategy: insisting, indeed, that military strategy is even counterproductive if 'We look too much to men and visible helps', for God is the general (Letter to the Committee of Both Kingdoms, 25 April 1645). Not to be outdone in claims upon God's particular care, royalists rejoiced when the Parliamentarian commander Lord Brooke, besieging Lichfield, was killed by an incredibly lucky shot from a sniper on the cathedral roof. In all respects this incident appeared to manifest the hand of a royalist God. Ironically, Brooke had prayed for 'some special token' of God's approbation of his siege; but (as a Cavalier described it)

> That enemy of our Church . . . was slain in his quarrel against our Church, by the God of our Church, with a shot out of the Cathedral, with a bullet made of Church lead, through the mouth which reviled our Church; and . . . the blow of death came from St Chad's Church on St Chad's Day.

So palpably the reverse of what Brooke had prayed for, this incident was frequently cited in contemporary royalist literature as a miracle. Neither side was prepared to relinquish its claims to God's support.

The fact that Puritanism was initially characterized as 'radical' by its opponents must be recalled if we are to understand the spectrum of post-war religious attitudes. Once we begin to consider the period of Civil War it is necessary to emphasize that the term 'Puritan' cannot be used with the same degree of precision as the terms Presbyterian, Fifth Monarchist, Baptist, Ranter, Seeker, Familist, Adamite or Quaker. Unless referring to a general attitude of mind, it is best to be more specific, for Puritanism is a tendency, whereas (for example) Muggletonianism – a cult centred upon the 'revelations' of Lodowick Muggleton – is a specific religious category. Of literary figures, the outstanding example of terminological difficulty must be Milton. Heterodox in several particulars, he was Arminian in his emphasis upon human free will, yet violently opposed to the 'Arminian ritual' of Laudianism. It is precisely the problem of classifying his position that renders the term 'Puritan' at once a useful description of Milton and a severely limited one.

After the Civil War sectarian groups like the Fifth Monarchists – who advocated the establishment of Christ's millennial kingdom by violent means – pressed for more radical religio-political reforms than most of the Parliamentarian gentry could countenance. Sectarianism flourished particularly in the army which had given those Parliamentarians their victory. From varied regional and urban backgrounds, thrown into new groupings and unfamiliar situations, listening to the army chaplains and discussing points of doctrine, heady with victory and encouraged to rethink the bases of authority – having by their own arms overthrown the old order – the soldiers often questioned more than their new masters wished them to question. As Levelling doctrines took hold upon some troops and their officers, so also Fifth Monarchism and Quakerism found converts. While social fluidities, class antagonisms and intellectual movements all played their parts in the dissemination of radical religious ideas within the army, so did something else which has been largely ignored. Like Winston Churchill at Omdurman, soldiers under fire have frequently been frightened into religious fervour. In precisely this manner a Quaker convert was made of Thomas Lurting by the dangerous naval action at Santacruz in 1657, for he was convinced that God had preserved him from five close shaves in order that he should recognize the error of his ways. Having beaten and abused the Quakers in the crew during the outward voyage, he now began to recognize that his hostility towards them had been a reflex of his fear – fear of the recognition and sympathy that God's power was forcing upon his heart.

Even as their army became a focus for religious radicalism and its rebellious or democratic impulses, parliament in the 1640s and 1650s made repeated attempts to discover and establish a new form for the national Church. In 1643 the body entrusted with this task, the Westminster Assembly of divines, issued a severely Calvinist 'Confession of Faith' which repudiated the Anglican reverence for Church tradition: 'Nothing is at any time to be added' to the scriptures, 'whether by new revelations of the Spirit or traditions of men', and by scripture is the Church to be ruled. By 1646 the Solemn League and Covenant had abolished episcopacy, the 'Directory' had replaced the Prayer Book, and the new church-government was in essence Presbyterian. Yet such a settlement could not command consensus, especially in view of the strength of Independency, or congregationalism, within the army, which had the muscle to make its dissatisfaction felt. Cromwell himself was an Independent, favouring a loose church-government in which local congregations would largely be left to order themselves. Once in power, he remained more inclined to the toleration of religious differences (except for atheism and 'popery') than most conservative Parliamentarians. Thus, in the 'Savoy Declaration of Faith and Order' in 1658, Independency won the argument: religious meetings were not to be regarded as formal, authoritarian events but as communal expressions of unity in faith. Any 'Pastor, Teacher or Elder' would be appointed by election. In sum, the Church was not an institution, but a gathering of godly 'societies' whose various inflexions of Protestantism would be tolerated providing that they did not disturb the peace. In practice, however, throughout the Commonwealth and Protectorate church-organization remained in a state of disarray. Continuing sectarian agitation irritated the government, and in the absence of obvious spiritual authorities prudent candidates for the clergy often sought out the ejected bishops for their blessing, just to be on the safe side. Just as the Laudians had before them, many ministers during the Interregnum echoed Edward Reynolds's complaint that men of God received precious little respect. Although many modern commentators may have thought that Puritan ministers were complacent in a new authority, clearly those ministers themselves often felt embattled. The theological democracy offered by sectarianism, and the tolerant emphases of Independency, both tended to erode spiritual authorities.

Under the Protectorate non-separating Independency thus became a centrist position. In 1649 the ministers of Banbury and Brackley had condemned 'that grand designe of the Devill and his Agents, to decry all religious and zealous [people] under the name of Sectaries and Independents'. By 1658 things had changed: opponents of the Protectorate were already complaining of the propaganda which labelled them 'enthusiasts'. After the Restoration the name which Cromwellian conservatives had used to revile radical religionists was appropriated by Stuart apologists and churchmen to condemn the whole spectrum of dissent, from the most sober Presbyterian to the maddest sectarian prophet. Such labels were constantly in flux, as the vagaries of political propaganda and religious polemic tossed them hither and yon.

Nevertheless, it is in the non-separating congregations that we can locate the most powerful residue of traditional Puritanism. Such Independents as Cromwell and his admirer, Marvell, regarded the activities of radical sectarians with dismay, as promoting both political and religious anarchy. 'The Shame and Plague both of the Land and Age', they hope 'That their new King might the Fifth Sceptre shake, / And . . . Quake', 'their Rant' a 'frantique Army' of heresies ('The First Anniversary of the Government', 294–307). Marvell's assault upon Ranters, Quakers, Shakers, Fifth Monarchists and Anabaptists is more than equal to the satiric invective launched indiscriminately upon Presbyterians and sectarians alike by the royalist satirist Samuel Butler in *Hudibras*. Indeed, we owe most of our 'definitions' of the sects, as of Puritanism generally, to their enemies' fulminations and caricatures. Among the most savage was *Gangraena* (1646) by Thomas Edwards, a Presbyterian whose hostility to the sects manifests the great divides within the Puritan tendency. It was easy enough for such royalists as Butler to accuse 'Puritans' of hypocrisy when they had managed to tar conservative Presbyterians and such sectaries as Lawrence Clarkson with the same brush: this was propaganist identification of all 'saints' with the notorious excesses of the Ranters.

In the case of the Ranters, particularly, more conservative Puritans fashioned a stick to beat their own backs. After the success of the revolution, the new government had to preserve itself against precisely those forces which had brought it to power. In the face of continued agitation, like many governments before and since they resorted to scaremongering and the exploitation of paranoia. Government propagandists railed against the Ranters, among others, to foster a general fear of subversion and imminent anarchy. (Precisely to resist this stratagem the Digger Winstanley, the Quaker Fox and the Baptist Bunyan all explicitly dissociated themselves from the Ranters.) Given that propagandist exaggeration, it remains difficult to tell precisely how large or significant a phenomenon Ranterism was. Nevertheless, the extant works of identifiable Ranters display an exuberant antinomianism, which did indeed suggest the overturning of received authority, whether spiritual or civil. The headlong prose of Abiezer Coppe describes a trajectory of pantheistic, millenarian, materialist ascent to the godhead of man. Heaven and hell are his earthly states of being. Hell's lure, moralism, is confounded by licence, releasing the energy of immanent godliness:

> Kisses are numbered amongst transgressors – base things – well! by bare hellish swearing, and cursing, (as I have accounted it in the time of my fleshly holinesse) and by base impudent kisses (as I then accounted them) my plaguy holinesse hath been confounded, and thrown into the lake of fire and brimstone.
>
> (*A Second Fiery Flying Roule*, 1649)

By affording such deliberate 'blasphemies' the 'oxygen of publicity' (to use a modern Prime Minister's phrase), Presbyterians and other conservatives themselves invented the terms of condemnation which were later redeployed by royalist writers to castigate dissent.

Their opponents were unable or unwilling to recognize that 'Puritans' might be sincere in their pursuit of godliness. From the comedies of Ben Jonson early in the century to the satires of Dryden and Howard after the Restoration, the same charge is laid against Puritans and sectarians, thus compounded – that they were canting hypocrites who condemned in others their own secret sins, assumed a spiritual superiority, and hence elevated simple egotism into a doctrine of election. Calvinism was easily caricatured in such portraits as Butler's: 'The Modern Saint, that believe's himself Privileg'd, and above nature, ingage's himself in the most horrid of all Wickednesses . . . [calling them] good workes.' Note the telling use of 'nature' to undermine what is presented as a perverted idealism, while simultaneously, 'natural' vices are denoted by a generalizing moralistic phrase ('most horrid of all Wickednesses'). Here 'nature' is already a word with positive value, abandoned precisely at the moment when its values might merge into those of antinomianism. It would be naive to take such propaganda at face value, without balancing against it the voice of Lucy Hutchinson, wife of the Parliamentarian colonel, complaining of precisely such deliberate calumnies that any who 'were . . . established in faith and holiness . . . [were] at court . . . hated, disgraced, and reviled, and in scorn had the name of Puritan fixed upon them'.

Charges that Puritans were joyless authoritarians were, and are, equally exaggerated. Butler spoke of Puritans as wedded to 'Fire and Sword and Desolation / A godly-thorough Reformation . . . As if Religion were intended / For nothing else but to be mended' (*Hudibras*, I.i: 199–204). However, as we have seen, Puritans had excellent reasons for demanding 'reformation' of the Laudian theocracy, and their desire for national reformation reflected the Calvinist attitude to individual experience: that, as the believer must guard against his naturally sinful tendencies to backslide, so must the Church be preserved from corrupting tendencies. After the Civil War a Presbyterian church-settlement (which had proved on occasion to have strongly authoritarian aspects in Scotland) encountered considerable resistance, especially from the army. Nor was the post-war church-government as thoroughgoing or oppressive as it has been painted. On the contrary, the re-establishment of the Anglican Church after the Restoration was so swiftly effected partly because parliament had had neither the will nor the means completely to overhaul Church organization throughout the nation. And if, before and during the Civil War, Puritanism had an authoritarian urge to impose 'moral order' upon the nation, it must be said that the Laudian Church's policy of 'Thorough' had been equally rigorous and comprehensive, and more successful. Equally, it had implemented a form of social control with significant political implications, reflected for instance in its directions for preaching on the topic of 'royal supremacy'. Evidently there was popular anticlericalist backing for Puritan complaints against Laudian alterations in churches; *soi-disant* Puritan iconoclasm was not essentially an aesthetic objection against such features as decorated windows, but a reassertion of the pre-Laudian character of the church building. Laudian treatment of the communion table, sanctifying it as an altar and railing it off from the congregation, privileged the priestly function at the eucharist above the congregation. This was a valid doctrinal issue. And in many cases Puritan iconoclasm was limited, when it came to windows and sculpture, to removing only the heads of figures represented there, since these alone offended antipathy to popish 'idolatry'. More extensive damage in churches and cathedrals tended to be the effect of mere vandalism and looting – phenomena common in most conflicts – rather than of religious fanaticism. Popular support for the removal of Laudian innovations is reflected in the alacrity with which parishes responded to parliament's edict in the 1640s, even though later and more contentious parliamentary reforms were resisted.

The popular commitment to Anglicanism (rather than to Laudianism) is particularly evident in affection for those traditional calendar festivals whose spirit animates such poems as Herrick's 'The Ceremonies for Candlemasse Day', and which were interlocked with the traditional social organization, as portrayed in his 'Hock-cart'. Even in London, centre of Parliamentarian and Puritan support, Anglican services were still celebrated in the 1650s using the Prayer Book, and attended by such traditionalists as the diarist John Evelyn. Their occasional disruption by soldiers gave episcopalian religion a new savour of danger. Those Anglican clerics who took refuge within aristocratic houses were able, in the novel role of the underdog, to lay the foundations of an alliance between episcopate and Cavalier which, after the Restoration, would force through a church settlement of unprecedented rigidity, indiscriminately excluding all colours of nonconformists or 'dissenters', as well as Catholics. The Restoration alliance between Cavaliers and High Churchmen was unattractive both to Charles II and to Clarendon, both of whom sought to reward those Puritans and other groups who had helped to effect the Restoration, and to achieve a religious unity which might stabilize the nation. They were unable to resist a backlash in which old Cavaliers saw the Church of England as an ally in the reimposition of the former social order. If the Cromwellian regime had sought to control sectarian activity, imprisoning on occasion such itinerant preachers as the Baptist Bunyan or the Quaker leader George Fox, the Restoration regime allowed a new vigour in episcopal repression, under which Bunyan (for instance) would spend the greater part of twelve years in prison.

Between 1661 and 1670 the Clarendon Code and further Acts attempted to exclude noncomformists from all public offices and to silence their preachers by exiling them from the urban nonconformist populations. Ministers with a record of Puritan sympathies were ejected from their livings. Conventicles, religious meetings independent of the Established Church, were banned, on the premise that they provided focuses of insurrection 'under colour or pretence of [the] exercise of religion'. By such means religious dissent was treated as a form of treason. And, *mutatis mutandis*, Quakerism in particular was now reviled and persecuted in the same paranoiac terms which had once been applied to the Ranters.

Certainly the Protectorate parliament had displayed an hysterical barbarity in its punishment of the Quaker leader James Nayler, accused of blasphemy when he adopted messianic airs (see p. 38); but Cromwellian policy omitted to observe the full rigour of parliament's measures against Quakerism. Under the Clarendon Code, however, their refusal to swear oaths provided the strongest theoretical challenge to the legal system by which the Code itself was enforced. Their conviction of humankind's innocence questioned the whole prescriptive philosophy which lay behind seventeenth-century institutions, just as their refusal to remove their hats in the presence of authority reflected their rejection of all hierarchies: only God merited the respect of any man. Inevitably, then, they became especially symbolic of the 'treason' of dissent. Hundreds of Quakers were arrested under the Conventicle Act, and many were sentenced to transportation. Ironically, by 1664 Quakers had already espoused pacificism, partly that they might be allowed to survive, but the exigencies of government decreed that they be treated as revolutionaries and potential terrorists.

Now nonconformists and recusants were subject to the same legislation, a fact bitter to those who had always regarded 'popery' as the doctrine of the devil. Yet the imposition of the Test Act in 1673 in fact struck at the highest in the land, for by then the Duke of York, the king's own brother and the future James II, was known to be a 'papist'. When he succeeded to the throne, his attempt, in the 1688 Declaration of Indulgence, to link toleration for recusants with that for nonconformists was inevitably regarded as an act of bad faith, preparatory to the re-establishment of Roman Catholicism. In 1689 William III's Toleration Act, while relieving dissenters of most of their legal burden, excluded Roman Catholics. The most urgent reason for this Act was political, since it was intended to maximize Protestant support against James's attempts to regain the throne. In the same year the philosopher John Locke published his first *Letter on Toleration*, which provided the culmination of many arguments already aired by nonconformist writers, that the state had no business to compel men's consciences in the matter of religion. Yet this argument had its price, for when Christianity is deemed to live behind boundaries its basic premise, that nothing can be a merely 'secular' matter, is denied. Upon the universal effects of the spiritual view had depended the crisis of the mid-century, with consequences both fortunate and unfortunate: but religion was never more influential than in that crisis.

The period between 1660 and 1700 is often popularly regarded as one in which the religious sense was losing ground – a view which exaggerates change – yet it is also a period when the Anglican Church ossified in intolerance. Part of the price it paid for this power in ecclesiastical jurisdiction was to become a limb of political conservatism in a manner that Laud had sought to avoid. While he had attempted to maintain the Church's doctrinal independence of the state, after the Restoration the

Anglican Church gradually became much more effectively erastian. A Church which is seen to be under government orders has, to all intents and purposes, given up its claim to be God's and become man's. In that sense post-Restoration Anglican hegemony was, in religious terms, a fatal weakness, rendering Anglicanism susceptible to the inroads of rationalism, utilitarianism and materialism.

The potential weakness of a quasi-erastian Church was, by the 1670s, rendered more problematic by changes in the perception of the monarchy itself. In the reign of James I the monarchical title 'Defender of the Faith' was justified by James's writings against popery and his taste for theological disputation. It was no accident that, in the context of a court where persons ecclesiastical and matters theological had a high profile, Lancelot Andrewes and John Donne should have perfected the art of the witty, intellectual High Anglican sermon. Charles I was much less theologically accomplished than his father, and his ecclesiastical preferences did not encourage the art of the sermon – Laud was a clumsy preacher – but, despite suspicion of his crypto-popery, it was sufficiently evident that Charles was pious. He and Henrietta Maria encouraged in the court a high moral tone attached to Neoplatonic ideals, reflected in the court masques' celebration of their marital chastity as the fountainhead of a righteous royal power. Puritans like William Prynne protested against the court masque not so much on aesthetic as on ideological grounds, which recognized in this costly form of entertainment both absolutist propaganda and an extravagance which sorted ill with Charles's fiscal exactions from the nation. Just as offensive to anti-papist feeling was the smack of pagan idolatry in the courtly mode of compliment, as in Waller's 'Of His Majesty's receiving the news of the Duke of Buckingham's Death' (1628), where Charles is addressed as 'this mix'd Divinity and Love'. After Charles's execution *Eikon Basilike* (1649), purporting to be written by the king but probably compiled from his notes by the cleric John Gauden, portrayed Charles as a Christ-like 'Man of Sorrows' sacrificed to his people's error. The popularity of this hagiography is partly attributable to its exploitation of the messianic perception of kingship. One can see in the symbolism of its frontispiece, where Charles relinquishes the earthly diadem for a spiritual crown of thorns, that the sanctity now attributed to him was an ideological compensation (as it were) for his monarchical failure: he could be regarded by royalists as transcending rather than losing his earthly power. The image of the monarchy as divinely appointed and protected, although apparently discredited by defeat and regicide, was thus restored to sanctity: a process formalized when at the Restoration Charles was afforded the Anglican equivalent of a saint's day in the ecclesiastical year.

As the reign of Charles II progressed, however, the sanctified image of the monarchy became increasingly untenable. Although the ceremony of touching for the 'King's Evil' continued into the eighteenth century, the ideology of monarchy which underlaid it was eroded by the licentiousness, crypto-popery and cynicism of Charles II's court. Lucy Hutchinson equally articulates the crucial difference between the Restoration and Caroline courts when she remarks upon the moral improvement of Charles I's court from that of James; that 'King Charles was' despite his other faults 'temperate, chaste, and serious . . . and the nobility and courtiers, who did not quite abandon their debaucheries, yet so reverenced the king as to retire into corners to practise them'. The contrast with his son's libertine court could not be more marked, so that when Dryden set out in *Absalom and Achitophel* to state the conservative case against Exclusion his biblical parallel for Charles II, the Old Testament King David, had to be based upon David's promiscuity rather than (as the parallel had been used in his grandfather's day) upon David's sanctity as the psalmist.

> In pious times, ere priestcraft did begin,
> Before polygamy was made a sin; . . .
> Then Israel's monarch after Heaven's own heart,
> His vigorous warmth did variously impart
> To wives and slaves; and, wide as his command,
> Scattered his Maker's image through the land.
>
> (1–10)

Dryden's sophistic apologia for Charles II's sexual peccadilloes – that he imitated the Creator by making human beings 'in his own image' – is a rhetorical strategy which cannot conceal the damage Charles has done to the religious dignity of his office. In *The History of Insipids*' sarcastic address to this king as a 'true . . . Gods Viceregent', what conservative writers were disposed to see as Charles's providentially miraculous Restoration is seen as rather the nation's 'Curse and Punishment', because he is a travesty of the 'Chast, pious, [and] prudent' monarch. His attempts to implement religious toleration are portrayed as the result merely of a cynical atheism: 'Never was such a Faith's Defender', who 'Gives liberty to Conscience tender,/ And doth to *no* Religion tye us.' When the titular head and defender of the Church could be thus discredited, ecclesiastical deference to the monarchical state was the more damaging to Anglicanism's claim upon the hearts of his subjects.

II

Within this religio-political context we can begin to examine doctrinal differences, and their literary manifestations, more closely. Had there really been a sea change in religious attitudes by the end of the century? And if there had, did it amount to the disablement of religion as a major force in the history of this island and the minds of its people? I would suggest that changes did occur, but that contemporary witnesses overreacted to them, as people habitually do, because change produces fear. Yet these changes did not amount to a decisive disablement.

By 1700 the dominant religious ideology, in terms of the literate culture, was one of temperate rationalism expressing the principles of 'natural religion'. Thus the deistic John Toland's *Christianity Not Mysterious* (1696) insists that religion has now emancipated itself from superstition, and emerged into the high clear uplands of simple certainty. Religion is a matter not of faith but of knowledge. Indeed 'Faith *is* Knowledge', since religion does not require 'Assent to anything above Reason'. Toland's arguments essentially subordinate 'revelation', the scriptures and their authority, to a person's inner sense of what is true: 'Reason is not less from God than Revelation; 'tis the Candle, the Guide, the Judg he has lodg'd within every Man.' His words imply that Reason had now eclipsed or acquired the deity himself, who had customarily been described as the 'light of the world', 'the Guide', 'the Judge'. Statements of this kind in the works of prominent divines at the turn of the century look suspiciously like a claim for man's right to be his own god. In this sense extremes meet, for the sectaries had been accused of exactly this. Are both, or neither, to be regarded as 'irreligious'?

Locke also argued, in *The Reasonableness of Christianity* (1695), that God's existence was verifiable by reason, and that therefore the 'truth' of Christianity was a function of its reasonableness. This was an attempt to square religion with empiricism and 'enlightenment', and Locke is indifferent to doctrinal squabbles or denominational variety. On the one hand, this rationalist view tends to render most theological concerns as trivial, and hence might appear to erode the religious sense. On the other hand, Locke himself was in thrall to the eschatological ideas which, in an earlier manifestation, had fuelled millenarian fervour. Similar ideas had influenced the secularist Hobbes, even though *Leviathan* (1650) had been received with shock and dismay, as an impudently confident manifesto for atheism. And although Newtonian science depicted a mechanical universe, Newton himself was an eschatologist. The history of ideas is shockingly untidy, at least for those who love tidiness above all things.

Nor does the Restoration provide a watershed. The religious sense remains crucial in literature from Herbert at the beginning of our period to Bunyan after the king's return, and it is in the subsequent decades that those two great testaments to faith, *Paradise Lost* (1667) and *The Pilgrim's Progress* (1678–84), are published. In literary terms, then, the erosion of the theocentric view cannot be dated at 1660. Equally, the rationalist tendency of thought which is observable by 1700 has origins in, among other things, theological developments of the first half of the century. In the Restoration period literature, religion and rationalism are inter-involved in a manner which merges continuity with change.

In examining doctrinal development we must begin with Puritanism, and specifically with Calvinism. Calvinism is Augustinian in its emphasis upon the depravity of postlapsarian man, which he may escape only in the experience of 'conversion' from unregenerate (or 'natural') to spiritual man, living in Christ. This process is emphatically affective and irrational, for by a catalytic consciousness of sin the individual is reduced to a state best described (in our terms) as a nervous breakdown. From this nadir God rescues him by an act of grace, reviving the patient to a sense that he may indeed be one of those selected for salvation. This slow and painful progress is most memorably described in Bunyan's autobiographical *Grace Abounding to the Chief of Sinners* (1666). Written while Bunyan was incarcerated, *Grace Abounding* reveals that the only substantial prison is that of sin, and the only true liberty resides in voluntary submission to God's will. 'I never had in all my life so great an inlet into the Word of God . . . those Scriptures that I saw nothing in before, are made in this place and state to shine upon me; Jesus Christ also was never more real and apparent than now' (Section 321). His conversion was fully effective only when he recognized that the world was insubstantial, while Christ was 'real'. Conversion is an utter transformation in which the saint is brought 'to live upon God that is invisible' (326). Having recognized that this apparently irrational neglect of the world and of external realities is fundamental to a true faith, Bunyan brings his rational faculty into the service of faith's suprarational commitment: he 'reasoned with myself' that instead of fearing further persecution for his faith he must learn to live as if he were already dead – dead to the world (326). Whether or not God decided that Bunyan must undergo the ultimate penalty for his faith, 'I might not therefore choose whether I would hold my profession [of faith] or no: I was bound, but he was free' – the whole point of faith is that he does not act in expectation of reward. True freedom is liberation from self-interest, a launching of the spirit into eternity. Whatever happens 'I am for going on . . . I will leap off the ladder even blindfold into eternity, sink or swim . . . Lord Jesus, if you will catch me, do; if not, I will venture for thy name' (337). In this commitment to a liberty within God's will, the freedom from mere self-hood, Bunyan speaks for the very essence of the Puritan attitude. Certainly man must be rational, that being the dignity of Adam's race (*PL* VII: 505–10), but when reasoning became self-interested – as it would have done had Bunyan acted in the interests of self-preservation – it deteriorated into 'carnal reasonings', as Cromwell put it. Reason was a faculty bounded by postlapsarian limitations, for man was no longer capable of uncorrupted thought. In this Augustinian subordination of reason to faith, Puritanism was traditional in its emphasis.

Entrusting himself to God's will, Bunyan's commitment to 'venture' himself informs the narrative adventure of his *Pilgrim's Progress*, which adapts traditional romance narratives of the wandering or errant knight to the experience of the Christian who must be 'errand in the wilderness' of this world, the central metaphor of Puritan thought. That emphasis upon the resolved, isolated, and venturing saint, meeting both temptation and grace, exemplifies Puritan individualism and its rigorous demands upon the psyche. The reality of the psycho-spiritual realm, contradicting appearance, is formalized in Bunyan's allegorical method; while the psychological naturalism of Christian's encounters with such characters as Mr Worldly-Wiseman owes much to the acute psychological insights which the self-analysis of conversion encouraged, and which are reflected in Bunyan's autobiography. Indeed, the autobiographical genre is best served in this century by such writers as Bunyan and Richard Baxter, who in their different ways infuse it with Puritan affectivism and hence avoid the dangers of formlessness and tedium which are inherent in mere chronicle. A difference is immediately apparent in the autobiographical writings of Margaret, Duchess of Newcastle, wife of the royalist general, and Lucy Hutchinson. Whereas the former begins her self-justifying *Memoirs* with the bare chronicle of her patriarchal origin, 'My father was a gentleman . . .', Hutchinson's fragment begins with God – 'The Almighty Author of all beings' and director or their destinies, each human life a 'book of providence' like the Book of Nature or the Bible itself: so must biography be, in which the human author is concerned to articulate this divine author's shaping of events. This theocentric conception of writing at once reflects Puritan scripturalist reverence and provides a principle of literary structure. Equally, it liberates Lucy Hutchinson from a purely social definition of her identity in terms of her father and her husband, for the stress upon individual spiritual responsibility encouraged a surer sense of identity in Puritan women.

The literary repercussions of Puritanism were considerable. Insistence upon the 'plain sense' of scripture, and the avoidance of religious formalism or embellishment and elaboration in churches, are reflected in Puritan preaching style, which – in contradistinction to the witty complications and elaborate exegesis of Andrewes' High Anglican mode – favoured a vigorous directness designed for maximum communication to the auditor. Unless scriptural, metaphors are avoided and their rhetorical power substituted by that of resounding quasi-biblical phrases like 'the shaking of the nations' or 'Desolation and Reformation'. At its best, in the sermons of Thomas Temple or Stephen Marshall, this style attains poignancy and force. Its influence did not recede with the defeat of the Puritan cause. Whereas literary historians in particular tend to ascribe the unembellished prose of the post-Restoration sermon to the influence of Bacon and the Royal Society, it should also be remembered that in the propaganda war of the 1640s Puritan preachers had proved the more effective, and a sensitivity to that success may have played a role equal to that of more secular pressures in the fashioning of the favoured post-Restoration preaching style. Episcopalians learnt many useful if unpleasant lessons from their mid-century experience.

The influence of Baconian science was itself far from exclusively secular, since part of the impetus for scientific advancement in this century was provided by Puritans who – like many others – thought this to be the 'last age' of time, in which God would reveal the secrets of the natural world and enable men to control their environment. During the Interregnum such Cromwellian appointees as John Wilkins forwarded scientific studies in the universities, and such men were among the leading lights in the Royal Society. While Milton incorporated some of the new discoveries into the cosmography of *Paradise Lost*, some Puritans retained an Augustinian suspicion which is voiced in Marvell's diatribe against horticultural sciences as a tool of man's original sin of pride. Man's corruption, vitiating Nature by the Fall, now extends to a Faustian manipulation of her processes: still 'Man, that sov'raign thing and proud', seeks 'Forbidden mixtures' in the 'Tree' ('The Mower Against Gardens', 20–2). That note of doubt about scientific progress is neither exclusively Calvinist nor confined to the mid-century. In his adulatory address to the Royal Society in 1667 the conservative poet Abraham Cowley celebrates the defeat of scholastic 'Authority' by Baconian 'true reason', but refuses to identify 'that scarecrow deity' of Aristotelian scholasticism with religion itself. Nor had the Society managed to discredit the irrational attraction of alchemy, in which Newton, among others, dabbled. Earlier in the century, similarly, Paracelsian influence upon Samuel Hartlib had harnessed alchemical interests to the reforming projects canvassed in Parliamentarian circles. Evidently there was a dangerous tension in that alliance of scientific advance and political conservatism which was signified by Charles II's patronage of the Royal Society.

Nor did Newton differ from that earlier natural philosopher, the doctor Thomas Browne, in regarding scientific investigation as enhancing human perception of God's 'Book of Nature' (*Religio Medici* I: 48). In Browne's 'scientific' critique of popular superstitions, the issue of whether the first human beings possessed navels is referred both to obstetrics and to theology, evoking a spiritual meditation upon 'Adam's umbilicality even with God himself' (*Pseudodoxia Epidemica* V: 5). In the history of science's relation to religion in this period Browne is a piquantly transitional figure. The title of his *Religio Medici* (*RM*) challenges the contemporary assumption that doctors were atheists (otherwise how would they dare interfere with the bodily 'image of God'?). While it would be tempting to assume that a sceptical scientific tendency informs Browne's proponence of religious toleration – even of the dreaded Catholics – he evidently regards his resolute belief in witches as a cardinal index of his supernatural belief, since only 'Atheists' deny the existence of evil spirits (*RM* 1: 30). While he too believes that the world is approaching its end, he rejects Jacobean 'melancholy' and its gloomy insistence upon the world's decay (so evident in Donne's reaction to the 'new Philosophy') in favour of a faith in epistemological progress. Browne is aware that the spirit of scientific inquiry may lead to a dependence upon naturalist rather than supernaturalist explanations of phenomena, and that 'whilst I labour'd to raise the structure of my reason, [Satan] striv'd to undermine the edifice of my faith'. However, his recognition of man's increasing need to live in 'divided and distinguished worlds' informs his advice that, since faith is necessarily an irrational quantity, 'a moderate . . . discretion' will acknowledge that faith and reason operate in different categories of experience, each 'exercising his Soveraignty . . . in a due time and place' (*RM* I: 34; I: 19). In religious matters Browne is an enthusiastic exponent of Tertullian's apophthegm 'Certum est quia impossibile est'; whereby 'I can answer all the objections of . . . my rebellious reason' to the miraculous and enigmatic aspects of Christianity. Indeed, hereby Browne forges a link between the spirit of scientific enquiry and the questing theological sense, between mystery and reason: 'the deepest mysteries [our faith] containes, have . . . been . . . maintained by . . . the rule of reason: I love to lose myself in a mystery, to pursue my reason to an *o altitudo*' (*RM* I: 9).

In fact seventeenth-century conceptions of reason were not confined to the realm of science as distinct from religion but, rather, often developed within doctrinal contexts. While traditional Puritanism emphasized the rationality of simple religious doctrine and practice, given man's incapacity for definitive knowledge of 'unrevealed' matters, this could be linked by a monarchist Independent like Marvell to a diagnosis of England's elect role as a nation 'reasonable' in both religion and constitution (*An Account of the Growth of Popery* . . .). At the sectarian extreme of the spectrum, however, 'reason' was for the Digger Winstanley a ratification of man's dignity and liberty, his right to a socialist freedom on the model of primitive Christian communism. For him 'Reason' 'is truth and love and peace', not merely God's presence in man but coterminous with the Deity (*If Reason, king, do rule in thee* . . .). In this context reason signifies something approximate to 'humanity', and certainly some of the more radical religious thinkers of the Civil War period anticipate humane notions of legality, polity and social justice that we tend to regard as distinctly modern. Winstanley was a passionate advocate of certain basic human rights, for which it was metonymic that God 'made the earth to be a common treasury of livelihood to whole mankind without respect of persons' (*A New-Yeers Gift*, 1650). In 1662 Hester Biddle, a Quaker, demanded of a court notorious for wasteful excess, 'did not the Lord make all men and women upon the earth of one mould, why then should there be so much honour and respect unto some men and women, and not unto others, but they are almost naked for want of clothing, and almost starved for want of bread?' (*The Trumpet Of the Lord Sounded Forth*).

Between Calvinistic Puritanism and High Anglicanism lay the moderating humanist emphases of Cambridge Platonism, which, growing in Cambridge during the 1620s, under the guidance of Nicholas Ferrar found its home in a private community at Little Gidding. One of its exponents in the public sphere was Peter Sterry, a fine preacher and tolerant religionist, who became one of Cromwell's chaplains in 1650. Like many moderates, however, Ferrar's colleagues were susceptible to attack from both flanks. Many Puritans were suspicious of Little Gidding's formalist observance, and Calvinistic Cambridge Platonists, like Sterry, could not follow those of his colleagues who settled comfortably into latitudinarianism after the Restoration. At the other extreme, arcane hermeticists interested in alchemy and the cabbala – Thomas Vaughan, brother of the poet, for one – were too mystical in tendency for orthodox Cambridge Platonism: which, while assimilating the influence of Hermes Trismegistus' mystic books (see p. 10), balanced this element by an insistence that reason was 'the candle of the Lord', the very heart of religious experience. This mystical conception of reason, as the vessel of a godly enlightenment and access to revelation, narrowly avoided the ecstatic potential of Neoplatonism, and the aridity of rationalism, by regarding reason as a co-operation of will and feeling (or 'affect'). Thus Henry More, contesting Vaughan's proponence of magic with a rationalist argument, is vulnerable to Vaughan's riposte that More's is tantamount to a denial of the supernatural. Attempting to get out of this one by affirming his belief in demonic witchcraft, More thereby renders illogical his denial of white magic's efficacy – if black magic works, why not white?

This difficult and narrow course between the rational and the mystical appears to have an etiolating effect upon the literary products of the movement. While Sterry retains vigour, most of these range within a limited affective compass. The tedious doggerel of More's philosophical poems (a genre which outlived its uselessness) is equalled only by the predictable vapidities of Benlowes's staggeringly long *Theophila* (1652): a Neoplatonic allegory of the soul's ascent, stanza by stanza as it were, to God. Even when enthused by hermetic nature-worship and its 'soul's ecstasy', as also in Mildmay Fane's 'To Retiredness', this religious experience is drained of emotive power by poetic ineptitude. Only Henry Vaughan, influenced by Herbert as much as by hermeticism, seems able to modulate transcendent mysticism effectively. His own poem on 'The British Church' visibly reflects the distance between Herbert's 'plainness' and a hermeticist flavouring from *Canticles*. Whereas Herbert's poem articulates the 'joy in moderation' that he finds in Anglicanism, Vaughan's register is more hieratic and mystical in the Canticlean echo, 'My glorious head / Doth on those hills of myrrh, and incense watch' (3–4). That essential difference in these poets' use of scriptural models reveals why – despite his celebration of such 'idolatrous' features as church-windows, and his commitment to a liturgical framework for personal spiritual experience – Herbert's poetry was admired even by some Puritans. His ability to convey the affective spiritual dimension while retaining a scripturalist purity of diction and allusion, his insistence in *The Country Parson* upon the preacher's avoidance of rhetoric and elaboration in the service of effective communication with his flock – all render him more sympathetic to the Puritan consciousness than the arcana of hermeticism and the philosophical interests of Cambridge Platonism.

These interests, and its affective deficiencies, may explain the contribution of Cambridge Platonism to the growth of rationalism and its tendency ultimately to subvert religion into utilitarianism. Some of the most prominent Restoration divines, like Tillotson and Wilkins (flatly described by Pepys as a Latitudinarian), were heirs of Cambridge Platonism. Prefacing John Wilkins's *Of the Principles and Duties of Natural Religion* (1675), Tillotson clearly manifests the utilitarian tendency inherent in this doctrine when he remarks that wise men will be convinced of religion once it is impressed upon them that 'Religion and Happiness, our Duty and our Interest, are really but one and the same.' This worldly inducement to belief is like a negative image of Bunyan's expression of the Puritan (and Augustinian) conviction that self-'Interest' is actually the negation of self, liberty consisting in God's will. Rationalized, reduced and dulcified along utilitarian lines, this form of religion allows the spiritual realm to disappear into the material. When religion's defenders were so anxious to relinquish their ground to common sense and pragmatism under the name of 'reason', it is no wonder that the spiritual power of religion receded before the forces of sceptical rationalism. The Lockean attempt to assimilate religion to 'reasonableness' was effectively to disable religion by ignoring the irrationality of faith, which is fundamental to it. The Restoration regime's attack upon dissent as 'enthusiasm' allied Anglicanism with forces which denied imagination, inspiration and emotional commitment in their religious manifestations. The consequent affective vacuum in established Anglicanism can be measured by the popular response to the Methodist Revival in the eighteenth century. In contrast, the way in which religious 'enthusiasm' could release the literary imagination is evident in those cultural exiles of the Restoration period, Milton and Bunyan.

In this respect it is necessary to recognize that Puritanism was not, as it has often been assumed to be, opposed to the aesthetic. In the first half of the century Puritan criticism of the theatre was motivated largely by concern about social disruption by audiences whose rowdiness was perceived as comparable to that of modern football crowds, and by a moral objection to the libertinism of Cavalier comedy, which anticipated that of the Restoration stage. On the other hand, the dramatist Middleton benefited from Puritan patronage; Cromwell loved music, and concerts were regularly performed at his court; Milton saw his vocation as a poetic service to his God in which commitment to artistry was a prerequisite. In that respect there is nothing to choose between the aesthetics of Milton and Herbert, whatever their doctrinal differences.

But we do not need to consult Puritanism for the damaging effects of rationalism upon either the affective or the literary aspects of life in the late seventeenth century. Rochester – himself a libertine product of sceptical tendencies – sufficiently articulated both the folly and the cost of an unquestioning faith in 'Reason' in his 'Satyr Against Reason and Mankind' (c. 1675), a product of his insight that *in extremis* reason became a new Idol of the Tribe, of the kind which Baconian notions were supposed to dispel: 'an *ignis fatuus* in the mind' (12). However, for Anglican divines of the Tillotsonian stamp, if faith were to be transformed into 'Reasonableness' God must be made reasonable too: which required that not only the arbitrariness of predestination but also the rigour of eternal punishment must be abandoned. In the traditional concept hell was at once an 'actual' place of torment in the afterlife and a state of mind in which the sinner's wretchedness anticipated that future punishment. It has been claimed by some that after the Restoration Puritanism, forced by its marginalization into introspection, 'internalized' the heaven and hell which it had been accustomed to envisage as actual entities. But it has not been understood that Milton's 'paradise within thee, happier far' than the lost Eden (*Paradise Lost* XII: 587) is the spiritual anticipation, within the converted saint, of the millennial 'new heavens and new earth' (Revelation 21), which 'Shall all be paradise, far happier place / Than this of Eden'(*PL* XII: 464–5). This conception of spiritual reward as at once internal and external, available here and hereafter, was reflected in the traditional notion of hell's punishment as well, and in this duality the sixteenth-century Marlowe is echoed by Milton. Within *Doctor Faustus*'s soul 'Hell strives . . . with grace', for 'Hell hath no limits . . . where we are is hell'; while Milton's Satan states flatly that 'My self am hell' (*PL* IV: 75). Where emphases on hell did alter in the late seventeenth century was among rationalist divines, who sought to deny the notion of eternal torment by emphasizing rather the notion that 'hell' consisted merely in the groanings of conscience in this life. Yet even in the eighteenth century traditionalist believers like Samuel Johnson were resisting this mitigation of religion's minatory aspect. A similar debate remained in force on the topic of witchcraft, for which the last conviction as a capital offence occurred in 1712. Wesley, for instance, reasserted the once common tenet that belief in demons was a cardinal point of faith. Before condemning seventeenth-century demonology as uniformly purblind, we must call to mind such works as *The Witch of Edmonton* by Dekker, Ford and Rowley (1621: pub. 1658) in which it is made clear that the witch was initially an innocent scapegoat of communal fear and distress, and that her pact with the devil is her form of protection and retaliation against her community's preconception that she *is* a witch. Especially in religious matters, the seventeenth-century mind is often more acute and discriminating than it is generally assumed to be. Equally, in the conception of hell – as in other issues – the process of 'dulcification' in later decades originated in ideas active in the first half of the century, in this case those of the Cambridge Platonists.

While it would be erroneous to see Puritan thought as generally more 'introverted' in doctrinal matters after the Restoration, it was natural that in the face of rigorous exclusion and persecution (no 'dulcification' in the Anglican Church in this respect!) both traditional Puritans and sectarians turned with renewed devotion to their central myth, that of a permanent spiritual 'warfare' against the forces of darkness and oppression. Embodied most effectively in the New Model Army during the Civil War, this galvanizing militancy became, after the imposition of the Clarendon Code (1661–5), the backbone of dissenting resistance. Just as Bunyan saw his obstinate refusal to refrain from preaching as similar in kind to apostolic persistence under the Judaeo-Roman persecution, so George Fox was unflagging in his certainty that persecution (whether by Protectorate or Restoration regimes) merely confirmed his missionary status. His *Journal* begins with the determinative proposition of the work, that it will describe 'the various exercises, trials, and troubles through which [God] led me, in order to prepare and fit me for the work unto which He had appointed me'. Like Bunyan's Christian, he begins his spiritual journey by cutting himself off from family and friends, leaving familiarity behind in order to fashion himself into the 'stranger in a strange land' (Exodus 2: 22): he who is estranged from the world by experiencing the true reality which is godliness. The life of the itinerant preacher is for both writers (despite Bunyan's hostility to Quakerism) an enactment of godly 'wayfaring' and 'warfare'. In both cases this isolationism is intended to serve an ultimately communal experience of godliness: the pilgrimage of Christian is recapitulated in the familial and communal pilgrimage of *Pilgrims Progress II*, and Quakerism becomes the Society of Friends. But that initial alienation from the world is for Fox a consequence of the decision to become 'fools for Christ's sake', impervious to worldly counsels so that in godliness 'we might become truly wise'. This divorce from the canons of worldly wisdom, pragmatism and common sense in favour of a different order of being is obviously refined and strengthened by an atmosphere of persecution (and, it may be, by an antagonistic rationalism). Certainly in the early 1660s Quakers abandoned their militarily and politically active profile of the 1650s in favour of pacificism, but political quietism is not equivalent to religious introversion. Ideals remained, as for Milton too, but their affective force was redoubled as political means dwindled. Something like the heterodox Quaker insistence upon the possibility of recuperating original innocence is evinced in Thomas Traherne's ecstatic poems, in which a spiritual return to childhood effects a recognition of and *rencontre* with the true self, at once pristine and all encompassing:

> little did the Infant dream
> That all the Treasures of the World were by.
> And that himself was so the Cream
> And Crown of all which round about did ly
>
> ('News', 43–6)

Despite its moments of Blakean power, however, Traherne's mystical verse is reminiscent of the limitations of earlier hermetic-mystic poetry in its resolute disjunction from reality. As Milton's militant stance towards the world exemplifies, the Puritan spirit could not countenance so complete a withdrawal from the realm of action. Apart from any other element, it is this commitment to life in the world (rather than *of* the world) which informs the vitality of the great Puritan epic, in contrast to the recessive *Theophilas* of this period. Equally, the spiritual distinction between Traherne and Herbert has much to do with the earlier poet's transmutation of the mundane, from the biblically inspired legal and commercial imagery of 'Redemption' to the sweeping of 'The Church-floore'. Whether High Anglican or Puritan in origin, the best religious writings of this period are those which integrate the spiritual life with the earthly conditions of its existence.

The difference between Herbert and Traherne in this respect has nothing to do with their relative chronological setting or the menace of an impinging rationalism. Mystic escape from the world is a traditional strand of Christian thought, especially when admixed with Neoplatonism. Throughout the seventeenth century the theme of solitudinous meditation and contemplation is enshrined in poems of hortulan retirement, ranging from Fane's earnest naturist ecstasy to Marvell's witty treatment of Christian *contemptus mundi* in 'The Garden', where 'Society is all but rude, / To this delicious Solitude'. In contrast, the Cavalier tradition preferred the 'country-house poem' genre as inherited from Jonson's celebration of ancient moral and social virtues, symbolized by rural estates like *Penshurst*. That poem's proponence of Christian charity and fellowship is recalled in Herrick's 'A Country Life', but most oddly imitated – because infused with the more familiar libertine emphases of Cavalierism – by Carew's 'To Saxham', where the beauties of house and garden evoke the poet's erotic disappointment that 'I might not all thy pleasures know'. The hollow ring of this Jonsonian exercise is not unusual in the context of Charles I's exile of his gentry to their country estates, and Fanshawe's 'Ode' upon the proclamation of 1630 is evidently making a virtue of necessity: 'Nor let the Gentry grudge to goe / Into those places whence they grew, / But thinke them blest they may doe so' (81–3). That sense that the pastoral garden is 'blest' is more convincingly represented in the tradition which informs

Marvell's 'Garden', that God himself was the first 'skilful Gard'ner'; and that in the creation of an earthly garden and the contemplation of its beauties one might recapture an Edenic innocence while imitating God's own great action. Husbanding a garden was an active emulation of God's nurturing of world and spirit. Equally, the poet who celebrated hortulan experience imitated both the creative and the authorial functions of the deity, while reciprocating his gifts in emblem and in praise. (In Milton's epic, indeed, such resonances combine with the Puritan emphasis upon action to make Adam and Eve gardeners, Edenic workers.) This fusion of Christian and classical traditions, supported by the meditative habits encouraged in popular emblem-books such as those of Quarles and Wither, reflects also the belief that the frequenting of gardens could be spiritually improving. In John Evelyn's *Sylva* and its appended essay, originally written for the Royal Society, this hortulan philosophy is readily merged with a manifesto for the scientific improvement of horticulture.

Evelyn's devout eclecticism recognizes no antagonism between the Society's aims and the fundamentals of his religion, for to him a scientific academy would ideally represent a modern extension of Solomon's glorification of God by means of natural philosophy. In this manner Evelyn's millenarian Baconianism contributed to a Society which, as its first historian and major apologist indicates, was not totally unaware of its own sceptical implications. According to Sprat, 'The true and certain interest of our Church is to derive its doctrine from . . . the Scripture expounded by reason'; therefore it need fear nothing from an equally rationalizing and reforming science, as long as it is mindful of its limitation to rational exegesis of only the 'unquestion'd parts' of Scripture, 'and to keep itself in due submission to the civil magistrate'. In other words, religion is safe as long as it commits itself to an erastian and rationalist alliance of which the monarch, patron of the Society and head of the Church, is the linchpin. In this declaration of the conservative hegemony of progress the common enemy is explicitly identified as 'The extremes [of] implicit faith and enthusiasm'. Of this political definition and rationalist proscription of 'faith' such devout men as Evelyn were ironic agents.

III

At this point significant continuities and alterations in the relationship between doctrinal issues and individual experience can be focused by a juxtaposition of the apparently 'personal' genres of biography and autobiography with the seemingly 'public' mode of satire. In the religious context neither is quite what it seems.

Evelyn did not devote himself wholly to works of natural philosophy, expressing his religious preoccupations more directly in his *The History of Religion* and his spiritual biography, *The Life of Mrs Godolphin*. While

Puritanism best expressed its affective individualism in autobiography, Anglican biography tended to address the same objective: the communication of an exemplary religious experience. The Baptist Bunyan and the Quaker Fox both open their 'journals' with the assertion that each is a case-history whereby God's glory 'may be the more advanced and magnified before the sons of men'. Similarly, Herbert's *The Temple* is a didactic analysis of spiritual development by means of personal history enacted within a liturgical framework. His readers responded appropriately, for throughout the century *The Temple* was regarded almost as a contemporary scripture, subsuming devotional and aesthetic edification and delight. Hagiographical devotion to the poet, as exemplified in Izaak Walton's *Life of Herbert* (1670), and the use of *The Temple* as catechistical reading in private households, testifies to the popular survival of a more traditional religious bent than that favoured by ecclesiastical utilitarianism. To such paradigmatic religious significance Evelyn's spiritual biography also aspires, its introduction culminating in the express hope that 'the reader [might] in a better day learn in secret, for himself, those lessons of heavenly wisdom which adorned the life and glorified the death of Margaret Godolphin', who died at the age of 26, but according to Evelyn was already saintly at the age of 7!

Despite this broad similarity across the denominations in the didactic designs of biographical writing, the publication in 1680 of Bishop Burnet's *Some Passages in the Life and Death of John Earl of Rochester* marks a signal change in the ambience of such works. The difference between the deathbed chronicle of the notoriously atheistic Rochester and that in 1648 of the deist Lord Edward Herbert of Cherbury, brother of George, is instructive. Anticipating eighteenth-century deism, Edward Herbert sought to refine religious belief to 'the most certaine and unfallible Principles' and found these in the five common denominators of all known religions. These boil down to little more than that there is a God and that 'there is reward and punishment both in this life and after it'. While this hardly forms a body of doctrine, and is incapable of generating much spiritual gratification, in its day it was naturally regarded as offensively close to atheism. According to Aubrey's *Brief Lives*, on his deathbed Lord Herbert, deciding it might be better to be safe than sorry, sent for Bishop Ussher because 'he would have received the sacrament [but] The Primate refused it, for which many blamed him'. Lord Herbert managed to expire 'very serenely' none the less. By 1680 the deathbed repentance of a famous libertine demanded very different treatment by the attendant bishop, for in accepting and endorsing Rochester's conversion Burnet could trumpet this admonitory example to what he regarded as a sceptical society. He claims that Rochester himself, unable at this fatal juncture to express the sincerity of his conversion in good works, insisted that to supply this deficiency Burnet must advertise his case as a reforming example to others. The value of such advertisement is explicit in Burnet's assertion that 'my only design [in this] writing . . . is doing what I can towards the reforming a loose and lewd age' by this 'signal instance'. While debate over the efficacy of a deathbed repentance extended well into the next century, it is evident that those ecclesiastics who professed certainty of it in Rochester's case often did so in consciousness of its polemical value at a time when religion required defence. Such a motive was not so pressing in Lord Herbert's day.

In essence the polemical or didactic intention of this biographical mode is similar to that of satire, the major post-Restoration literary genre. Both are ultimately 'public' in address, but equally each expresses in its own way a personal interaction with society. In their relation to religious experience the similarity is very striking. Of the Restoration ambience Marvell remarks that 'the times are something criticall' (Letter to Mayor Shires, 21 October 1675) referring at once to current religio-political crises and to the satirical temper. It is a common if often implicit assumption that the literary dominance of satire after 1660 reflects a sceptical society. However, it can be argued that, while satirical raillery may express the reproof of folly by 'reason', the dignity of the satirical mode was defended by Dryden and others rather on moral grounds, that its purpose is 'to avert men from vice and incline them to virtue'. In that sense satire assumed its place within the tradition of edificatory aesthetics exemplified by Sidney in his *Defence of Poetry* (1595), and is broadly comparable to Dryden's 'improving' essays in the heroic drama or Milton's objectives in his epic. In such a view the major Restoration satirists – including Rochester, who defended satire as a corrective operation against the worst of men – are not far from the Ciceronian moralism of Ben Jonson's satirical works or the obliquities of Jacobean tragedies such as *The White Devil*, where evil is rendered ridiculous. The point is not merely that faith and satire are not necessarily contraindicative, but rather that in the Restoration they are signally conjoined in John Oldham and Andrew Marvell. Marvell's Restoration satires in prose and verse maintain his Puritan reformist concerns of the 1650s; Oldham's nonconformist background earths his sense of poetic vocation and fuels his use of satiric invective, whether in his *Satyrs upon the Jesuits* or on other topics. Indeed, it is probable that the congeniality for Oldham of the Juvenalian satiric mode consisted precisely in its approximation to that tradition of religious invective (drawn from such biblical models as the fulminations of 2 Timothy) of which Quakers had made such effective use in the 1650s. Yet Oldham was conscious enough of his marginal existence in Restoration society, seeking for the accommodation of faith and reason in contradistinction to 'the mere fanatics, and enthusiasts in poetry, / (For schismatics in that, as in religion be)' ('Upon the works of Ben Jonson'). There is a complex irony in this observation, for it was the libertine Rochester whom Oldham would criticize as 'unreasonable', rather than the dissenters, or 'fanatics' (as they had come to be called). Nevertheless, a sensitivity to accusations of 'enthusiasm', evoked by his nonconformity, naturally made for a tension in Oldham's aesthetic formulations for the satiric voice of faith. His problem is one of expression within an atmosphere hostile to dissent in particular, against which Marvell indeed insisted upon the 'reasonableness' of his 'true religion'. What he meant by that was something at a great distance from the fashionable rationalist tendency in Anglicanism, but in a Puritan sense it was accurate enough, and the stylistic restraint with which his assertion is articulated is precisely intended to address an age suspicious of passion in the religio-political sphere. In contrast to Oldham's emotive satirical style, Dryden's no less committed 'faith in satire' is eventually matched by his authoritarian religious stance in Catholicism. Restoration satire, then, is no less illustrative of the religious spectrum than was the mid-century's contrast between the baroque sensibility of Crashaw – who moved from High Anglicanism to Catholicism – and the direct simplicity of Winstanley's prose.

If the dominant culture was hostile to religious passion, it compensated with the sexual libertinism of the court. To rationalism Rochester opposed a different species of materialism, sensual or epicurean 'right reason'. Given the similarly libidinous if, in philosophical terms, more traditional spirit of pre-war Cavalier love-lyrics, it is tempting to see post-Restoration courtly libertinism as a liberation from Puritan prudery. In this too Puritanism and the Cromwellian regime have sometimes been misrepresented. Although it is true that female adultery became for the first time a capital offence in 1650, we have reason to believe that such social legislation was rarely implemented. More significantly, as against the fundamentally exploitative sexual attitudes of Suckling's and Carew's lyrics, the Puritan attitude to the spiritual dignity of women in godly marriage seems distinctly more attractive. Colonel Hutchinson was initially drawn to Lucy by her learning; the difference between her awareness of self-definition and that of the Duchess of Newcastle was, as we saw, instructive. Puritan influence helped, in the 'conduct-books' which dispensed advice, to stress the necessity of real marital affection as opposed to that materialist and contractual view of marriage which was the aristocratic norm. For Puritanism reckoned marriage both a sexual and a spiritual issue, incompatibility damaging equally the legitimate pleasures of the conjugal bed and the spiritual amelioration provided by godly partnership. Milton took the argument further, in order to press the case for divorce. In this light we can see how his poem liberated sex from its proscription by the more ascetic vein of Christian tradition. In *Paradise Lost* Eden comprehends sensuous delights (IV: 206); nakedness is juxtaposed with hypocrisy and prurience, 'dishonest shame / Of natures works' (313–14); and Adam and Eve enjoy the pleasures of sex,

> Whatever hypocrites austerely talk
> Of purity and place and innocence,
> Deforming as impure what God declares
> Pure . . .
> Perpetual fountain of domestic sweets,
> Whose bed is undefiled and chast pronounced.
>
> (*PL* IV: 744–61)

In such a view the point is that sexual joy, available in a happy marriage, is denied to courtly libertinism: 'not in the bought smile/ Of harlots, loveless, joyless, unendeared, / Casual fruition . . . in court amours' (765–7). When balancing either Cavalier or extreme sectarian proponence of complete sexual liberty against the traditional Puritan stress upon 'wedded love' as the context for sexual enjoyment, we should remember that in the absence of reliable contraceptive methods sexual freedom was really limited to the male. Women alone paid the price of libertinism. It is no accident that nonconformist and Whig attitudes to Charles II's court often associated its libertine features with its repressive and 'popish' tendencies.

Christian doctrine had traditionally derogated women, the guilty descendants of guilty Eve. There was no more spectacular example of male hegemony than the Church. But the growth of sectarianism had provided new opportunities for women's self-expression. Already women had been prominent in the Anabaptist and Familist movements, and in the 1630s the deranged prophetess Lady Eleanor Davies had made her mark at court. Among other things she had predicted the assassination of Charles I's favourite, the Duke of Buckingham. During and after the Civil War, however, female sectarians from humbler backgrounds became a voluble presence. Some were itinerant preachers, a vocation particularly favoured by the Quaker repudiation of Pauline strictures against women's right to speak in religious contexts (1 Corinthians 14: 34). In 1667 Margaret Fell (who married Fox in 1669) would summarize the arguments against Paul in her *Womens Speaking Justified*: 'God hath put no such difference between the Male and Female as men would make', and 'God hath said, that his Daughters should prophesie as well as his Sons.' Convinced that God required her to preach in New England for the Quakers' sake, Alice Curwen was prepared to abandon her husband and family if need be. More public, mass action was taken by those women petitioners to parliament who protested against the imposition of tithes, and at the incarceration of the Leveller John Lilburne. The prophetess Anna Trapnel also made a public intervention for her Fifth Monarchist colleagues when they were imprisoned for sedition. She could not fail to attract attention, for when in a state of trance, she would pour forth prophecies in verse.

Such a rapid surge in women's activities was possible only because some sectarian theologies asserted the spiritual equality of men and women. Women could also, like Alice Curwen, claim that inspiration demanded their autonomous activity, and defy their husbands. Traditionally regarded as intuitive and hysterical creatures, women the more easily assumed the role of involuntary prophetic eloquence, and could excuse their 'forwardness' by appeal to a power higher than any earthly authority. Of course, prophetesses offended and alarmed conservatives, who frequently complained in popular pamphlets that any old London fishwife now felt able to pronounce on matters of national importance. In this sentiment royalists were joined by many Puritan writers whose misogyny must be read to be believed. That same ignoble impulse had once added savour to attacks on Charles I's 'popish' consort, and still enjoyed itself most in lipsmackingly lubricious rants against the 'Scarlet Whore' of popery. Perhaps the most telling example of the kind of theological logic involved in the misogynist position is provided by John Leake, a Lincolnshire cleric ejected by parliament for persistent immorality. He had attempted to argue one woman into bed on the basis that, as women did not possess souls, fornication afforded no spiritual problems. Clearly the sexual casuistries of John Donne were not witty fantasies, but strictly functional! Or rather, they expressed in accomplished literary form the excesses of wish-fulfilment to which misogynist theology had always been prone.

That had not changed by the end of the century. It was the insulting misogyny of a sermon by John Sprint, a nonconformist, which provoked Mary Lee (1656–1710) into writing a satiric dialogue, *The Ladies Defence*, and Sarah Fyge Egerton wrote her *The Female Advocate* (1686) in answer to Robert Gould's poem, *A Late Satyr Against the Pride, Lust and Inconstancy of Women* (1683). Egerton pours scorn on

> my Antagonist's Fancy, that all Men are Good, and fitting for Heaven, because they are Men; and Women irreversibly Damn'd, because they are Women: But that Heaven should make a Male and Female, both of the same Species, both indued with the like rational Souls, for two such differing Ends, is the most notorious Principle, and the most unlikely that ever was maintain'd by any rational Man; and I shall never take it for an Article of my Faith.

One consequence of women's disaffection with male religious attitudes, and the deficiency of their educational opportunities, was a return to Catholic models: in the 1630s Lady Lettice had considered establishing a 'female retreat', a kind of Protestant nunnery, to foster learning and religion, and Mary Astell's *A Serious Proposal to the Ladies* (1694) proposed a similar cloistered freedom from the interference of men. The tradition of Christian retirement had become a vehicle for female separatism.

For women, then, the consequences of religious controversy were paradoxical. On the one hand, sectarianism inspired many women and enlarged their sphere of activity, with such literary consequences as the distinctive genre of 'confessions' produced by incarcerated Quaker women. After the Restoration Martha Simmonds, Dorothy White and Elizabeth Redford, all Quakers, were among those publishing theological tracts. Nor was the liberating capacity of religion limited to the left wing. More conservative religionists, most significantly Mary Astell, also wrote extensively on theological questions and engaged in lively topical debate. The number of women writers in this period has generally been underestimated precisely because such a significant proportion of their works was theological, and largely forgotten because of the modern distaste for their subject-matter. This is particularly true of conservative women's writings. Yet, whether conservative or radical, women writers were emancipated by religious opportunity: God's authority for writing provided a bulwark against male criticism of their presumption. Thus in *A Treatise of Magistracy* Mary Pope, a loyalist, asserted that she had 'good warrant out of God's word' to express her opinions about government. On the other hand, male criticism could always fall back upon the traditional religious justifications of patriarchy. As Lee and Egerton had insisted, no man congratulating himself on rationality should be allowed to enjoy such a prejudice, and sometimes rationalism could indeed forestall misogyny. John Locke was prepared to engage in a spirited correspondence with Elizabeth Burnet, wife of the bishop, about his *Reasonableness of Christianity*.

If we regard the gradually rationalist trend of the dominant culture and established religion within a purview of late seventeenth-century literature, the damage inflicted by the proscription of 'enthusiasm' is evident. Apart from Dryden and Rochester – the latter a passionate materialist and then a convert, never a mainstream rationalist – the finest writers of this period, outside the drama, were the 'fanatics' Milton, Bunyan, Marvell and Oldham. For the conservative alliance against enthusiasm Cowley praised Hobbesian 'Reason' as 'like the Shield from Heaven' (70), impervious to assault; whereas for Bunyan such 'security' is the great spiritual enemy, which 'Atheists' and sectarian extremists equally 'use to help themselves withal' (*Grace Abounding*, 161) and 'security, blindness, darkness, and error' form a spectrum of comfortable evils (162). It is possible to take Bunyan's point, not least in the sense that an unquestioning faith in human capacity for rational judgement, and the complacency consequent thereon, are at once contraindicative of spiritual energy and unhelpful to literary creativity. By the late seventeenth century 'fanaticism', 'enthusiasm' and 'imagination' were interchangeable terms.

FURTHER READING

Claire Cross, *Church and People 1450–1660* (London, 1976).
I.M. Green, *The Re-Establishment of the Church of England, 1660–1663* (Oxford, 1978).
M. Heinemann, *Puritanism and Theatre* (Cambridge, 1980).
K.V. Henderson and B.F. McManus, *Half Humankind: Contexts and Texts of the Controversy about Women in England, 1540–1640* (Urbana, Ill., 1985).
C. Hill, *The World Turned Upside Down: Radical Ideas During the English Revolution* (London, 1972).
J.P. Kenyon, *The Popish Plot* (Harmondsworth, 1972).
W.M. Lamont, *Godly Rule: Politics and Religion 1603–1660* (London, 1969).
B.K. Lewalski, *Protestant Poetics and the Seventeenth-Century Religious Lyric* (Princeton, NJ, 1979).
W.F. Mitchell, *English Pulpit Oratory from Andrewes to Tillotson* (London, 1932).
J. Morrill, 'The religious context of the English Civil War', *Transactions of the Royal Historical Society* 34 (1984).
C.A. Patrides (ed.), *The Cambridge Platonists* (London, 1969).
M. Stocker, *Apocalyptic Marvell: The Second Coming in Seventeenth-Century Poetry* (Sussex, 1986).
K. Thomas, *Religion and the Decline of Magic* (Harmondsworth, 1971).
H.R. Trevor-Roper, *The European Witch-Craze of the Sixteenth and Seventeenth Centuries* (Harmondsworth, 1969).
N. Tyacke, *Anti-Calvinists: The Rise of English Arminianism* (Oxford, 1987).
D.P. Walker, *The Decline of Hell* (Chicago, 1964).
C. Webster, *The Great Instauration: Science, Medicine and Reform 1626–1660* (London, 1975).

Chapter 4

The book of nature

Ken Robinson

> Nature and Nature's laws lay hid in night,
> God said: 'Let Newton be', and all was light.

Pope's witty celebration of the *fiat Newton* expresses a commonly held view of the development of scientific and philosophical thinking in the seventeenth century, the view that the century witnessed a quantum leap forward. Newton is not the only candidate for the role of the period's intellectual deliverer from ignorance and darkness. Abraham Cowley saw Francis Bacon, for example, as a Moses figure who had led forth his countrymen from the intellectual wilderness to 'the very border . . . of the blest promised land' which Newton went on to cultivate. Or there was Thomas Hobbes who, again in Cowley's words, had proved 'the great Columbus of the golden lands of new philosophy'. But whether the honours are accorded to Bacon, to Hobbes, or to Newton, to Galileo or to Descartes, the model is the same, one of sudden discontinuity born out of genius. The model is misleading. There is no doubt that Newton's *Principia* (1687) and *Opticks* (1704) were major landmarks, but their foundations were laid earlier. The archaeology of Newton's masterpieces would take us back not just to Descartes, Bacon and Galileo but to, for example, Nicholas of Cusa's assertion of infinity and the gradual rediscovery of the major texts of Greek mathematicians and science in the medieval and Renaissance periods. Or, to take another example, when the sceptical chemist Robert Boyle played a prime part in establishing matter as the proper sphere of physical investigation and in exploding the medieval notion that qualities can be regarded as entities, he drew on the work of both the early atomists and, odd as it may seem, the work of the alchemists who had bequeathed to the seventeenth century not only a body of empirical knowledge but also a methodological emphasis on hands-on experience. The western world's way of perceiving the world did not change suddenly on 10 November 1619 when Descartes realized the full significance of mathematics for man's knowledge of the natural world, nor in the autumn of 1665 in Newton's garden at Woolesthorpe when he supposedly recognized that there was a special providence in the fall of an apple; the change is part of a complex map of shifting conceptual perspectives. What is more, the unquestioned scientific geniuses of the past did not any more than those of the present voyage 'through strange seas of thought alone', as Wordsworth thought Newton to have done (and as Hobbes had according to Cowley). The intrepid deliverers and explorers drew on a context in which others pursued similar ends. Bacon's emphasis on the importance of co-operation in scientific endeavour played a significant role in the formation of the group of virtuosos which began meeting at Gresham College in London around 1645, of John Wilkins's Philosophical Society which met at Wadham College in Oxford from 1648, and of the Royal Society itself. Such groups provided a network of connections with fellow thinkers. Their stimulus could be supplemented through often extensive and international correspondence or through working in partnership. Newton was indebted in his *Principia* not simply to those who in both the distant and recent past had helped lay the necessary foundations for his achievements. He owed much, too, to co-workers like Robert Hooke (even if his relationship with Hooke did become acrimonious), to Huygens and to Leibniz who shared with Newton the distinction of working on a differential calculus. It may have taken someone of Newton's mathematical originality to find the answer to basic questions about celestial motion, but the questions had been focusing for some time.

If what might be called the 'Newton's apple model' of development needs qualification, so does the idea that the period saw a steady development in its scientific and philosophical thinking. If generally speaking the period became more empirically minded as it moved on, the new empiricism did not simply supersede earlier modes of thought. Old and new rubbed shoulders together in often extraordinary ways. Joseph Glanvill who rewrote his *Vanity of Dogmatizing* (1661) as *Scepsis Scientifica* in 1665 to bring its style more into line with the new mathematical plainness of expression appropriate to treatises by members of the Royal Society, clung on to a belief in witchcraft, as did Sir Thomas Browne who was otherwise keen to spot vulgar errors. Newton himself devoted enormous energy and time to arcane theological speculations. New ideas are assimilated slowly, even by intellectuals. It can take considerable time for older ways of seeing the world to be discarded once they have been theoretically deconstructed. There is no better example of the slowness with which truly radical thinking finds acceptance than Copernicus's displacing of the Ptolemaic view of the earth as the centre of a finite universe in favour of a heliocentric and infinite universe. If it had its learned adherents, like Thomas Digges in the sixteenth century and John Wilkins in the seventeenth century, there were also those less enthusiastic. Sir Thomas Browne sat on the fence, while Burton kept counsel and Milton, who met and admired Galileo, contrasted the old and new cosmologies in *Paradise Lost* as unfallen and fallen respectively. In

1661 Glanvill could remark that though he and others 'of the learned world' accepted the Copernican, the rabble took it as 'proverbial' that 'the Earth rests as the world's centre, while the heavens are the subject of the universal motions'. Not until 1692 could Richard Bentley announce confidently in his Boyle Sermons that 'we do now generally believe the Copernican system'. Glanvill's swipe at the 'proverbial' wisdom of the rabble is a timely reminder that even Bentley's 'we' was an educated elite. It is difficult to be sure what assumptions the illiterate and silent majority lived by, even though we might want to stress that the prevailing ways of seeing and structuring the world do not find their expression in learned treatises alone but are inscribed across the whole range of discourses. English historiography has not produced for the seventeenth century any equivalent to Ladurie's *Montaillou*.

If these two models do not work, how else should we view the period? We might attempt to synthesize the models, or we might try a more radical approach. Traditionally, accounts of the course of scientific and philosophical ideas in the seventeenth century have tended to assume that we see in the period a movement towards a generally correct modern scientific thinking, towards, that is, objective empirical science. Its method is to employ objective observation to establish facts which various theories offer explanations for, theories on which are founded testable predictions which can be evaluated through experiment. Science, on this view, develops by building up neutral observations with their confirmed hypotheses. Its end is to advance towards more and more inclusive theories. This method is, however, no longer the unchallenged received view of modern science. Relativity theory, Heisenberg's Uncertainty Principle and current advances in particle physics have led recent philosophers of science to de-emphasize the objectivity of scientific observation and to think about observation instead as theory-laden. Science is perceived now not as the pursuit of the Truth but as concerned with problem-solving within the context of an agreed theory. What is seen, even what is taken as fact, is determined by the theory with which the observer operates. At any point of its history science depends upon a community of scientists who share a language and premises, a model according to which they structure not just their activities as scientists but their conception of the world. If we take this view back to the course of seventeenth-century thought, we can understand the century's development not as a progression towards empirical objectivity but as a process in which one interpretative model replaces another and one conception of reality gives way to an alternative. We do not have to limit this approach to strictly scientific and philosophical thinking; it covers all knowledge, all discourses. The question of whether the march of seventeenth-century thought is marked by discontinuity and continuity is itself a product of an evolutionary model of intellectual enquiry. The idea of a model or paradigm places its emphases differently. It frees us to look at seventeenth-century thought not in terms of evolution but in terms of the transition from one major conceptual framework to another, at the strategies employed to keep models intact in the face of new data and at the way in which models have social and political as well as intellectual power.

The two different conceptual perspectives, or, to appropriate a once fashionable term, different *Weltanschauung*, which mark the century share a common image, the image of nature as a book that can be read and understood by humans exercising their reasoning powers. What distinguishes the perspectives is not that they offer different interpretations of the same book but that the book which they see is quite different. It is determined by their reading tools. On one view, which carries over from the Middle Ages to the Renaissance, the book is a remarkable tissue of correspondences or resemblances which require allegorical, mystical-religious reading; on the other it is written in the language of mathematics, not in the language of Pythagorean and Neoplatonic number symbolism which Renaissance architects had spatialized to embody in their creations the pristine harmonies of the music of the spheres, but in the new mathematics which sharply divided qualities from quantities and saw its province as the latter. Although the two perspectives provided alternative hermeneutic models, the empiricists thought of their activities not as interpretative but as observational and neutral; interpretation was left to the more subjective allegorists. Both books and both sets of readers are to be found throughout the seventeenth century, though the empirical book came to be more standard reading.

Let us look briefly at the earlier of the two conceptual frameworks. When George Herbert remarked that God's word is all if we could spell and searched for correspondences between man and nature, he assumed the world to be a heiroglyphic text everywhere marked with God's signature, a text that in the spring of faith and greenness people could read and a text that in the winter of doubts they might be unable to comprehend. When later in the century Sir Thomas Browne discovers the quincunx wherever he looks in the natural world, or Thomas Traherne sees the world in a grain of sand, they are reading the same book. In it is to be found a plethora of similitudes between apparently unrelated and seemingly discordant phenomena, patterns of symmetry on earth consonant with those in the heavens, sympathies between man and nature (whether planets, plants or animals). Man felt himself part of a symbolic world whose final cause was God. He even felt himself, as 'a little world made cunningly', to represent it. 'Is not the rhubarb found where the sun most corrupts the liver; and the scabies by the shore of the sea, that God might cure as soon as he wounds?' asks Jeremy Taylor in a mid-century sermon. If Taylor contributed to a more rational theology he had not shaken off the habit of mind which thinks in terms of resemblances – indeed South attacked him for his 'starched similitudes'. It is worth looking more closely at his mind at work. He sets up a two-fold resemblance. First, rhubarb and corrupt livers are connected geographically through location and medically through sympathy, and second their relation of disease to remedy is analogous to that between sinful man and God's mercy. If humans can read aright, they will see in the scabious the redemption that follows anger. But humans will never be able to fully comprehend, Taylor believes, because the number of God's mercies has no measure, 'for they that descend on us, we see and feel; but by what order of things or causes, is as undiscovered as the head of Nilus, or a sudden remembrance of a long-neglected and forgotten proposition'. It is not just the infinity of resemblances that makes readings of the book of nature necessarily partial; it is also that the clear propositions that Adam saw in the world before the fall are long-forgotten, reachable only through provisional interpretation. One embodiment of such interpretation is the emblem poem. In his *Collection of Emblems* (1635) George Wither celebrates a resemblance between the pelican and Christ, using as an emblem of the Christian sacrifice a picture of a pelican wounding its breast to feed its young with its blood. Below the picture are explanatory verses and above it the lines:

> Our pelican by bleeding thus
> Fulfilled the law and cured us.

Another and more remarkable expression of correspondence is the so-called metaphysical conceit. Samuel Johnson's famous complaint that the conceit 'yoked heterogeneous ideas by violence together' is the complaint of one habituated to empirical reading. For those whose book of nature was symbolic, for Jeremy Taylor who could see redemption in a stick of rhubarb, the correspondences were not in themselves ingenious though they required ingenious interpretation to be recognized. Sometimes, however, it can seem that the conceit is used not so much to celebrate heiroglyphic order as to deny disorder. Some of Donne's poetry might be read as attempting to assert resemblance, to hang on to the received *Weltanschauung* in a world in which 'new philosophy calls all in doubt'; or later Dryden's outrageously baroque treatment of smallpox pustules as 'the cabinet of a richer soul within' in his elegy on the death of Lord Hastings, his first printed poem, in 1648, might be taken to represent an unconvincing, if understandable, claim that there is a symbolic beauty in the foulest of deaths. For those who had already begun to read a different book, like Cowley, the conceit could be no more than decorative.

This earlier conceptual perspective allows room for many different inflections, influences and exponents; but whether Neoplatonists, Neo-Aristotelians, Paracelsians, or whatever, they share not only the fundamental belief in resemblances but also a sense of the world as inextricably physical, moral and divine. Theology and science were traditional bedfellows. The world was studied to understand its purpose, with God as its final cause. The perspective was also highly eclectic. It may seem odd to modern eyes that rational discussion of the physical world can exist side-by-side in seventeenth-century texts with massive classical erudition and more mystical and magical interests. It may seem that writers so eminently intelligent should have known better. But for the contemporary mind there was no contradiction. The mind equipped to search out the meaning of signs in the physical world as part of a system of resemblances could just as easily be turned to the Bible or to the works of classical antiquity, to, for example, its typology and its mysteries. The task and the reading skills were fundamentally the same.

In a famous passage from his *Essay Concerning Human Understanding* (1690) John Locke distinguishes between wit and judgement. The province of wit is facile resemblances while in the realm of judgement the power of differentiation holds sway. The distinction marks out the nature of the fundamental shift from one *Weltanschauung* to another. Whereas the earlier interpretative model approached the world as a unified thesaurus of correspondences and affinities in which part parallelled part and part symbolized whole, the alternative model sought not to unify but to take apart, to distinguish part from part and to discover the taxonomies and laws that order the whole. Moreover, what constituted the part, the proper object of study, now changed. Quantity is distinguished from quality, primary qualities from secondary qualities; science is divorced from theology and matter is studied rather than mystery. In replacing resemblance with difference and identity the new *Weltanschauung* saw resemblance as trivial and worse than that as one of the possible sources of error. The new perspective sought not provisional interpretation but clarity and certainty. Although there are two quite distinct strains of thought within this model, the empirical and the rational, they agree in using systematic doubt about received ideas and opinions to arrive at, or at least move towards, greater certainty on a methodologically secure foundation. Whether like Descartes reasoning outwards from clear and distinct ideas or like Bacon sifting empirical data as a basis for either a specific taxonomy or general laws about the physical world, both schools put aside teleology as inappropriate to natural philosophy. As Descartes put it, 'we must examine not the final but the efficient causes of created things'. They concern themselves with the structure of the world not its substance. With this new perspective there began to crystallize a more modern concept of the physical, of a material something independent of observers and existing unaltered beneath the various changes in the form of things. And as part of the isolation of the material as the proper object of investigation there came the dualistic distinction between mind and body.

Whereas within the older *Weltanschauung* the task had been to read resemblances, to crack the riddle of the book of nature through the exercise of wit in a fundamentally subjective way, under the newer dispensation the watchwords were objectivity and disinterested neutrality. Subjectivity came to be feared for that way lay madness. For John Locke the madman simply took his fancies to be reality, failing to check on their conformity to reality; he trusted his own wit instead of rational, discriminatory judgement. The reverse side of an immense trust in reason and order was a profound suspicion of the private spirit wherever it operated, whether in politics, in religion or in literature. It is a suspicion which finds expression in, for example, Dryden's attacks on Shadwell's bad poetry and Shaftesbury's bad politics. The days of the poet who like Milton thought of himself as inspired or vatic were numbered. Instead the poet was more likely to see himself as a representative figure concerned with 'what oft was thought but ne'er so well expressed'. Where the prediction for resemblances is embodied in the metaphysical conceit, difference and identity found their expression in that most rational of verse forms the heroic couplet. Bravura displays of correspondence are replaced by carefully measured antitheses. When Dryden mourned the death of his fellow satirist John Oldham in 1684 he felt no need to explain away the fact that he like Hastings died of smallpox. In place of the conceit he turned to allusion, allusion to Oldham's own poems by way of tribute to his art, and allusion to Virgil and Catullus to place both the nature of his relationship to the younger poet and his own feelings about mortality. Where there is often a sense in Milton's allusions that mythological analogues can only approximate to the Christian truth, in Dryden's poem the allusions leave nothing unsaid.

Under the new dispensation nothing could be taken to be true simply on the authority of an earlier thinker. Only successfully tested hypotheses or clear and distinct ideas held authority. All else had to be doubted. We should not, however, think of the new perspective as wholly sceptical. It used scepticism as part of an optimistic epistemology, as part of a conviction that knowledge and the advancement of human learning are possible. Pessimistic epistemology, the doctrine that all that we can know is that we can know nothing (and not even that), was not unknown in the century. It saw, for example, two major translations of Montaigne's essays, the most popular exposition of the hard-line scepticism associated with Pyrrho, one by John Florio (1603) and another by Charles Cotton (1685); and there are distinct strains of pessimistic scepticism in the poetry of John Wilmot, Earl of Rochester. But the dominant strain in the *Weltenschauung* based on difference and identity was optimistic, even if there is at times such a thoroughgoing gloominess about human capacity for error that it amounts almost to pessimism in the works of Bacon and those like the satirist Samuel Butler who were influenced by him. The belief in the possibility of progress marked a major departure whose emergence forms part of the transition from one model of reality to the other. One of the ideas that it helped put paid to, the notion that the world was decaying and even close to its end, was in part a product of a strategy of accommodation practised within the older model to preserve it in the face of uncomplimentary data. The idea that the world was still in a process of decaying from a perfect golden age was axiomatic in Renaissance thought. It is fed by Plato's thoroughly Greek fixation with the permanent and eternal and abhorrence of flux as well as by the Augustinian conviction that mankind has degenerated morally since the fall. What optimism the doctrine of decay left room for was largely channelled either into the theory of *ricorsi* or cycles according to which there is a continual cycle of decay and renewal or into the conventional Christian belief in progress towards an eternal paradise outside space and time in heaven. Whereas the finite Ptolemaic universe, ordered by divine fiat offered a physical and teleological compensation for mutability, the infinite heliocentric system opened up by Copernicus struck at the very heart of the idea that the universe was a finely structured symbolic whole. Its threat was compounded by a series of astronomical observations including Galileo's discoveries through the telescope of 'imperfections' on the moon's surface (which Milton associated with Satan in *Paradise Lost*) and an infinity of stars in the Milky Way. The string untuned, discord threatened. The problem was where did these deviations from a perfect pattern lead? One way of answering the question was to embrace the full but shattering implications of the discoveries and with Galileo to relinquish the model which they brought into question. Another was to deny the challenge as the church authorities sought to do with both Copernicus and Galileo and as the youthful Donne tried to in *Ignatius His Conclave*. Or there was a compromise solution which attempted to accommodate the inconvenient facts to the received model. This was the strategy adopted in one of the most famous expressions of seventeenth-century pessimism, Godfrey Goodman's *Fall of Man, or the Corruption of Nature, Proved by the Light of our Natural Reason*, first printed in 1616 and again in 1618 and 1629. Goodman simply tried to marry the new observations in astronomy to the Augustinian perspective. They were fresh evidence of the gradual demise which had been initiated by Adam's fall and which was now drawing to its close. They were signs in the book of nature that could be read in terms of resemblance:

> thus being mortal of ourselves, we dwell in houses of clay, the roof of this world, as well as the foundations shall together be moved; for wherefore serves the diversity of seasons, the day and night succeeding each other, summer and winter, the rising and setting of stars, the different and contrary motions, the various aspects and oppositions? but that in some sort they partake of our nature, and shall have their part and portion with ours?

Important in itself, Goodman's treatise is also important because it prompted an equally famous rebuttal in George Hakewill's *An Apology or Declaration of the Power and Providence of God in the Government of the World* (1627) which though opposed to Goodman represents a further attempt at accommodation. Here pessimism is replaced by an optimistic trust in providential progress. Just as on the larger scale we have the providential pattern of creation, fall and redemption, or, in the individual's life, birth, death and the rebirth into a new life in heaven, so the history of the world is governed by 'a kind of circular progress'. All things 'have their birth, their growth, their flourishing, their failing, their fading, and within a while after their resurrection and reflourishing again'. What might seem like decay is only a stage in this ever-onward cycle of progress. To prove the point, Hakewill's massive folio documents at length the progress made in all aspects of human endeavour. Modern people are not dwarfs by the side of the giant Ancients, able to seem to progress only because they stand on their shoulders. According to Hakewill's cyclic theory human intelligence and human abilities are constants. If Hakewill recognizes that the idea of modern people as dwarfs is a construct of the received view of decay, his attempt to defend and promote progress is no less conducted within a received conceptual model. Hakewill's *Apology* does not mark a point of discontinuity but is a determined effort to demonstrate providence at work in a world of rapid change by applying the secular theory of progressive cycle which had been recovered from antiquity by Italian Renaissance historians. The cycle would continue until the final conflagration of the world. Although his treatise was widely read and widely plundered for material, the attempted conflation of an eschatological pattern ending in the Day of Judgement and the more secular pattern of *ricorsi* is forced and uneasy.

Perhaps the most significant aspect of Hakewill's rejection of the theory of decay is his conviction that nature is always the same. This was an idea fundamental to the new *Weltanschauung*. As Spinoza put it, nature

> is always the same and everywhere one. Her virtue is the same, and her power of acting; that is to say, her laws and rules, according to which all things are and are changed from form to form, and everywhere and always the same; so that there must also be one and the same method of understanding the nature of all things whatsoever, that is to say, by the universal laws and rules of nature.

But whereas Hakewill's conception of progress is cyclic, that of the new thinking is linear. It is clear from Descartes's method or from Bacon's and later Newton's that the advancement of knowledge about a constant nature is a matter of building on secure foundations, on a coherent methodology and on trustworthy data and tried hypotheses, all organized on the basis of difference and identity. Hakewill had rejected the Augustinian view but clung to a still traditional finite Christian epic; the new perspective also cut loose from the Augustinian but in addition it left teleology to the theologians, freeing itself from the contradictions that outcrop so clearly in Hakewill's treatise. In so far as the new thinkers interested themselves at all in God's place in his creation, it was, as we have seen, as efficient not final cause. If they scrutinized the book of nature for signs of God, it was his wisdom not his mysteries on which they focused. God, the divine geometer, was by inference behind the structure of the universe; they did not see his mystical signature in nature.

The newer *Weltanschauung* is also marked by contradictions which are thrown up by a strategy of accommodation. Bacon's work, for example, shows a pronounced ambivalence, preaching progress on the one hand but stressing human susceptibility to the forces of error on the other. This janiformity may be understood as Bacon's attempt to reconcile a lingering and uncomplementary aspect of the older conceptual perspective, for the conviction that interpretation could be no more than provisional provided a fertile ground for pessimistic epistemology. Bacon seems to have been caught between a hope that humankind may regain Adam's prelapsarian 'pure knowledge of nature and universality, a knowledge by the light whereof man did give names unto other creatures in paradise as they were brought before him according to their properties' and a recognition that the fall is irreversible and language irredeemably opaque. The contradiction filtered down to Bacon's disciples. It occurs, for example, in Glanvill's otherwise optimistic treatise *The Vanity of Dogmatizing* in the notion that 'Adam needed no spectacles' to see what is now 'muffled up in mist and darkness'. A more pervasive attempt at accommodation sounds through the apparent inability of, for example, Descartes and Newton to separate the physical and metaphysical, despite their removal of teleology from their science.

Since there were no giants and no dwarfs, authority had no power. What was true was true because it could be demonstrated not because Aristotle or anyone else, past or present, affirmed it. Everything was to play for. The utopian replaced the arcadian, a world to be aimed for rather than a world irretrievably lost. Bacon's unfinished *New Atlantis* (1627) with its society dedicated to natural philosophy spells out the dream, a dream that Thomas Sprat, the historian of the Royal Society, saw as at least partially realized in the Society. Bacon's optimism is echoed everywhere as the century progresses. It finds expression not just among scientists and philosophers but among theologians, politicians and poets. In his verse epistle to Dr Charleton, John Dryden, for example, celebrates Bacon for his contribution to the escape from Aristotle's 'tyranny' and for providing a basis for future progress. But the first in Dryden's pantheon of free thinkers was Columbus. Had he not broken away from homage to Aristotle ('which only God and nature justly claim'),

> The western seas had been our utmost bound,
> Where poets still might dream the sun was drowned:
> And all the stars that shine in southern skies,
> Had been admired by none but savage eyes.

If classical authority seemed to have written *ne plus ultra* at the boundaries of its knowledge, modern thinkers like Columbus, Bacon and Hobbes (that later 'great Columbus') had torn down the signs. The new watchword was *Plus Ultra*, the title of the prolific Joseph Glanvill's review in 1668 of the progress and advancement of knowledge since the days of Aristotle. The new thinking knew no bounds. Glanvill's Royal Society colleague John Wilkins could even conceive that the human capacity to boldly go where no one has gone before would lead to space travel.

There was good reason for optimism. The new emphasis on a physical world that could be measured and whose laws could be searched out brought very significant advances in the tools of measurement and observation. Scales were improved until accurate to within five-hundredths of a grain; Huygens invented the pendulum clock and slashed the daily error of the clock about a hundredfold, to less than one-tenth of a second; Galileo's bequest of the telescope and the invention of the microscope (celebrated in England in Robert Hooke's magnificently produced *Micrographia* [1664]) not only revolutionized astronomy and the biological sciences but also deeply affected the consciousness of their time. In mathematics the period saw the introduction of logarithms and slide-rules; eventually Newton and Leibniz produced the crowning glory of their systems of differential calculus. Such tools helped to facilitate major advances in all branches of science. In biology Nehemiah Grew explored and defined sexuality in plants in his *Anatomy of Plants* (1682) while John Ray (1628–1705) published a magistral taxonomy of plants in his *Historia Plantarum* between 1684 and 1704, extending his study to both birds and fishes in collaboration with Francis Willoughby. In the closely related fields of anatomy and physiology Harvey's discovery of the circulation of the blood laid the foundation for others to build on. Athanasius Kircher distinguished red corpuscles, Malpighi added the capillary system and Richard Lower (1630–91) performed the first experiment in blood transfusion in Oxford in 1655 using two dogs, repeating it before the Royal Society. Lower intended the experiment to show the possible usefulness of transfusion in the treatment of human disease, but not surprisingly he found it difficult to locate a human subject. It was almost three years before a volunteer came forward in the shape of an eccentric scholar, Arthur Cage. Lower conducted a successful transfusion on Cage before the Royal Society in November 1667. He was also active with Thomas Willis in anatomical research into the human brain. Willis, whose *Cerebri Anatome* (1664) contained plates by Sir Christopher Wren, deserves mention in his own right because he helped to steer abnormal psychology away from both the humoural pathology of Hippocrates and Galen and the symbolic equation of madness and devilish inspiration towards a more sophisticated science, though the alternatives that Willis and his contemporaries expounded still reduced the psychological to the physiological. Equally innovatory was the work of Robert Boyle (1627–91) and his sometime assistant Robert Hooke (1635–1703) who laid the foundations of modern chemistry. Boyle, for example, broke the strangle-hold of the traditional belief in the four elements (fire, water, earth and air) to arrive at something much closer to the modern conception of elements as 'primitive and simple or perfectly unmingled bodies, which, not being made of any other bodies, or of one another, are the ingredients out of which all those called perfectly mixed bodies are immediately compounded and into which they are ultimately resolved'. Boyle's *Sceptical Chemist* (1680) and Nicolas Lémery's *Course in Chemistry* (1686) were watersheds, bringing together the current advances in both theory and terminology. The names of Hooke and Boyle were important, too, in physics. Hooke designed the air-pump that Boyle used to explore atmospheric pressure, his investigations leading to the still current Boyle's Law.

One of the results of the improvements of lenses that went with the invention of the microscope and telescope was a theoretical interest in optics which was shared by some of the best scientific minds of the period, by Kepler whose *Dioptrice* (1611) gave a working explanation of lenses and refracting telescopes, by Descartes whose own *Dioptrique* was published in 1638 and by Huygens who made a significant contribution to the wave theory of light (as, too, did Hooke). Their work made Newton's *Opticks* (1704) possible, though he sometimes found himself in radical disagreement with their findings, advancing, for example, an atomistic and mechanical wave theory as distinct from Huygens's geometrical theory. Newton's own interest had begun with lens-grinding in 1663 and brought his first scientific publication in 1672 in the *Transactions* of the Royal Society, which plunged him into a controversy which made him reticent about publication for a considerable time.

Taken together Newton's *Principia Mathematica*, in which he synthesizes the scientific advances of a century and a half, bringing to them a prodigious mathematical skill, and his *Opticks* stand as the greatest monuments to the period's scientific progress. His motto in the *Principia* had been 'hypotheses non fingo' (I frame no hypotheses), but despite echoes of that motto in the *Opticks* he allows himself the luxury of conjecture in the later work, especially in a series of queries added at the end of the last book. Whereas the *Principia* was written in Latin and required a daunting mathematical competence, the *Opticks* was written in English and, as Einstein recognized, was more personal in style. Perhaps because it was more accessible, perhaps because it was more expansive, it was the *Opticks* which most caught the imaginations of Newton's eighteenth-century contemporaries, as it did Pope's. There he added an inter-atomic force to gravity, magnetism and electricity. The structures of the vast heavens and the minutest particles were explained alike by his concept of attractions and repulsions:

> And thus nature will be very conformable to her self and very simple, performing all the great motions of the heavenly bodies by the attraction of gravity which intercedes those bodies and almost all the small ones of their particles by some other attractive and repelling powers which intercede the particles.

Not only was nature uniform, but also it was stable. Atoms were immutable. If there was change or decay it belonged only to the form of things, not to their substance:

> All these things being considered, it seems probable to me that God in the beginning formed matter in solid, massy, hard, impenetrable, moveable particles of such sizes and figures, and with such other properties, and in such proportion to space, as most conduced to the end for which he formed them; and these primitive particles being solids are incomparably harder than any porous bodies compounded of them; even so hard as never to wear or break in pieces; no ordinary power being able to divide what God himself made one in the first creation.
>
> While the particles continue entire they may compose bodies of one and the same nature and texture in all ages; but should they wear away, or break in pieces, the nature of things depending on them would be changed. Water and Earth composed of old worn particles and fragments of particles would not be of the same nature and texture now with water and earth composed of entire particles in the beginning.
>
> And therefore that Nature may be lasting the changes of corporeal things are to be placed only in the various separations and new associations and motions of these permanent particles; compound bodies being apt to break not in the midst of solid particles but where those particles are laid together and only touch in a few points.

Newton's scientifically grounded optimism is a far cry from Goodman's belief in decay. This was the universe which so excited Pope's imagination.

There was considerable technological progress, too. Bacon had been convinced, as had Descartes, that there had been more successful technological than scientific advance in the Middle Ages because those concerned with the 'mechanical arts' were closer to nature and less given to the cobweb speculations of scholastic logic. He emphasized that proper scientific advance offered control over not just understanding of nature. Given his influence on the century it is not surprising that the new spirit was turned to practical use. Under the terms of its second charter of

22 April 1663 the Royal Society's efforts were 'to be applied to further promoting by the authority of experiments the sciences of natural things and of useful arts, to the Glory of God the Creator and the advantage of the human race'. At the government's request the Society investigated problems in navigation and mining and on its own initiative it examined a variety of mechanical arts. The diarist John Evelyn presented a *Discourse of Forest-Trees and the Propogation of Timber* and Sir William Petty reported from first-hand knowledge as an ex-clothier on dyeing and the use of sheep's wool in textile manufacture. Petty is best known now as a demographer, for his *Political Arithmetic* (1676, published 1690) and for his analysis of the origins of wealth in his *Treatise of Taxes* (1662), but like many of his contemporaries he was multi-talented. In Petty we have a prime example of the Royal Society's commitment to the practical. It is worth pausing a while to look at his career. Born the son of a clothier, Petty (1623–87) had shown a precocious interest in technology. John Aubrey records that his 'principal amusement [was] to look on the artificers, e.g., smiths, the watchmakers, carpenters, joiners etc.; and at twelve years old he could have worked at any of these trades'. Instead he went to sea. His precociousness did not endear him to his fellow sailors, who deserted him on the French coast with a broken leg. Staying in France he earned enough to pay for his education and eventually began to study medicine in Leyden in 1644. Moving to Paris he became a member of a group that met at the home of the mathematician Father Mersenne and struck up a friendship with Thomas Hobbes. Returning to England he took his place as a clothier in the family business at Romsey before going up to Oxford to resume his medical studies. There he became a Doctor of Physic in 1649 and a member of Wilkins's Invisible College. Appointed as physician-general to Cromwell's armies in Ireland he ended up overseeing the mapping and assessment of forfeited estates in Ireland. By intellectual training and practical background he was well equipped to be a founder member of the Royal Society. He received his knighthood at its first incorporation on 22 April 1662. His papers to the Society show a remarkable range, but they always draw on his practical experience. As we have seen he put his knowledge of textiles to good use; he capitalized, too, on his time at sea. Among other things, he devised a ship with two keels to cope with the winds and tides of the Irish Channel and with Sir William Spragge he attempted to equip a ship with an engine. In his *Political Arithmetic* and later works he turned the Society's emphasis on measuring to demography, building on the statistical methods which he and John Graunt (1620–74) had used to analyse London bills of mortality to provide statistics for the population by class, religion, occupation, age, marital status and origin. It is difficult to generalize about the heterogeneous membership of the Royal Society, but it is safe to take

Petty's application of the new objectivity as an expression of its Baconian spirit.

This is not to say that everything done in the name of the Society was carried through in this spirit. Self-interest, rivalry and egotism are not the exclusive province of any particular conceptual framework. They led to controversies within the Society as well as without, controversies which the satirists were quick to seize upon. Samuel Butler's burlesque satire 'The Elephant in the Moon' suggests that it was not scholastic logic alone which set men together by the ears. Its virtuosos are equally skilled in obfuscation, putting their reputations before the truth. 'The Elephant in the Moon' caricatures a meeting of the Royal Society at which the fellows gather to view the moon objectively, 'by her own light', using a telescope. Flies within the telescope are seen as the warring armies of two races which inhabit the moon, the Privolvans and the Subvolvans, and a mouse that has infiltrated the 'long star-gazing trunk' presents a golden opportunity for a fresh discovery and for reputations to be made or enhanced. The mouse is taken to be an elephant. The virtuosos approach nature *by their own light*, they

> greedily pursue
> Things wonderful, instead of true;
> . . . in their speculations choose
> To make discoveries strange news;
> And natural history a Gazette
> Of tales stupendous and far-fet.

Behind Butler's satire there lies an essentially Baconian set of convictions, that neutral observation is the proper route to the truth, that worthwhile knowledge has practical implications and that the human mind is easily misled into error. While the scientists are writing up their discovery, two footboys wander over to the telescope and look at the moon through it. Because they are disinterested they see at once the simple truth that there is something inside the telescope,

> And, viewing well, discovered more
> Than all the learned had before.

By a rich satiric irony the footboys represent the proper scientific method. But it was not simply the human capacity for error which attracted the satirists of the Royal Society and its scientists. It was the indiscriminate collecting of data and curiosities for their own sake which is characteristic of Shadwell's Sir Nicholas Gimcrack in his play *The Virtuoso* (1676). Beneath the failings which Shadwell caricatures lies a severe shortcoming in Bacon's own work. In his *Novum Organum* Bacon represented the proper philosophy of nature as steering a middle course between experiment and dogma:

Those who have handled sciences have been either men of experiment or men of dogmas. The men of experiment are like the ant; they only collect and use: the reasoners resemble spiders, who make cobwebs out of their own substance. But the bee takes a middle course, it gathers its materials from the flowers of the garden and of the field, but transforms and digests it by a power of its own. Not unlike this is the true business of philosophy; for it neither relies solely or chiefly on the powers of the mind, nor does it take the matter which it gathers from natural history and mechanical experiments and lay it up in the memory whole, as it finds it; but lays it up in the understanding altered and digested.

But as the historian of the Royal Society, Thomas Sprat, admitted, there was something of the ant in Bacon himself. His natural histories, which form the basis of his scientific methodology, appeared 'rather to take all that comes than to choose, and to heap rather than to register'. And despite Bacon's own fulminations against the idols which lead the mind into error, he himself took material for his natural histories from unreliable sources. But the sniping of the satirists should not obscure the period's very real sense of pride in its scientific progress.

There was good reason for it to take pride in philosophical advances outside science, too. Descartes's systematic doubt led him to a method which was widely influential. It was a method that inverted Bacon's empirical emphasis on establishing progressively general laws by induction. Doubting all it was possible to doubt, he arrived at the bedrock certainty of the self-evident truth 'cogito ergo sum', 'I think therefore I am'. And from there he argued outwards to the existence of God and the dualistic distinction between the objective primary qualities of extension and motion and the subjective secondary qualities of colour, taste, smell and sound. Descartes's thinking drove a wedge between the mind and body, reason and experience, the inner and the outer life; a wedge that it was to take centuries of philosophical endeavour to begin to dislodge. As the century went on, his influence grew, reaching into the work of the Anglican rationalists as well as into the empirical stronghold of the Royal Society. Despite Newton's disapproval of Descartes's method, he took over the salient features of the earlier thinker's metaphysics as part of the explanation of the universe that Pope was to celebrate.

Another but very different thinker who came afresh to central problems in philosophy was Thomas Hobbes. Hobbes's ethical naturalism, based on a mechanistic epistemology, presented the natural state of man as unenviable. According to Hobbes in his *Leviathan* (1651) it is 'solitary, nasty, brutish and short'. In this state humans seek to gratify their own desires and find themselves at war with one another. Co-operation not war is necessary if anyone's needs are to be fulfilled. People therefore strive towards an ordered and peaceful society which will lay down rules backed by a sovereign power. Hobbes's thinking was nothing if not bold. His contemporaries found it controversial and often misunderstood him. He was variously charged with atheism, with robbing humans of their free-will, and with advocating political absolutism. In his naturalism the rakish courtiers of the court of Charles II found a convenient prop for their own brand of egotistic hedonism. In complete contrast the philosophical writings of John Locke set the foundations for a liberal tradition of political thought which stressed that humans are born 'with a title to perfect freedom and uncontrolled enjoyment of all the rights and privileges of the law of nature'. If Hobbes's thinking grows out of the turmoil of the mid-century, Locke's looks forward to the relative stability of the next century. On his view a stable society is cemented by a social contract grounded in the defence of property. More generally, at the end of our period his *Essay* synthesizes the age's empiricism, taking in Newtonian physics (though Locke himself could not understand the mathematics of the *Principia*) and setting down the basis of the philosophy of mind and philosophy of language for the succeeding generations.

These were remarkable minds, and we must not expect others to have adopted the newer conceptual framework with the same clarity. If we remember, however, that the models we are considering are not simply alternative ways of approaching the same reality but structure different realities, it is not at all surprising that old habits of thought should die hard. Although the two models are discontinuous, vestiges of the earlier hang over into the thought of many of those who embrace the newer. They are found in the heartland of the new thinking, in Bacon's own willingness to admit that the Ancients were naturally more gifted, in Hooke's sneaking interest in resemblances in his *Micrographia* (1665), and in another Royal Society member, John Dryden's allegiance to the Ptolemaic system. Whether they wrestle to accommodate the old to the new or the new to the old, the writers of the period will often need to be read with both the conceptual frameworks in mind. Thomas Traherne's *Centuries*, for example, describe his education in the new science at Oxford in the time of Hooke, but they are also deeply Augustinian and seeped in a Renaissance mysticism. Traherne is hard put to reconcile the empirical to his more dominant interest in the Neoplatonists and Hermes Trismegistus.

One of the most fiercely contested fronts in the transition between the two *Weltanschauungs* centred on the rival claims of the Ancients and Moderns. In a society whose education system was based on the classics in both humanities and sciences, the threat to the status of authority was understandably felt as radical, though in fact the classics were not being proscribed. The battle of the books raged at its strongest over literature rather than science, probably because the reader who had come up through the still fundamentally humanist grammar school system was best educated in classical literature. Beginning in Italy with Tassoni's advocacy of the case of the Moderns against the Ancients in his *Dieci Libri di Pensieri Diversi* (1612–20) the controversy spread slowly to England prompting Sir William Temple's defence of the Ancients in his *Essay on Ancient and Modern Learning* in 1690 and William Wotton's riposte in *Reflections upon Ancient and Modern Learning* in 1694. Temple had been stung by the promotion of the modern in both Thomas Burnet's often anachronistic *Sacred Theory of the Earth* (1684–9) and Fontenelle's state-of-the-art popularization of modern science, *Entretiens sur la pluralité des mondes* (1686) translated by Glanvill in 1688. Like Burnet's *Sacred Theory*, Temple's treatise is a hotch-potch. Here it cites instances of progress as if self-evidently worthless, here it takes a more balanced line; and here it wheels out the theory of compensation familiar from Hakewill. It is difficult to extract a coherent theory from Temple's argument. At root it seems driven by an unthinking allegiance to the classicism that generations of humanist teaching had instilled into its pupils. Wotton's response is impressive. Wotton is concerned not with taking one side or the other but with making two important distinctions, first that the arts and sciences need to be treated separately since only in the latter can there be said to be incremental progress, and second that since in general men have the same capacities in all ages, superiority whether of Ancients or Moderns does not point to decay or meliorism but depends on the social and cultural context. He could agree with Temple 'that former ages made greater orators and nobler poets than these later ages have done' but he could also argue 'that the present Age, with the same advantages, under the same circumstances, might produce a Demosthenes, a Cicero, a Horace, or a Virgil'.

Similar arguments are found almost twenty years earlier in John Oldham's praise of Homer. The sort of commonsensical line taken by Wotton, or by Dryden in his probabilistic view of the classical rules, allowed praise to be given where it is due, whether to ancient or seventeenth-century writers. Being a Modern did not rule out admiration for classical literature. Oldham could eulogize Homer as the source and paradigm of 'authentic wit' in poetry, but he could also praise Ben Jonson for steering a course 'beyond the narrow bounds that pent antiquity' and for making 'Rome and Greece [his] humble tributaries'. Since classical and seventeenth-century writers observed fundamentally the same nature, Oldham could translate Juvenal's satires on Rome to London (as Jonson had done in *Epicene*) to help him to focus his response to contemporary society. Oldham's imitations provide a remarkable example of the neo-classical Modern at work. They place him in a classical tradition but leave him free in making Juvenal 'speak as if he were living and writing now' to adapt his model 'to the relish of the present age'. The increased popularity of the imitation in the later seventeenth century is not surprising if we consider that it represents an exercise in establishing difference and identity for both writer and reader through an extended and perspicuous comparison.

With hindsight we can see that the skirmishes between Ancients and Moderns, often inspired as much by social grouping or political affiliation as by deep conviction, easily obscure the real relation of the classical to the contemporary. The major exponents of 'new' scientific thinking went back to the Greeks for their starting-points, not the Greeks as filtered through the distorting lens of scholasticism but the Greeks in their pristine form as freshly discovered by the humanists. Galileo had brought mathematics to the atomism of Democritus, and Harvey saw himself as working within the traditions of Aristotle and Galen. Bacon's attacks on Aristotle's scientific procedure should really have been directed against those Aristotelians who misappropriated their master's method, for Bacon's and Aristotle's procedures are fundamentally similar. In the title of his *Novum Organum* Bacon had proclaimed a new departure which would supersede the *Organon*, the medieval anthology of Aristotle's work; but both thinkers regarded scientific method as an inductive-deductive movement from observation to general principles and back to observation. Bacon's procedural divergence from Aristotle is more a matter of revision than replacement. What was new was, as we have seen, his part in ridding scientific enquiry of teleology, his insistence on the practical application of scientific advance in place of Aristotle's interest in knowledge of nature for its own sake and his conviction that if humankind was to recover the control over nature lost with Adam's fall science must be a co-operative enterprise. Similarly, Descartes's deductive method, his ideal of a deductive hierarchy of propositions, draws on Archimedes; the corpuscular theory or atomism of Robert Boyle and his colleagues in the Royal Society takes its inspiration from classical atomists, notably Democritus and Lucretius. Thomas Creech's translation of Lucretius's *De Rerum Natura* demonstrates the interpenetration of ancient and modern. Creech dresses Lucretius in fashionable, often Hobbesian, clothing, and in his notes he marshals a dialogue between the Latin author and his seventeenth-century successors. It is not until Newton's conception of immutable atomic particles held together by binding forces that the early atomists are truly left behind.

Since this account of the period's thought is aimed primarily at those concerned with literature, it seems appropriate to conclude by glancing at the conceptions of language which belong to the two *Weltanschauungs*. The earlier perspective, with its emphasis on the book of nature as containing an infinite store of resemblances, treasured forms of the figurative language which mirrored those resemblances, forms like the conceit which could reveal hidden sympathies. If the world as given to humans seemed marked with physical signs which they must read, if peaches could be interpreted with all seriousness as helpful to baldness because they have that quality which bald people do not have (hairiness), the world also revealed itself to humans as structured by words. Somehow, somewhere inscribed in those words lay further clues to the nature of things, perhaps in their etymology, perhaps in their structural relation to each other. George Herbert's joy at realizing that the meaning of 'Jesu' is 'I ease you' is more than a display of wit. He expresses a serious, if artfully naive, celebration of being able to spell, of recognizing through the homophonic pun the meaning of a resemblance in a particular linguistic sign. The empiricists complained that words came before things in this model; but they might have objected more radically that it contained no notion of a thing as independently knowable. Things and words were both signs of an ultimately unreachable deeper meaning open to no more than provisional interpretation. For Adam it had been different. Before the fall the language of the book of nature was transparent. The names which Adam gave to the animals did not stand in need of interpretation: they embodied the essence of the animals. With the fall language became opaque. The view of language which underlies the book read by Galileo, Descartes, Bacon, Hobbes, Newton and Locke is radically different. Theology and science are now separated and the physical world no longer needs to be scanned for signs of a final cause. Nor does language, whose relation to things is regarded as arbitrary rather than natural. As Samuel Parker put it in 1666 attacking Platonism and much besides, words are not 'names [that] have in them a natural resemblance and suitableness to things and [that] are peculiarly expressive of the several natures and properties of those things they are used to represent'. Where the guarantee of meaning in the older model lay with God, for Parker and those of like mind it rests with rational consensus:

> the office of definitions is not to explain the natures of things but to fix and circumscribe the signification of words; for they being notes of things, unless their significations be settled their meaning must needs be equivocal and uncertain.

Now that the world had ceased to be read as a text whose meaning each man could imaginatively unravel for himself, now that it had become a physical thing which could be weighed and measured, language had to be correspondingly perspicuous. In Thomas Sprat's words, it had to take on a 'mathematical plainness'. In his *Essay towards a Real Character and a Philosophical Language*, which was published with the Royal Society's blessing in 1668, John Wilkins argued for a close correspondence between words and things; and Hobbes, Parker and Locke all remarked forcefully on the dangers of the various forms of figurative expression, especially 'metaphors and senseless and ambiguous words [which, according to Hobbes,] are like *ignes fatui*; . . . reasoning upon them is wandering amongst innumerable absurdities'. These figures belonged to the earlier *Weltanschauung* based on resemblance. Parker brushed aside 'emblems, fables, symbols, allegories' as no more than 'pretty poetic fancies . . . infinitely unfit to express philosophical notions and discoveries of the nature of things'. Empiricism found little room for imagination – Locke went so far as to exhort parents to stifle any interest their children might show in poetry – and the new attitude towards language brought correspondingly little trust in the non-literal. Figurative language was fit for ornament but not for truth, and even for ornament the more perspicuous simile came to be preferred to the more pregnant but less immediately clear metaphor. It is not surprising that Bacon and Descartes should have been interested in schemes for a universal language or that the Royal Society should have set up a committee for improving the language. The implications for literature are fundamental.

FURTHER READING

Of the many studies of science and philosophy in the seventeenth century, the following may be found helpful. R.T.T. Gunther's twelve-volume *Early Science at Oxford* (Oxford, 1920ff.) is useful for primary material. For a general survey of the development of scientific thinking there is A.C. Crombie's *Medieval and Early Modern Science*, 2 vols (New York, 1959) or S. Toulmin and J. Goodfield's *The Architecture of Matter* (London, 1962). And for an overview of the course of seventeenth-century philosophy it is worth consulting W. Von Leyden, *Seventeenth-Century Metaphysics* (London, 1961). A.O. Lovejoy's seminal *The Great Chain of Being* (Cambridge, Mass., 1936) is still useful for the earlier conceptual perspective, as, on a narrower front is L. Babb, *The Elizabethan Malady: A Study of Melancholia in English Literature from 1580 to 1642* (Michigan, 1951). The later *Weltanschauung* is well-served by E.J. Dijksterhuis, *The Mechanisation of the World Picture*, trans. C. Dikshoorn (Oxford, 1961), R. Briggs, *The Scientific Revolution of the Seventeenth Century* (London, 1969), and C. Webster, *The Great Instauration: Science, Medicine and Reform 1626–1660* (London, 1975). For a more detailed study of the Royal Society there is M. Hunter's *The Royal Society and its Fellows, 1660–1700: The Morphology of an Early Scientific Institution* (British Society for the History of Science, 1982). R. Foster Jones's *Ancients and Moderns: A Study of the Rise of the Scientific Movement in Seventeenth-Century England* (Berkeley and Los Angeles, 1961) remains the standard account of the ancients and moderns debate in the context of its contemporary science. And for studies of science and cosmology in relation to literature there are several contributions from M.H. Nicolson, among them *Science and Imagination* (Ithaca, NY, 1961) and *The Breaking of the Circle* (Columbia, NY, 1960). Finally, there are two very different but equally challenging approaches to the period's thought in K.R. Popper's *Conjectures and Refutations: The Growth of Scientific Knowledge* (London, 1963) and M. Foucault's *The Order of Things: An Archaeology of the Human Sciences* (London, 1970).

Chapter 5

The visual arts and architecture in Britain 1625-1700

T.G.S. Cain

I

The next day was the first of March, and when I awoke, rose, and opened my curtain, I saw the risen sun struggling through fog. Above my head, above the house-tops, co-elevate almost with the clouds, I saw a solemn, orbed mass, dark-blue and dim – THE DOME.

For Lucy Snowe in Charlotte Brontë's *Villette* St Paul's is *the* symbol of London. Even today, when it is more nearly co-elevate with City offices, Wren's cathedral still has that dominant and symbolic status. We cannot help being aware of it. The relationship of our society to Wren's buildings, our use or abuse of his great legacy, is the subject of current, indeed perennial argument. We are, however, less conscious of the marks left by other great seventeenth-century masters. Many hundreds of eighteenth- and nineteenth-century buildings (culminating, it might be unkindly argued, in twentieth-century Dulwich neo-Georgian) are the legitimate and illegitimate issue of Inigo Jones, for example. Less obviously the portrait, so dominant a genre in English painting and photography, frequently echoes the poses developed by Van Dyck for the Caroline court, or the head and shoulders format used by the great miniaturists. Byron, for example, is best known from George Sanders's portrait in a pose taken straight from Van Dyck, while many an Edwardian amateur cricketer leans casually on his bat to be photographed in a pose derived from those used by Van Dyck nearly three centuries earlier to convey the confident ease, the nonchalant lack of pomposity, which he established as defining characteristics of the ideal English gentleman.

Wren, Jones, Van Dyck: it seems inevitable that any account of this century should begin and end with these three artists. Art historians usually present them as dragging English painting and building out of their provinciality and abreast with continental trends, moving towards (and perhaps achieving) an English version of baroque. This process is invariably seen as being grievously set back by the Civil Wars and by an iconoclastic Commonwealth government, with new artistic life re-emerging with the Restoration of Charles II.

Like all conventional accounts, this one contains elements of truth, but almost as many inaccuracies. In architecture, for example, there is a danger of locating as most important that which looks most European, particularly Italian, with a consequent downgrading of more 'provincial', but not necessarily less talented architects. This is especially true in the earlier Stuart period: Inigo Jones was indeed the most innovative architect at work during those years, but his effort to adapt Italian models did not take root easily, and much of the building of distinction carried out in the years before the Civil Wars developed instead the English Elizabethan style seen at its finest in such houses as Longleat (1568–80) and Hardwick Hall (1590–7).

In painting the dominance of Van Dyck is a factor less open to dispute. Native British painting in the century before his arrival had almost all been provincial in the pejorative sense. Almost, but not quite: in the hands of Nicholas Hilliard and Isaac Oliver, the strong English tradition of limning, or painting in miniature, had reached by 1600 a standard of excellence unrivalled in the rest of Europe. The tradition of the portrait miniature was carried on into the Stuart period by painters of great competence such as Isaac's son Peter, and John Hoskins, who was probably trained by Hilliard, and who in turn trained Hilliard's greatest successor, Samuel Cooper. The influence of the miniaturists extended also to the work of the one native painter in oils who stands out from the surrounding mediocrity of the 1620s, Cornelius Johnson, a painter whose work is only now receiving the attention it deserves.

Conventional accounts of the period label it baroque, but the strong if theoretically problematic links which tie the baroque style to political absolutism and Roman Catholicism mean that Stuart England was never a fertile field for the development of full-blown baroque art. There are, as will be seen, painters and architects whose work it is meaningful to call baroque, but a more circumspect approach is needed than that which, taking over an essentially continental label, indiscriminately describes all work done in Britain in the seventeenth century as 'baroque'.

Another distortion in the orthodox view of the period, and the one that passes with the least question, is the account of the Interregnum period as one barren and hostile to the arts. So deeply embedded is this view that the evidence against it, though clear enough, is rarely given weight. The idea of the arts going into hibernation between 1640 and 1660 is given a fortuitous symmetry by the death in 1641 of Van Dyck; his death had no connection with the imminent conflict, but it left a huge gap in English artistic life in the following years, as it would have done at any time. Painting in fact continued throughout the 1640s and 1650s much as it would have done if Van Dyck had died at the beginning of a period of peace. His two greatest successors, William Dobson and Peter Lely, worked through the

Civil Wars, as did the young Samuel Cooper. Though Dobson died young in 1646, Lely and Cooper flourished during the 1650s: Cooper's most justly celebrated miniature is that of the Lord Protector himself (Plate 14), while Lely was at first patronized by such opposition magnates as the Earls of Northumberland and Pembroke, men who had also been leading patrons of Van Dyck. During the 1650s Lely would travel to country houses to paint the portraits of those who had retired there after the execution of the king and the abolition of the House of Lords. These men, excluded from political power, or not caring to work with Cromwell's regime, also spent their time improving their estates, so that a good deal of building work went on. The old Inigo Jones certainly advised on, if he did not design, the south wing of Wilton House for the Earl of Pembroke, who also commissioned a magnificent new interior for Wilton from Jones and his assistant Webb in 1647–8, built to accommodate the Earl's Van Dycks. Webb was hard at work elsewhere throughout these years, while Coleshill, one of the most graceful and influential of all English country houses, was also built during the 1650s by the gentleman amateur Sir Roger Pratt (Plate 2).

Ordinary life continued, and with it commissions for buildings and portraits (for the demand for paintings in Britain was almost exclusively for portraits). Only the patronage of the court diminished: but Cromwell's court, though incomparably less extravagant in its patronage than that of Charles I, was not notably inferior to Charles's predecessors. Nor did Charles II's patronage differ greatly from Cromwell's as far as painting was concerned: Lely and Cooper in fact continued as the leading painters of the Restoration court. The great change that certainly did come about after 1660 was in public building. Even this, however, was in part fortuitous: the Great Fire of 1666 necessitated a huge programme of rebuilding, and would have done had it occurred in 1646 or 1656. Charles II was immensely energetic in this, but (though he hankered after it) he was never in a position to build the great new palace of Whitehall that had been one of his father's most cherished projects. Wren's Chelsea Hospital, Charles's most successful piece of secular patronage, was largely forced on him by events, while the palace Wren built for him at Winchester was left unfinished after Charles's death, left to decay by successors unwilling to pay for its completion.

II

Changes in the climate of patronage were as important as the emergence of new artists in the earlier years of the century. The greatest English painter of the sixteenth century, Nicholas Hilliard, suffered financially and artistically from the lack of discerning patronage at Elizabeth's court. A few Elizabethans had begun to form collections, but none of them remotely rivalled that started in the early Stuart period by one of the most important figures in the history of patronage in Britain, Thomas Howard, 14th Earl of

Arundel (1585–1646). Howard, his wife Aletheia, and his secretary, the humanist scholar Franciscus Junius (François du Jon), formed a triumvirate whose impact on the development of British art and architecture in this and subsequent centuries was immense. It was the Howards who took Inigo Jones on the Italian tour of 1613 from which he returned with an understanding of the principles of Italian Renaissance architecture which was to transform building in Britain over the next two centuries. It was the Howards who first attracted Rubens, Mytens and Van Dyck to England, the latter also included on an Italian tour with the Countess which deeply influenced his mature style. It was probably Arundel who, as adviser to James I's eldest son Henry, most guided and encouraged the collection which passed, on Henry's death, to Prince Charles; probably in emulation of the haughty and patrician Arundel the arriviste Buckingham began to form his own important collection in the 1620s. It was the Countess of Arundel who began negotiations over the collection of the Gonzaga Dukes of Mantua, and then (either out of extraordinary self-denial or financial and political realism) passed on to Charles I the opportunity to buy the richest single collection ever to be bought by one person. It was the Howards who brought to England the famous collection of Leonardo drawings now at Windsor, and who took into their employment the Bohemian topographical artist and engraver Vaclav Hollar, to whom we owe much of our knowledge of the appearance of seventeenth-century London. The Arundel collection included classical sculpture and inscribed marbles (the famous 'Arundel Marbles' described by the lawyer and antiquary John Selden) and the Pirkheymer library, which had belonged to the kings of Hungary. It also contained numerous Holbeins, Titians, Tintorettos and many other important paintings. The Howards were drawn in particular to Northern European and Venetian painting, and the large Venetian component in the collection influenced both other collectors – especially Charles I, who nevertheless disliked Arundel intensely – and also those painters, notably Mytens and Van Dyck, who probably had their first comprehensive view of the great Venetians in Arundel House. Arundel's secretary, Junius, wrote a distinguished treatise on *The Painting of the Ancients* which probably reflected his patrons' enlightened views, and which later in the century greatly influenced the French Academy. Rubens, who was not easily impressed by aristocratic patrons, said of Arundel that he was 'one of the four evangelists' of art, and painted a number of portraits of him, two of which can be seen in the National Gallery and the National Portrait Gallery. Van Dyck, who can justly be called the Earl's greatest protégé, also painted several portraits, one of the best of which, at Arundel, shows the Earl with his grandson 'my little Tom bye me', a complex mixture of tenderness and the *hauteur* which Clarendon described when he called him 'a proud man, who lived always within himself and to himself, . . . so that he seemed to live as it were in another nation'. Difficult though Arundel's pride may have made him, his influence on the course of British art is difficult to overestimate. The only criticism that can be made of him is that his discerning patronage of foreign artists may have encouraged less critical collectors in the fixed belief that foreign art was necessarily superior to the native product.

The other great patron of the period was Charles I. He inherited a passion for collecting art from his elder brother, together with the nucleus of a collection already formed under Arundel's influence. Though Charles's personal relations with Arundel were at best strained, he shared his tastes, and received via the Howards not only the entire Gonzaga collection, but also the services of the great artists patronized by the Howards – notably Rubens, Van Dyck and Jones. The king's enthusiasm led other courtiers to build collections and patronize major European artists on a scale unknown to their parents and grandparents. Of these, the 10th Earl of Northumberland's importance as a patron, and as a prominent political figure, has never been adequately recognized. Apart from the king, he was second only to Arundel as a patron, as the collections at Alnwick, Syon House and Petworth still testify. The young Lely, painting the children of Charles I, to whom Northumberland was guardian during the king's imprisonment, probably found himself working in Northumberland's London house in a room full of paintings by Van Dyck. In such ways, as well as through simple financial support, discerning patronage had its effects: the Titians which Van Dyck saw in the collections of Arundel and Charles I helped him to move away from the dominating influence of Rubens, while William Dobson was probably to learn more from the royal collection than from the minor master to whom he was apprenticed, Francis Cleyn.

The patronage of Cromwell's court cannot be compared with that of Charles I: one source of popular discontent with the crown during the 1620s and 1630s had been the ostentatiousness of such patronage, particularly in the shape of Inigo Jones's extravagant masques in 'the Queen's dancing barn', and in the encouragement given to foreign and (much worse) Roman Catholic painters like Van Dyck or the Gentileschis, father and daughter. This hostility had the compensating effect of encouraging native-born painters like Walker, Cooper and the younger Hoskins, but, along with the need to raise money, it provoked the Parliamentary Commissioners' sad decision to sell Charles I's collection, bar the two great sequences of Raphael and Mantegna cartoons. Religious objections too played their part: the damage done to churches, especially in London, by such men as the Presbyterian Sir Robert Harley, was savage. But most Parliamentarians were far from being philistines, and the habit of many guidebooks of ascribing all vandalism dating from before 1700 to a miraculously ubiquitous Oliver Cromwell has as much truth to it as the widespread belief among European Jews that Oliver was the Messiah. In fact, after the king and Arundel, the greatest of Van Dyck's patrons during the 1630s, Northumberland, the Earl of Pembroke, and Philip, Lord Wharton, all took the side of Parliament, while in the field of sculpture one of the most dramatic portrait busts of an Englishman of any period is Bernini's of the Parliamentarian Thomas Baker (Victoria and Albert Museum), who was willing to pay far over the odds to persuade Bernini to execute it. Cromwell's passion for music is well known. Less so is his willingness to allow the performance of simple masques at his court, or his continuing employment of Lely and Cooper as court painters.

Conversely, court patronage of painters after the Restoration is not accompanied by the discernment of Charles I and his agents, nor are there aristocratic patrons of the stature of Arundel or Northumberland. The fashionable taste of the post-Restoration court was easily satisfied first by Lely, and then by Kneller, painters whom Arundel or Charles I would probably not have found quite as satisfactory as Van Dyck. The social base of patronage did widen to include merchants and professional men, but few patrons of the later years of the century demanded more than to have their portraits painted in the fashionable manner. Where larger decorative schemes were in question the decline between early and late Stuart standards was even more marked. In place of Rubens's magnificent paintings for the ceiling of the Banqueting House, or Gentileschi's less ambitious ones for Greenwich (now in Marlborough House) we have the ambitious but incompetent staircase by Verrio at Hampton Court, or the rather better executed designs of Laguerre at Blenheim.

III

As was so often the case in British painting before Hogarth, these were all the work of foreign artists. The most important native artist to emerge in the discerning and artistically favourable atmosphere of the early Stuart period was a painter turned designer and architect, Inigo Jones (1573–1652). But Jones did not stand alone. His Palladian innovations, though much to the taste of Anne of Denmark, scarcely swept all before them. Instead, Jones's work coexisted alongside some neglected but inventive building that both developed the English styles of the previous generation, and adapted other foreign models than those of Palladio. One of the greatest of all Renaissance houses, Hardwick Hall, had been completed only at the turn of the century. The 'Elizabethan' style of Robert Smythson's Hardwick, 'more glass than wall', and the earlier Longleat developed out of the English perpendicular style of the fourteenth and fifteenth centuries. The perpendicular and its Elizabethan and Jacobean descendants were unique in Europe, a vigorous and sophisticated native tradition confident enough to resist European innovations, Renaissance or mannerist, before and during Jones's lifetime. Lanhydrock in Cornwall (1620–58), Aston

Hall, Birmingham (1618–35) and Blickling Hall, Norfolk (1616–27) are good examples of the continuing distinction and variety of this tradition, as are a number of Oxford and Cambridge colleges of the 1620s and 1630s. A related but highly idiosyncratic phenomenon is Bolsover Castle (1612–34), built in a mixture of styles ranging from neo-Gothic to baroque, for the Cavendish family. John Smythson (*d.* 1634), and possibly his father Robert (*d.* 1614), the creator of Hardwick, were the architects primarily involved, and Bolsover on its own is sufficiently impressive to demonstrate that Jones is not the only architect of genius working in England during the 1620s.

A related group are the London-based 'Artisan Mannerists', masons and sculptors as well as architects, among whom the leading figures are Nicholas Stone (1586–1647) and Edward Marshall (1598–1675). Though indebted to Jones in many ways, they work in an idiom that mediates the English Elizabethan tradition with an eclectic range of neo-classical features derived in part from the Netherlands rather than Italy. They were particularly associated with the City, building the halls of the great livery companies, and houses, town and country, for merchants and for those many landowners with strong City connections. Their earlier City houses are all lost, but good examples of their work may still be seen at Swakeleys, Middlesex (1638) or the 'Dutch House' at Kew Gardens (1631). The scrolled gables associated with these buildings do not tell the whole story, however: in Lindsey House, Lincoln's Inn Fields (1638–40), now attributed to Stone, we can see a mastery of a more academic neo-classicism that would have satisfied Inigo Jones. Stone reappears later in this chapter as a sculptor of genius: here it is enough to emphasize that there is not such a huge gulf between his achievement as an architect and that of Inigo Jones as the conventional account would have us believe.

Jones himself first appears in 1605 as a designer of masques for Queen Anne. He was in France in 1609, as, interestingly, was Arundel. His drawings show greater confidence after this trip, and the still more important visit to Italy in 1613–14 with the Arundels. The fluency with which he could sketch out ideas for costume and scenery for masques was a factor in his success at the Stuart court. More important was the confidence with which he approached his Italian models, first of all in his masque designs, and increasingly in his architecture. As has been said, 'Italian' does not necessarily equal 'good': English painters and architects of the sixteenth century had praised and written on Italian Renaissance art, and quoted Italian Renaissance motifs in their buildings. But Jones was the first English architect to understand the implications of Renaissance neo-classicism. He was deeply interested in Neoplatonism, in mathematical and musical harmony and their application in both masque and building. He read and assimilated Vitruvius, the theorist of classical Roman architecture, and the modern Italian theorists Palladio, Scamozzi and Serlio. In the seriousness and sophistication of his commitment to neo-classical ideals, and in the philosophical underpinning of his art he is strikingly similar to his collaborator in the masques, Ben Jonson. Both men offered, in their different arts, an opportunity for the Stuart court to place itself within that timeless, civilized tradition which, in theory, stretched back to Augustan Rome. On a more practical level, the flamboyant court masques designed by Jones and written by Jonson enabled James I and his son to present the new British (as opposed to merely English) monarchy as being on equal terms in its sophistication and splendour with any in Europe, and gave both kings the opportunity to liken themselves, however implausibly, to Augustus Caesar.

Though the masques constituted his most spectacular and ideologically influential contribution to the life of the court, Jones had two other roles in which he made a more lasting impact than in those expensive but ephemeral entertainments. One was as connoisseur: we shall never know just how much impact Jones's expertise had in the formation of the great collections of Arundel and of Charles I, but his advice was certainly sought and valued. The other, of course, was as architect, and it was here that he left his most inalienable mark on the culture not only of his own time but also of the following century, when with the publication of Colen Campbell's *Vitruvius Britannicus* (1715-25) his particular brand of Italianate neo-classicism came to represent the ideal. That it could come to do so was largely due to the strongly philosophical basis of Jones's architecture, especially his belief in the relationship between mathematics and ideal proportions in building. This was a belief he shared with Vitruvius, Palladio and other theorists. Many of the annotations in Jones's 1601 copy of Palladio's *I Quattro Libri Dell'architettura* are on the detailed proportions of Palladio's examples, the mathematically harmonious relationship of the parts of a building to each other and to the whole. This intellectual bent was also the source of the admiration of his contemporaries, who saw in him, as they saw in his collaborator Jonson, a man whose scholarship allied to his genius, could give to his art the authority of a reborn classicism. Jonson, who describes Jones in the *Masque of Augurs*, as 'full of noble observation of Antiquitie', once described a poem of his own as 'having somewhat in it *moris antiqui*', and Jones might have accepted such a description of his architecture. Though Jonson's envy at Jones's success was to make them enemies, Jones sounds a thoroughly Jonsonian note, that of the classical plain style, in the best known of his theoretical statements: 'in architecture, the outward ornaments ought to be solid, proportionable according to the rules, masculine and unaffected' (*Italian Sketch Book*, 20 January 1615).

None of his work illustrates these principles better than the two religious buildings by Jones which can still be seen in London, the Queen's Chapel at St James's Palace (now attached to Marlborough House), and St Paul's Church, Covent Garden. The Queen's Chapel is a double cube – a recurring proportion in Jones's work – and though small, the relatively plain exterior gives an effect of weight and dignity that is evidently intended to suggest an austere Roman temple. The much richer interior confirms this, for its superb barrelled ceiling imitates that of the Roman Temple of Venus as it was restored by Palladio.

The Queen's Chapel was a private commission for a Roman Catholic queen: but for Covent Garden in 1631, Jones had to design the first new church to be erected in London since before the Reformation. Throughout the century artists and architects had to confront the challenge posed by ascendant Protestantism: it is obvious enough that in painting and sculpture this meant the eschewing of the religious subject matter that was a staple part of the practice of most continental artists, and sculptors like Stone found themselves limited to tomb effigies, secular statues and chimney pieces. For architects the Protestant emphasis on preaching, on a certain plainness and simplicity, and antagonism to such popish amenities as side chapels and chantries, meant a whole new approach to the design of churches. Jones was brilliantly radical within the confines of the classical tradition in his answer. For Covent Garden he turned to the Tuscan style, a style rather despised by some Italian theorists because of its plainness. Jones used Tuscan, which had always been associated with rustic building, to make, as he said, 'the handsomest barn in England'. The powerful primitivism of the architecture was probably conceived of as analogous to the simplicity of the primitive church before it was corrupted by Roman Catholic deviations. The interior is a simple double square in plan, but it is the portico, which still dominates the Covent Garden piazza, that is most striking. Here the Tuscan order is at its most simple and impressive: four massive columns, two round and two square, support a cantilevered roof, with eaves which project several feet on huge timber beams. Originally this 'masculine and unaffected' portico stood several feet above ground-level, not as now on a level with the surrounding paving. Jones designed the whole square for the Earl of Bedford, with houses standing above open arcades on the north and east sides: the houses in this first London development scheme have all been demolished, but some idea of their appearance is given by Bedford Chambers, an 1880 reconstruction on the north side of the square. Even in its contemporary form, much restored, surrounded by bistros and with the eighteenth-century market buildings (also appropriately Tuscan) filling the centre of the square, Jones's aggressively plain portico still broods impressively over Covent Garden.

However, even Covent Garden was eclipsed by the huge Corinthian portico Jones built on the West Front of the old St Paul's Cathedral. Measuring fifty by a hundred feet, it seemed to many his finest achievement, but to others its cost made it a source of bitter complaint, another grievance to be stored up against Charles's administration. It survived the Great Fire of 1666, and stood, a charred remnant, for some years more while Wren began the long and difficult task of demolition from the east end.

A still more extravagant project was that for a new palace of Whitehall. This grandiose scheme was in gestation for many years, but the earliest extant design dates from the late 1630s. Jones planned a huge rectangular block containing eleven courts, influenced as ever by the designs of Scamozzi and Palladio, but also by Philip II's Escorial, and probably also by conjectural reconstructions of Solomon's temple. Its scale is vast: the shortest side of the rectangle, fronting on to the river, would have been as long as the present Houses of Parliament; the longer sides would have stretched back three hundred yards or more into St James's Park. The political implications of such a massive scheme are obvious, and nothing shows more clearly how obstinately unrealistic Charles I remained than that he was still discussing this tactless project well into the 1640s – though doubtless by then such plans had a mainly therapeutic function for the beleaguered king. No great royal palace ever was to be built in Britain: no monarch was ever again to aspire to the absolute power that such a building would symbolize. Instead, the old palaces were restored, added to, demolished, until, two centuries later, Barry's new palace of Westminster was built to house not the monarch, but parliament.

In the end, the only surviving building that Jones designed for Whitehall was the Banqueting House of 1619–22 (Plate 1). In his later Whitehall plans, the Banqueting House was to have been incorporated as a small part, but as it stands now in modern Whitehall it is triumphantly self-sufficient, with its smooth columns and pilasters set off against the deeply cut stone of the wall. The recently restored interior is one of the most magnificent in London, and yet one of the least visited: a huge double cube, with a cantilevered gallery, it provides an elegant, austere setting for Rubens's apotheosis of James I and its accompanying paintings set in the ceiling. This austerity would have been offset when the Banqueting House was used by the king, as intended, for major state occasions: ironically, the most momentous of these was to be in January 1649 when Charles stepped from one of its windows on to his scaffold.

Of the houses that Jones built, all but one have disappeared: that built at Greenwich for his first royal patron, Anne of Denmark, now framed majestically by Wren's Greenwich Hospital buildings. The Queen's House was Jones's first major architectural achievement. He began it in 1616, echoing both Palladio's Palazzo Chiericati and Giuliano da Sangallo's earlier Villa Medici at Poggio a Cajano, which is built in two halves like Greenwich. The two halves of the house at Greenwich were connected by a bridge, under which went a public road. Each half was a rectangle, the elevations simple, slightly severe, and lower and longer than his Italian models. As with all Jones's buildings, one is reminded of Jonson's creative *imitatio* in the discriminating use of sources. Much altered now, it is still easy to see the simple serenity of Jones's design in the main north and south elevations. The first major neo-classical building to be built in England, it is still one of the finest, so influential on later design that it could almost as easily belong to the eighteenth or early nineteenth centuries as to the early seventeenth.

The Queen's House was a country villa; there are surprisingly few designs by Jones for larger country houses, and no actual buildings survive. The nearest thing to a major country house designed by him is Wilton. Here rebuilding was carried out in the 1630s by Isaac de Caux, son or nephew of Salomon, the great hydraulic engineer who had been Prince Henry's mathematical tutor, and who is credited by some with the invention of the steam engine. Isaac may have built the houses at Covent Garden to Jones's design, but the south front at Wilton, though clearly inspired by Jones, was probably designed as well as built by de Caux himself. Inside the house the famous double cube room, which was rebuilt in 1648 with advice from Jones (then aged 75) is of a higher standard. Even this room, however, built to house the Earl of Pembroke's Van Dycks, probably has more to do with his pupil John Webb than with Jones. The type of the ideal English country house of the seventeenth century was to be created not by Jones, but, significantly in view of the future development of English architecture, by a gentleman amateur of genius, Sir Roger Pratt (1620-84).

Pratt built Coleshill, Berkshire (Plate 2) for his cousin Sir George Pratt. It was burnt down in 1952, but photographs confirm that Coleshill was a major architectural achievement, and one that gives its creator a prominent place in the history of English architecture. Until the discovery of Pratt's notebooks in the 1920s Jones was assumed to be its designer. With hindsight it can be seen that Coleshill was more original than any building by Jones, who always based his designs on one or more models. Pratt certainly consulted Jones, but he also used his travels in Italy, France and the Low Countries to study developments there. In drawings for country houses Jones uses a sloping roof with dormer windows, and Pratt did this at Coleshill, keeping the roof skilfully in harmony with the rectangular building below. The plan of the house was a Jonesian double square, and although the exterior looks simple enough the simplicity was, as so often with neo-classical art, deceptive. The spacing of the windows, for example, the use of rusticated stones on the corners of the building and the daring use of the tall chimneys are all extremely sophisticated. Indeed, simple but graceful sophistication is what photographs of Coleshill most convey, and this quality is said to have extended to the detailed carving on both exterior and interior; photographs, especially of the magnificent hall, are particularly eloquent in this respect, and a salutary reminder that skilled master masons such as Nicholas Stone or Wren's mason, Edward Pearce, who worked on Coleshill, were almost as rare, and as crucial for success, as the architects for whom they worked.

1 Inigo Jones, Banqueting House, Whitehall (1619–22)
Photo: University of Newcastle upon Tyne

2 Sir Roger Pratt, Coleshill, Berkshire (1649–61)
Photo: University of Newcastle upon Tyne

3 Sir Christopher Wren, St Paul's Cathedral, West Front
Photo: RCHM, England

4 Antonio Canaletto, *The Thames from Somerset House Terrace*
Photo: HM The Queen, Royal Library, Windsor Castle

5 Sir Christopher Wren, Hampton Court Palace, Fountain Court (1689–1702)
   Photo: RCHM, England

The visual arts and architecture 123

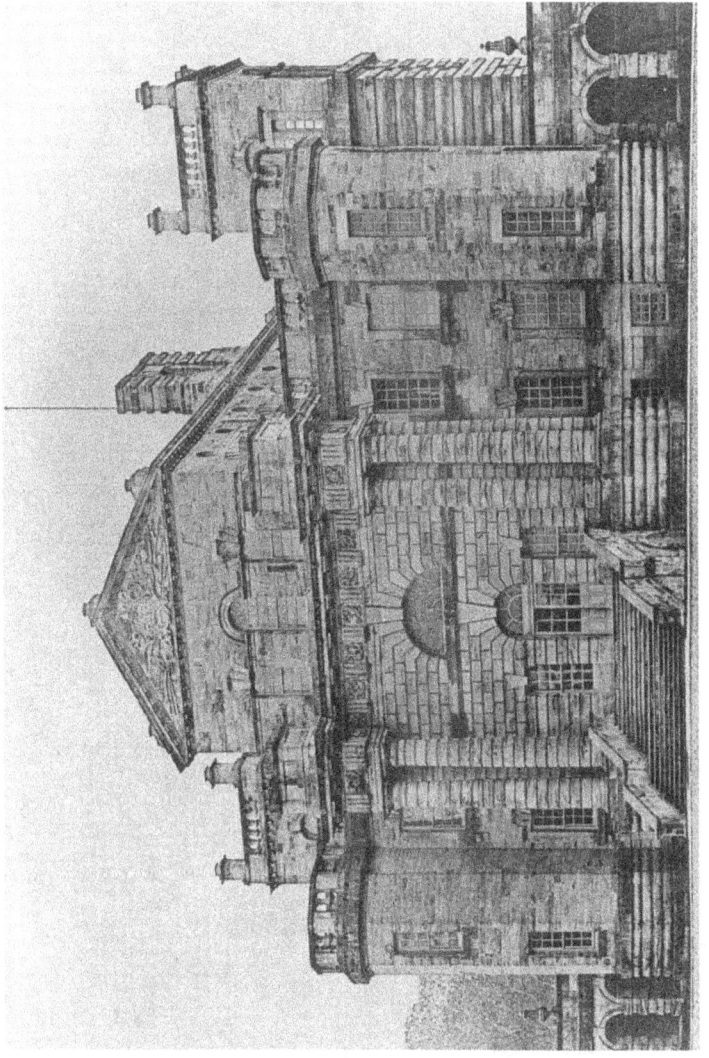

6 Sir John Vanbrugh, Seaton Delaval, Northumberland (1720)
 Photo: University of Newcastle upon Tyne

124 T.G.S. Cain

7 Nicholas Hawksmoor, The Mausoleum, Castle Howard (1732)
Photo: RCHM, England

8 Nicholas Stone, *John Donne*, St Paul's Cathedral (1631)
Photo: Courtauld Institute

9 Edward Pierce, *Sir Christopher Wren*
   Photo: Ashmolean Museum

10 Daniel Mytens, *Algernon Percy, 10th Earl of Northumberland* (c. 1620)
Photo: Viscount De L'Isle, Penshurst Place Collection

11 Sir Anthony Van Dyck, *Algernon Percy, 10th Earl of Northumberland* (c. 1640)
Photo: The Duke of Northumberland

The visual arts and architecture 129

12 Sir Anthony Van Dyck, *The Five Eldest Children of Charles I* (1637)
Photo: HM The Queen, Royal Collection, St James's Palace

13 William Dobson, *The Artist with Sir Charles Cotterell and ?Nicholas Lanier* (c. 1646)
Photo: The Duke of Northumberland

14 Samuel Cooper, *Oliver Cromwell* (c. 1650)
Photo: The Duke of Buccleuch and Queensberry

15 Samuel Cooper, *James Scott, Duke of Monmouth and Buccleuch* (c. 1664)
Photo: HM The Queen, Royal Collection, St James's Palace
(12.5 cm x 10 cm)

The visual arts and architecture 133

16 Sir Peter Lely, *Self-Portrait* (*c.* 1660)
 Photo: National Portrait Gallery

Pratt began building Coleshill in the year of Charles I's execution, and work continued until just after the Restoration. Nothing could show more eloquently than these dates how mistaken is the assumption that the arts stood still during the Interregnum. Jones died in 1652 (apparently in Somerset House, which suggests that he was not wholly out of favour with the new regime) but his devoted pupil John Webb continued to work throughout these years, building Lamport Hall, Northamptonshire (1654–7), Gunnersbury, Middlesex (1658–63) and redesigning much of The Vine, Sherborne. Other notable houses built during these years included Wimborne St Giles (*c.* 1650), Thorpe Hall (1651–6), Tyttenhanger (*c.* 1654) and Wisbech Castle (1654–8), all built for prominent Parliamentarians. Clearly the Civil Wars themselves held up building work, but only in large-scale state building projects can the Interregnum be seen as an architecturally barren period. Cromwell may have been tempted to accept the crown, but he was never likely to build himself a grand palace. He continued to use the old palaces of Whitehall and Hampton Court, and the Banqueting House remained as the sole product of the earlier plans for a new palace.

IV

As has been said, the Banqueting House was the setting not only for Charles's execution, but also for Rubens's paintings celebrating the apotheosis of his father. Painted for Charles I between 1630 and 1634, they form the only decorative scheme by Rubens which is still in its original place. Only a minor part of his prodigious output, they are nevertheless the most impressive single product of the patronage of major foreign artists by the English crown, and one of the few which can unequivocally be described as baroque. As always Rubens's preparatory oil sketches are more vibrant than the finished canvases, which may be partly studio work, but the confident, massive composition, the radiant colours, and the broad, free brushwork of the finished product give exciting realization to that dream of absolute but benevolent political power which the Stuarts were never to see realized in any other form than that of art.

Despite his respect for the English court, and for Arundel in particular, there was never any real prospect that Rubens might be induced to remain in England, his knighthood notwithstanding. Even if nothing else had prevented him, the English obsession with portraiture and the restrictions on religious subjects would have been stifling for an artist of his range and ambition. Dr Johnson's remark 'I would rather see the portrait of a dog that I know, than all the allegorical paintings they can shew me in the world' sums up an enduring English attitude which has never been adequately explained. Protestantism certainly plays a part: not only did it exclude such staple commissions of the Catholic painter as altar panels, but it encouraged that individualism and introspection which only the portrait can serve. If we add to this the strong English sense of family, an almost laral worship of ancestors, we have at least part of the explanation for that dominance which led Hilliard to state in 1600 that of all forms of painting, 'the perfection is to imitate the face of mankind'. The literature of these years, it is worth noting, displays no comparable limitations of scope: analogies can be made with the inward-looking individualism of the meditative lyric, with the self-portraits offered by Jonson and Herrick, or the sophisticated psychology of the drama; but the ways in which seventeenth-century literature imitates the face of humankind extend far beyond anything Hilliard had in mind.

The first foreign painter of real if minor distinction whom Arundel did keep in England was the Dutchman, Daniel Mytens (c. 1590–1647), who entered Arundel's service in about 1618, and who became painter to Charles I on the latter's accession in 1625. From the outset Mytens's portraits have far greater realism and weight than the patterned, meticulously detailed work of his immediate predecessors in England. The sitter is placed in three-dimensional space, the body not only given weight but also seeming actually to occupy a place in a way that must have been deeply impressive to patrons who had grown up with the work of Larkins or Peake. These qualities are seen at their best in the portrait of the Duke of Hamilton in the Scottish National Portrait Gallery, or in that of the Earl of Northumberland (Plate 10). A close contemporary and rival of Mytens in the 1620s was Cornelius Johnson or Janssen (1593–1664), English born of Flemish parents. Though some of Johnson's work is difficult to distinguish from Mytens, his best paintings are of single heads or busts, rather than the groups or full lengths favoured by Mytens and Van Dyck. The modesty of Johnson's characteristic format has caused him to be underrated in comparison with Mytens, but he is always quietly sensitive to the personality of his subject, whose features, treated realistically and undramatically, are often set in a painted oval frame that makes the whole composition strikingly reminiscent of an enlarged version of an Isaac Oliver miniature. With Johnson should be mentioned another native-born painter, the amateur Sir Nathaniel Bacon who, though he painted only for himself, produced work of a comparable quality to that of Mytens. Largely unknown, he remains one of the most accomplished of all English amateur painters.

Mytens and Johnson, though, have to be seen as minor figures when compared with the greatest product of Arundel's patronage, Anthony Van Dyck (1599–1641). Van Dyck, described by Rubens as the 'best of my pupils' though never formally apprenticed to him, had first come to London in 1620, a well-established if precocious master. Though still under the overwhelming influence of Rubens, his paintings of this early period already show his preference for quieter, more graceful gestures and expressions, and a greater concern with purely surface patterns than is found in Rubens. These tendencies would have received partial encouragement from the many Venetian paintings he saw in London in the houses of Arundel and Buckingham. In 1621 he joined the Countess of Arundel in Venice and then accompanied her to Mantua, where she began negotiations for the purchase of the Gonzaga collection. When the Countess returned, Van Dyck stayed on in Italy, painting under the influence of the great Italians of the previous century, and of one in particular: at his death, Van Dyck owned nineteen Titians.

Van Dyck entered Charles I's service on his return to England in 1632, and for the nine remaining years of his life worked with intense industry and inventiveness on a series of portraits of such distinction that they dominated English portraiture for at least the next century and a half. These English portraits are large in scale, and usually dramatic in pose. A strong sense of movement, or of incipient movement, is given to the sitters, intensified by billowing curtains or flowing draperies. Classical columns often give a counterbalancing sense of both stability and nobility, their texture as well as their form contrasting, as so often in Rubens, with the smooth silks or satins. The settings and poses give a strong sense of the social status of the sitter at the same time as they project an ease that is sometimes wrongly described as languid. The paint is applied with gusto, its texture an integral part of the whole. All these characteristics are major ingredients of the baroque style: however, in all Van Dyck's great English paintings there is a marked grace and restraint that is quite untypical of the baroque. His portraits, even of the king, are less obviously aristocratic, less redolent of aggressive power, than those of the Italian or Spanish sitters of his earlier years: it is part of the triumph of the portraits of Charles I that he is made to seem majestic without being assertively so. The equestrian portrait of the king, in which he seems to ride forward out of the canvas, has none of the aggressive pomposity of Van Dyck's portrait of the Spanish Marquis of Moncada, now in the Louvre. The poses of horse and rider are identical, but the features and temper of the king's face are quite different: this is an image of wise and beneficent majesty, a convincing realization of the courteous and semi-divine monarch celebrated in so many Caroline masques.

Van Dyck's most profound achievement in this and other royal portraits was to transform the small, reserved figure whom Mytens had portrayed realistically as standing defensively on his dignity into the personification of a majesty that had no need to assert itself. This was not simply a matter of flattery: it was an image of good government, analogous to that presented in masques and court poetry. Moreover, Van Dyck was sensitive, as Mytens had not been, to the best qualities in the king, his sense of duty, his loyalty and courage, his air of quiet melancholy, and it was these aspects of his character that he distilled brilliantly into the series of paintings by which we now know the king who, from a less sympathetic point of view was a shy, obstinate yet unreliable man of unprepossessing appearance with a speech impediment that made him still more distant in his manner.

Something similar might be said of Van Dyck's presentation of Charles's queen, Henrietta Maria. Prince Rupert's sister, knowing the queen only from Van Dyck's portraits, was put out to find that she was 'a little woman with long lean arms, crooked shoulders, and teeth protruding from her mouth like guns from a fort'. These qualities are convincingly suppressed in Van Dyck's view of her as queen, loving wife and mother, a figure displaying the same air of self-possessed grace that is seen in the king.

What is true of the royal portraits is largely true of Van Dyck's portraits of Charles's court. The Countess of Sussex was unusual in complaining that she had been made to look more 'ill-formed' and fat than she really was. Van Dyck invests most of his sitters, especially the men, with an air of graceful dignity and sophistication. The difference between a highly competent portrait by his predecessors and one by Van Dyck can be seen by comparing his half-length of the 10th Earl of Northumberland (Plate 11) with the slightly earlier version of the Earl by Mytens (Plate 10). 'The proudest man alive' according to Clarendon, something of that pride can be seen in Mytens's portrait, which in its quiet realism is itself a great advance on a previous generation of English portraits; but in the Van Dyck the features of the great magnate, unmistakably the same man, display an altogether more sympathetically realized version of his pride. Restrained, sophisticated and sensitive, even when placed as Lord High Admiral against the vividly sketched scene of battle, Northumberland's portrait typifies (apart from its unusual shape) the view taken by Van Dyck of any number of English gentlemen. He certainly does not, as is often said, portray an elegant but doomed court that looks away from reality: the intelligence and awareness we see in Northumberland's features is there too in portraits of other supporters of the Parliament's cause like Philip, Lord Wharton (Hermitage, Leningrad), the Earl of Warwick (National Museum, New York) or Arthur Goodman (Chatsworth), and in the various versions of Strafford's troubled face. It is there too in the portraits of such archetypal royalists as Thomas Killigrew (Windsor Castle) or James Stuart, Duke of Richmond (Iveagh Bequest, Kenwood). These portraits of the English gentry and nobility, compared with Van Dyck's earlier treatment of the nobility of Genoa in, for example, *The Lomellini Family* (National Gallery of Scotland, Edinburgh), reveal that emphasis on autocratic pride and remoteness has given way to a less obviously baroque presentation of sitters whose stylish air, informal dress and natural pose do the opposite of suggesting that they are insensitive to political and social developments around them. The romantic view of Charles's court as fated but insulated from the world around has always been difficult to uphold, and Van Dyck's portraits help to confirm that its members were indeed aware of the growing tensions that were not merely around, but inside the court. Before Van Dyck's death in 1641, brothers like Warwick and Holland, friends like Northumberland and Strafford, had already begun to find themselves ranged on opposing sides in a contest that was to lead Strafford and Holland, like the king, to the scaffold.

As Van Dyck's treatment of his sitters changed during his English period, so did his palette. His earlier sitters are painted in a range of dark colours, often in black, whereas the English ones are presented in lighter colours reminiscent of Veronese, with blues, pinks, golds, silvers and whites used with a freedom and mastery of light and texture that gives the surfaces of the canvases a vibrant life of their own. Armour as well as cloth gains from Van Dyck's brilliant use of white highlights in particular, as in the portraits of Arundel and Northumberland. Occasionally it is a detail of the painting which seems to have received the greatest attention: in the double portrait of Dorothy, Viscountess Andover, and Elizabeth, Lady Thimbleby, in the National Gallery the two sisters are static, as is too often the case with his portraits of women from his English period. The figure of Cupid stands out in terms both of rich colour contrasts, and of the relish with which flesh, hair and wings are painted. The attention given to Cupid may owe something to the fact that Van Dyck rarely had a chance during these years to paint anything but portraits, from which this represents a partial escape. It also reveals a special enjoyment and skill in the painting of children which dates from his years in Italy, a mastery seen at its finest in the group of the five eldest children of Charles I (Plate 12).

Van Dyck died in December 1641, just two weeks after Pym's Grand Remonstrance had passed through the Commons to signal an intensification of the struggle between king and parliament. William Dobson, his greatest successor, found that the court he painted was a court on the move and at war with its own people. Dobson's more dramatic, less idealizing technique was splendidly suited to this task. Although he was inevitably influenced by Van Dyck, and borrowed poses and techniques of composition freely, he was nevertheless more independent of him in both technique and approach to character than any other major painter working in England in this period. Dobson's was a very original kind of genius: his earliest surviving works from the 1630s, portraits of himself and his wife, are quite unlike anything painted in England before that date: they recall Caravaggio in their dramatic use of light and aggressive realism, but their conception is the confident one of a great and original artist, not an imitator, and in them we see the emergence of the first native English painter of major stature since Hilliard. The heavy impasto technique, the robust realism and the sense of solidity and weight given to the sitter characterize most of Dobson's work, though in some of the later portraits done for the Royalist Court in Oxford the impasto disappears and the paint is laid on very thin, perhaps for the pedestrian reason that Dobson's supplies were low.

Dobson's best portraits show him as the most unequivocally baroque of all the painters discussed in this chapter, apart, of course, from Rubens. This is above all evident in the dramatic poses and brushwork, but it is there too in the backgrounds to his portraits, commonly landscapes of war or of impending storm, and in his use of learned and sometimes very striking accessories: classical sculpture, guns and armour, and – in the portrait of Charles II as Prince of Wales (Scottish National Portrait Gallery) – a startling head of Medusa, complete with vicious snakes, staring out from beneath a chaotic heap of standards and weapons. In this, as in many of his paintings, Dobson uses a three-quarter length format which is all his own, cutting the prince off at the knees as Van Dyck would never have done. This strategy gives the figure dramatic impetus by thrusting it to the very front of the painting in a way that would be impossible with a subject shown with feet planted firmly on the ground.

Many of the best and most original characteristics of Dobson's work appear in what is probably the last of his major paintings, a group portrait of the artist with Sir Charles Cotterell and a third man, probably the composer, connoisseur and amateur artist Nicholas Lanier (Plate 13). This early 'conversation piece' appears to record a moment of choice, in which the painter turns his back on Lanier to be embraced by his patron Cotterell. The half-length figures are invested with weight and movement. The treatment of the flesh, as usual in Dobson, is utterly convincing, as are the fabrics, particularly the rich material of Lanier's doublet, the white of which is vividly rendered by a mass of greys with white highlights, contrasting with the rich black of Cotterell's coat. Such mastery of paint, and such ease in handling an ambitious and complex composition, are not matched by any English-born painter 'in large' before Hogarth.

There was, however, an English contemporary of even greater stature than Dobson who was rightly famed throughout Europe as the greatest living master in his field, the miniaturist Samuel Cooper (1609–72). Cooper was the first English painter to see himself, and to be seen by others, in the special role of an artist of genius, whose clients paid almost as much for the privilege of personal contact with such a man as they did for the finished portrait (this was Pepys's experience). Cooper was the last great figure in the tradition of limning, or painting in miniature, which had flourished in England since the early sixteenth century. Nicholas Hilliard and Isaac Oliver had ensured that this was the one field of painting in which England led rather than followed the rest of Europe, and the tradition remained strong in the 1620s and 1630s in the hands of Peter Oliver, Isaac's son, and John Hoskins the elder. The craft was a 'mystery often handed down in families, and Cooper, Hoskins's nephew, together with the shadowy figure of John Hoskins the younger, carried on the mystery in the next generation. An attempt has been made recently to reconstruct the younger Hoskins's *oeuvre*, which emerges as lively and naturalistic, its best-known example the fine miniature of the Leveller Sir John Wildman (1647, Victoria and Albert Museum). But Hoskins the younger seems to have painted little, and to have stopped altogether after about 1660 (an inconvenient fact for those who see this as the date at which artistic activity resumes in England). In contrast, his cousin Samuel Cooper produced a stream of signed and dated works of extremely high quality that runs from the portrait of Margaret Lemon, Van Dyck's dangerously jealous mistress (she once tried to bite his thumb off to prevent him painting other women) in the 1630s, to that of Lord Clifford of Chudleigh in 1672, the year of Cooper's death.

The young Cooper was evidently close to Van Dyck in the 1630s, as the portrait of Margaret Lemon shows. Partly as a result of this contact, he moves away from the techniques and general approach of his uncle Hoskins, replacing the relative formality of the latter with the informal, intimate image which was one aim of the baroque portrait. With this illusion of intimacy he frequently combines, as did Van Dyck, that of nobility in those of his sitters to whom such a quality is appropriate. He can also, however, produce an altogether different effect, the illusion of unvarnished frankness, in portraits of men like Hobbes, scientists and philosophers for whom (the miniatures tell us) truth is a higher concern than social status. This moderately subtle form of flattery reaches its apotheosis in the great portrait of Cromwell (Plate 14), painted with the famous instructions to show 'pimples, warts and everything as you see them'. A recently discovered miniature shows that Cooper had in fact painted Cromwell as early as 1649 (National Portrait Gallery). Both portraits, and other Cooper images of the Parliamentarian leaders, are appropriately austere, but it is worth restating the fact that there is no evidence that Cooper was not in as much demand during these years of the Republic as later. In so far as there is any hiatus in English painting in these years (and it is in fact very largely bridged by the work of Cooper and Lely) it is due to the early deaths of Van Dyck in 1641 and Dobson in 1646, rather than to the crude picture of Puritan philistinism fostered by too many art historians.

The fame, indeed the very survival of the Cromwell portrait show how highly Cooper and his clients valued the *ad vivum* likeness. Cooper always painted his sitters from the life, and it is in his work that we first see in England the idea of the unfinished original master sketch, such as the Cromwell portrait, or that of the young Monmouth (Plate 15), being more 'authentic', because of the interaction between artist and sitter, than the many more finished copies that would have been made from it. Not only the Cromwell, but also other *ad vivum* sketches for portraits, were in greater demand than more highly finished miniatures when Cooper's widow sold them.

Cooper had few studio assistants, and used them only for making acknowledged copies of his own work. His clients could always be sure of what they were getting. This was not always true of Cooper's major contemporary in large-scale painting, Sir Peter Lely (1618–80), who was the organizer of one of the most busy and efficient studios known in the history of painting, and whose reputation has suffered as a result. Lely's assistants worked (after Lely had painted the head) from a range of catalogued and numbered postures ('Sir Ralph Verney 1/2 49', for example, meant a half-length portrait in pose number 49) so that the later portraits in particular tend to exhibit a certain similarity, explaining the remark of his English rival, Robert Walker, who 'swore Lely's pictures was all brothers and sisters'. Lely might well have replied that Walker's portraits were often illegitimate children of Van Dyck. Certainly he was technically much more accomplished than Walker or any other of his contemporaries, though another Dutch immigrant, Gerard Soest, and the Catholic Michael Wright were both painters of considerable ability, who seem to have had neither Lely's organizational ability, nor his willingness to modify his style to suit the tastes of his sitters, who apparently welcomed a technique which made their features correspond to a fashionable type. It is a mistake, however, to dwell on such limitations, for at his best Lely was a formidable and highly influential painter. When he first arrived in London in the early 1640s under the patronage of Northumberland he began to develop a style which echoed Van Dyck, but gave a greater weight to the forms of his sitters. His finest paintings of the 1650s are arcadian portraits of children, painted for two other 'noble defectors' Pembroke and Leicester: in them his draughtsmanship and dramatic sense of texture and colour come together in the service of subjects towards which he was evidently sympathetic.

The growing confidence shown in such paintings increases during the Restoration period. His earlier designs and figures had often been stiff, but the portraits that emerge from Lely's studio during the 1660s have an ease and luxuriousness about them which is highly distinctive: he uses clear, vibrant colours, a paint thicker than Van Dyck's, but laid on with equal fluency, and flowing, rich drapery. The drapery is an important element, adding to the baroque sense of movement in Lely's pictures, and at the same time allowing the use of large blocks of resonant, subtly varied colour. In the later work, the paint becomes thinner, the colours less bright, and many country houses display almost monochromatic portraits of ladies largely indistinguishable from one another, with the same heavy-lidded eyes, frequently in variations of the brownish gold that Lely (or was it court fashion?) then favoured.

These paintings, largely studio work, have damaged his reputation – it is a cliché that he became a victim of his own success – but it seems likely not only that his sitters were too numerous for him to give them proper attention, but also that they actually encouraged the stereotyped poses and facial expressions. It is significant that more care went into his self-portrait (Plate 16) than into most of his subjects. Late in his life he told his friend Sir William Petty and others that he was 'Ambitious to make us an immortal picture'. He never did, but he made some very good ones. He had a considerable range, from the arcadian groups and portraits of the 1650s to the voluptuous series of 'Windsor Beauties' (Hampton Court) to the austere, heroic portraits of the Flagmen at Greenwich (National Maritime Museum).

Of his contemporaries other than Soest and Wright, Lely's huge practice might only have been threatened by Isaac Fuller had he not, in Lely's words, dissipated 'so great a talent' through alcohol. Fuller's best-known paintings are the related self-portraits in the Bodleian and National Portrait Gallery: the latter is a splendid, flamboyant composition which wholly supports Lely's estimate of Fuller's potential. A more shadowy figure, perhaps a pupil or imitator of Fuller, is William Sheppard, whose portrait of the dramatist Thomas Killigrew exists in several versions; that at Dyrham Park dated 1650 is the work of a highly accomplished minor master.

Of the next generation, Lely's two best pupils, Greenhill and Wissing, died young, leaving John Riley and Godfrey Kneller to succeed to Lely's role as fashionable portrait painter. The prospect is a depressing one: Riley's court portraits are dull and undistinguished, while the German-born Kneller is in many ways a lesser version of Lely, whom Pepys described as 'a mighty proud man and full of state'. Contemporaries seem to have reacted in a similar way to Kneller, though he had less justification for his immense vanity. Both men established studios with a huge and often undistinguished output, and both are best known for series of portraits, Kneller's Hampton Court Beauties and the Admirals at Greenwich forming conscious parallels to Lely's Windsor Beauties and Flagmen. Kneller's most famous series, however, the Kit Cat Club (1702–17) (National Portrait Gallery) is consciously different from Lely, direct and relatively austere in conception. Even in the Kit Cat Club, however, there is a lack of inventiveness in Kneller's poses, the sense that even here the artist is engaging in routine work. At his best, Kneller can provide a compensating degree of psychological subtlety in his portraits, but no more so than his less successful rival in later years, the Swedish-born Michael Dahl (1656/9–1743), who now looks a portraitist of equal stature, handling paint with more vigour than Kneller and often presenting faces of greater psychological interest. In general, however, the period between the best work of Lely and that of Hogarth in the 1730s sees even portrait painting, that most English of art forms, at a low ebb.

Equally lacking in distinction is the other form which flourished during these years (in terms of square feet covered), decorative painting. English patrons wishing to compete with the great baroque interiors of France imported a series of notably second-rate artists, to the limitations of whose work they seem to have remained complacently unaware. Verrio, Laguerre, Pellegrini and the two Riccis, uncle and nephew, all received major commissions, though in the end they were displaced by the most competent of English decorative painters, Sir James Thornhill (1675/6–1734), soon to become Hogarth's unwilling father-in-law. Thornhill's commissions for Greenwich, Hampton Court and the dome of St Paul's, the latter probably the most familiar of all these large schemes, were significant victories for an English painter over foreign rivals, and prepared the way for the aggressive nationalism of his more talented son-in-law. Even Thornhill is no more than competent, however, and his and other decorative painting of the post-Restoration period is interesting mainly as an adjunct to that art form which did flourish spectacularly in the late Stuart period, architecture.

The same must be said, though with less force, of the sculpture of the period: neither Arundel nor Charles I had the kind of success in their patronage of sculptors that they did with painters. Both courted Bernini, who was, however, firmly tied to Rome, although he did carve a bust of the king, based on Van Dyck's study of him in three positions. Much admired, it was destroyed in the fire which burnt Whitehall Palace in 1698. One truly distinguished bust of an Englishman by Bernini, that of Thomas Baker, does survive, its bravura craftsmanship hinting at the quality of the lost one. Instead of Bernini, Van Dyck's sculpting equivalent in the English court was the Frenchman Hubert Le Sueur (active 1610–43), whose main claim to fame is his bronze equestrian statue of Charles I at Charing Cross, the fate of which is described in chapter 6 by P.W. Thomas (p. 154). Apart from his technical skill as a caster, the only explanation for Le Sueur's mediocre work gaining any respect in England is that it probably had a veneer of fashionable sophistication: now it seems merely stiff, dull and empty. It is significant that Arundel did not employ him, but turned instead to Francesco Fanelli and Francois Dieussart. Even these men, however, probably owed their appeal to their knowledge of baroque fashions: the more provincial-seeming Nicholas Stone, already mentioned as a mason-architect, was also responsible for some of the most dramatic English sculpture of the period. His best-known work is the statue of Donne in his shroud (Plate 8), rising from his urn on the Day of Judgement. Walton records in his *Life* of Donne how the latter got up from his deathbed and donned his funeral shroud to pose for this extraordinary composition. Pedants question Walton's account, but the statue, whatever its genesis, survived the Great Fire, and is still to be seen in the ambulatory of St Paul's, with the great poet, knees slightly bent, ascending towards Heaven. Stone had learnt much from his time as a journeyman with the great Dutch mannerist de Keyser, and from the classical sculpture in Arundel's collection. He was also able to draw directly on Michelangelo for the tombs of Francis and George Holles in Westminster Abbey, and was often very inventive in his treatment of the funeral effigy which was, in Protestant England, the staple product of his workshop. And yet subsequent centuries have largely accepted his contemporaries' evaluation of him as a relatively humble artisan craftsman, a mason who could turn his hand to carving or to architecture.

Just such another figure is Wren's master mason, Edward Pierce (d. 1695), whose skill can best and most appropriately be seen in his bust of Wren in the Ashmolean (Plate 9). It is not unworthy of Bernini, and the few other surviving works by him confirm a talent more considerable than those of such specialist rivals as John Bushnell, Caius Gabriel Cibber and (when he was carving in stone) Grinling Gibbons. Pierce's work for Wren, including the wood carving in the church of St Lawrence Jewry (bombed in 1941), and before that for Pratt at Coleshill, covered the whole range of the mason's craft. Only his artisan status and the range of demands made on him prevented from being recognized as the leading English sculptor of the century.

Working in wood, Grinling Gibbons (1648–1721) developed a distinctive freshness which escaped him in stone. The influence of Dutch realism, especially in flower painting, was a decisive factor in his development of that crisp mixture of naturalism and formality which characterizes his work: born in Holland of English parents, he was receptive to the Dutch tastes brought over during the Interregnum and reinforced after 1660 by the return of a court exiled in Holland for many years. It was as one of the finest woodcarvers who ever lived that Wren valued Gibbons; he could give exuberant, realistic life to decorative work, whether in a house like Petworth, in the library at Trinity College, Cambridge, the chapel of Trinity, Oxford, or the choir stalls of St Paul's. Despite Gibbons's prolific output much of the work commonly attributed to him in country houses is by other carvers of distinction. Among those working in a similar style were Samuel Watson, responsible for much of the 'Gibbons' carving at Chatsworth, and Edmund Carpenter, who filled the same role at Belton. They are part of a tradition of skilled provincial craftsmen in wood and stone which sadly has no counterpart in provincial painting, but which is manifest in countless parish churches and country houses, surviving, unlike painting, as a craft from early medieval times until its demise in the nineteenth century.

V

The *sine qua non* for the work of all these men was the setting provided by the architect. After the Restoration, Pratt continued to produce important buildings, notably Clarendon House, in Piccadilly, and Kingston Lacy in Dorset. Clarendon House (1664–7, now demolished) was deeply influential, described by Evelyn, who, though a friend, was an exacting critic, as 'The best contrived, the most useful, graceful, and magnificent house in England'. Clarendon House and Coleshill were the prototypes of many country houses, one of the most perfect surviving examples being Belton House near Grantham (1685–8), possibly designed by another 'ingenious gentleman', William Winde, but owing everything to Pratt.

Pratt retired as an architect in 1667 to manage his estates. The professional architect Webb, who had no estates to manage, looked in 1660 for the Surveyorship of the King's Works, which, as the pupil of Jones, he felt to be rightfully his. But this was not the age of the professional designer, a species, indeed, which Pratt warned prospective patrons against, and the Surveyorship went instead to yet another gentleman connoisseur, the poet John Denham. Webb's disillusioned protest is worded significantly: 'though Denham may have, as most gentry, some knowledge of the theory of architecture, he can have none of the practice'. Architecture was now part of the equipment of 'most gentry'.

Denham designed his own house (later Burlington House) in Piccadilly, but none of his buildings were of consequence: he was a better poet than an architect. However, his colleague at the Office of Works, Hugh May, was a skilful interpreter of the new Dutch styles which he had seen in Holland during the Interregnum. Eltham Lodge (begun 1663) is the product of this influence, a country house which, with its emphasis on the texture and colour of brick, moves away from Jonesian and Italianate models. Meanwhile the disappointed Webb was also moving away from his master, developing in the massiveness of the King Charles block at Greenwich the seeds of an English version of baroque which was to flower a generation later in the work of Talman, Vanbrugh and Hawksmoor.

All these men, even Pratt, are dwarfed, however, by another amateur of architecture, the Savilian Professor of Astronomy at Oxford and founder member of the Royal Society, Sir Christopher Wren (1632–1723). Wren's longevity, and the scale and quality of his later achievement make it easy to overlook Wren's origins in a tradition similar to that of Pratt, the tradition of the gentleman virtuoso; but in Wren's case we are dealing with a virtuoso rivalled only by Leonardo, one who would be remembered as a mathematician and astronomer even if he had never designed a single building. Evelyn heard of him in the early 1650s, 'that prodigious young scholar Mr Chris. Wren', but his serious intellectual career begins in his teens, when because of his knowledge of anatomy he was chosen by Sir Charles Scarburgh to assist in his pioneering lectures at Surgeon's Hall in the late 1640s. An interest in anatomy remained throughout Wren's life: he invented a method of blood transfusion in the late 1650s, and was working on an artificial eye at the same period. His other inventions, let alone his experimental interests at this period, are too numerous to be listed in full: of astonishing variety, they range from 'ways of submarine navigation' to mechanized methods of weaving. This range and originality of intellectual activity continued until the end of his life, an unparalleled creative career of almost eighty years; Titian, Bernini, Picasso and Matisse were of comparable longevity, but none of these can challenge the sheer variety of Wren's interests.

That architecture came to dominate Wren's life was partly a matter of chance, the extraordinary opportunity given by the destruction of so much of London in the Great Fire of 1666. But his friend Hooke's praise of Wren – 'since the time of Archimedes there scarce ever met in one man in so great a perfection such a mechanical hand and so philosophic a mind' – makes him seem destined as the perfectly equipped architect. He is often said to have started late, but it is probable that a strong interest in problems of building design existed, along with so much else, at an early date. The first extant buildings, however, appear in the early 1660s, the chapel of Pembroke College, Cambridge, and the Sheldonian Theatre, Oxford. While the latter was being built, Wren made his only recorded trip abroad, visiting Paris for six months. Here he had his brief meeting with Bernini, 'but the old reserv'd Italian gave me but a few minutes view' of his sketches for the Louvre. He returned with a wealth of first-hand experience of recent French architectural practice, and confronted the great opportunity of his career, the rebuilding of London. Seven-eighths of the City, including virtually all its churches and its cathedral, had been destroyed by the fire of 1666. Wren submitted a plan for restoring the whole City almost before the fire had burnt itself out, but costs and vested interests prevented his elegant scheme from being adopted, and he had to be content with the task of rebuilding St Paul's and fifty-one City churches.

Nowhere is Wren's longevity more important than in the evolution of St Paul's (Plate 3). He was 35 when he began to supervise the long task of demolition and site clearing in 1668: over 47,000 wagon loads of rubble had to be carted away, and gunpowder and battering rams used to remove the more stubborn remnants. He was 85 when political pressures forced his dismissal as Surveyor-General in 1718, the fabric of the cathedral completed, but the decoration of the cupola (which Wren wanted in mosaic) not yet done. The length of time that was spent on the building enabled him to modify his design again and again, to the fury of successive Deans, the final result having only a broad similarity to that approved at the outset. Wren's favoured design was rejected due to clerical pressures: it can still be seen in the form of the 'Great Model' in the cathedral, a very pure, chaste structure based on a Greek cross. Like the final product, it would have had a massive dome, but the lack of similarity to Gothic models forced Wren to compromise. He produced a cathedral which for all its classical spirit does echo the traditional ground plan of nave, aisles, crossing and choir.

Wren's creative borrowing and his inventive genius are evident throughout St Paul's. The famous ovoid dome with its massive lantern not only would have been too heavy to be carried by the building beneath were it a simple structure but also would have seemed much too high when viewed from inside. Wren therefore built a separate interior dome, over which he constructed a hidden cone to carry the weight of the great lantern, surrounded by the framework for the huge, lead-covered exterior. A less complex trick was used to overcome the problem posed by the single-storey aisles which had been forced on him: Wren wanted to retain a two-storey external wall all the way round the building. His solution was to build exterior walls on each side which look solid, but whose upper storeys are merely screens which conceal flying buttresses to support the two-storey nave behind them.

The same inventive ingenuity went into the adaptation of a variety of styles and influences to form a structure of overwhelming integrity and originality. Wren was on the whole drawn to classical models, but in St Paul's he incorporated several features derived from Roman baroque: the towers at the west end seem to draw on Borromini's smaller towers at Sant' Agnese in Rome (though it is worth adding that Wren had by this time more experience of designing steeples in every possible variation than any other architect). The curved entrances to the transepts echo designs by Pietro da Cortona and Bernini; even the dome, for all its ingenuity, has similarities to that of St Peter's. It is a vibrant, challenging building, dramatic in scale and ingenious in its execution, but the baroque elements are tempered by the classical spirit of the side walls, apse and portico, and the whole effect is more restrained than the baroque cathedrals of Italy, France or central Europe.

For all this classical spirit, the exterior stonework is richly decorated by Wren's master masons and carvers. Edward Pierce was responsible for much of the south side; others involved were Joshua Marshall, the Strong brothers and the Kempster brothers. Such mysteries, like miniature painting, ran in families: Edward Pierce's father had worked as a painter at Wilton, while Nicholas Stone's sons had succeeded to his practice. Inside the cathedral the most significant additions to this group of artists were the carvers Jonathan Maine and Grinling Gibbons, and the smith Jean Tijou. Tijou forged both the delicate wrought-iron gates in the choir and the huge chain which is built into the base of the dome as reinforcement, pulling the great structure together.

Many of these men also worked with Wren on the numerous projects under way during the long period of St Paul's rebuilding. The City churches in particular took much of Wren's attention. A small number of such buildings might have been a considerable life's work for many distinguished architects: Wren built fifty-one, while working on not only St Paul's, but also Chelsea and Greenwich Hospitals, Hampton Court, Trinity Library, Cambridge, the palace at Winchester (never to be completed) and numerous other buildings of only slightly less importance. The churches in particular provided experience which fed back into St Paul's, and vice versa: they were a field for Wren's extraordinary inventiveness both in his adaptation to the problems of the small, often awkwardly shaped sites, and, most famously, in his treatment of the steeples, no two of which were alike. Twenty-eight of these churches and five lone steeples survive, destroyed partly by Victorian vandalism, partly by German bombs. An impression of the impact they made, along with St Paul's, on the London skyline can be gained from Canaletto's drawings of the eighteenth-century city (Plate 4).

Most of this work, along with Greenwich, Tom Tower, Oxford, Trinity Library, Cambridge, and much else, is in stone. Something should be said, however, about Wren's work in brick, in which at Chelsea and especially at Hampton Court (Plate 5), he uses the rich colours in contrast with stone pillars and facings to produce an effect altogether distinct from his work in stone. Chelsea Hospital is one of the most underrated and least visited of London's great buildings. Viewed from the river, it does not have the splendour of its naval counterpart at Greenwich, but the latter group is not wholly Wren's: he had to take into account Jones's Queen's House, and the king's block built by Webb, while there are later additions by Vanbrugh and Hawksmoor. Though on a huge scale, Chelsea is more modest, more austere, but not less graceful. Here and at Hampton Court a principal consideration in choosing brick may have been cost, but it seems equally likely that the ever inventive and eclectic genius of Wren was attracted by the exploration of the very different effects, more classical than baroque, that the mixture of brick and stone offered.

The austerity of the great Figure Court at Chelsea was not repeated at Hampton Court, where Wren's first designs for a new palace for William and Mary were on a grand scale. Royal economy dictated something less extravagant, and prevented wholesale demolition of Wolsey's old palace. It would be wrong, though, to conclude that the additions to Hampton Court were modest: the mulberry brick and Portland stone of the two garden fronts convey a richness which amounts to magnificence. This is not, as has sometimes been said, an enlarged version of a gentleman's house: more reminiscent of the Renaissance Louvre than of the newer baroque palace of William's enemy, Louis XIV, it is emphatically a royal palace, with motifs of William as Hercules repeated in its decorative programme. Despite this rather unlikely identification, Hampton has none of the aggressive grandeur of the Sun King's palace: significantly, in view of the changing role of the monarchy during the Stuart period, it was the general who defeated Louis XIV's armies who was, just a few years later, to be rewarded with a palace, Blenheim, that in its scale and grandeur rivalled Versailles.

At Hampton Court, as in most of his work, Wren controls the weight and mass of his building with ornament and line. The baroque exploitation of mass to emphasize the weight and solidity of the stone is first seen consistently in a follower of Wren, William Talman at Chatsworth (1686), Dyrham Park (1692) and Drayton, Northants (1701). At Chatsworth, the south front of an otherwise undistinguished design anticipates in its monumental qualities the more exciting designs by Vanbrugh and

Hawksmoor for Castle Howard (1701) and Blenheim Palace (1705). Blenheim was built by Vanbrugh and Hawksmoor not just as a house for Marlborough; it was conceived as a monument to British victories. The nation, not an absolute monarch, was celebrated, and Marlborough, its not unworthy representative, seems to have taken a level-headed view of the prospect of living in such baroque splendour. Even here, though, Wren had a hand, for as at Castle Howard, the two architects were in fact developing Wren's beautiful, unfulfilled plans of 1695 for Greenwich Hospital. A great central portico and hall is joined by curved arcades to Kitchen and Stable Courts to left and right. These frame the central building, and are subtly related to it by the repetition of a number of features, notably the rusticated stonework of four huge pavilions standing at each corner. The effect of receding courts, of massiveness and weight, is truly dramatic.

With the work of Vanbrugh and Hawksmoor at Blenheim the short-lived phase of English baroque reaches its climax. It is true that their great houses, and Hawksmoor's City churches, were all built after the turn of the century, but it would be pedantic to disregard them here for that reason. In all cases, even in the relatively small scale of Seaton Delaval (Plate 6), there is the same essentially baroque delight in the sheer mass of the building, a sense of the weight of stone and a use of planes and proportions that, if it is different in spirit from Wren, is still more removed from the Palladianism of the eighteenth century. There is an increasing disregard for classical rules, which have been almost entirely abandoned in the composition of Seaton Delaval, just outside Newcastle upon Tyne, a building whose design was exclusively Vanbrugh's. Nowhere does Vanbrugh's work for the stage feed more obviously into his parallel career as architect than in this remarkable house.

Hawksmoor's share in Castle Howard and Blenheim can only be conjectured, but he did deliver the last dying kick of English baroque in his design for the Mausoleum at Castle Howard (1732). Burlington, patron of the new Palladianism which the ascendant Whig establishment of the eighteenth century favoured, disapproved of Hawksmoor's grim and majestic temple, with its dramatic peristyle of Doric columns (Plate 7). There was no classical precedent for such a building, and the columns were too close together. The lack of communication between Wren's greatest pupil and the patron of the new enlightenment signals the end of an age in English art and architecture. Burlington's patronage was of a more prescriptive kind than Arundel's: the Palladianism which Jones had brought to Britain at the beginning of the seventeenth century had returned as an orthodoxy.

FURTHER READING

Baker, C.H. Collins, *Lely and the Stuart Portrait Paint)ers* (London, 1912).
Beard, Geoffrey, *The Work of Sir Christopher Wren* (Edinburgh, 1982).
Brown, Christopher, *Van Dyck* (Oxford, 1982).
Cabanne, Pierre, *Rubens*, trans. Oliver Bernard (London, 1967).
Campbell, Colen, *Vitruvius Britannicus* (London, 1715-25).
Colvin, H.M., *A Biographical Dictionary of British Architects, 1600-1840* (London, 1978).
Downes, Kerry, *Sir Christopher Wren and the Making of St Paul's* (London, 1987).
Foskett, Daphne, *Samuel Cooper and his Contemporaries* (London, 1974).
Girouard, Mark, *Robert Smythson and the Architecture of the Elizabethan Era* (London, 1966).
Gombrich, E.H., *Studies in the Art of the Renaissance: I Norm and Form* (London, 1966); *II Symbolic Images* (London, 1972); *III The Heritage of Apelles* (London, 1976).
Hauser, Arnold, *Mannerism: The Crisis of the Renaissance and the Origin of Modern Art*, 2 vols (London, 1965).
Hervey, Mary F.S., *The Life, Correspondence and Collections of Thomas Howard, Earl of Arundel, 'Father of Vertu in England'* (Cambridge, 1921).
Hilliard, Nicholas, *The Arte of Limning*, ed. R.K.R. Thornton and T.G.S. Cain (Ashington, Northumberland and Manchester, 1981).
Hook, Judith, *The Baroque Age in England* (London, 1976).
Lees-Milne, James, *The Age of Inigo Jones* (London, 1953).
Little, Bryan, *Sir Christopher Wren: A Historical Biography* (London, 1975).
Millar, Oliver, *Rubens: The Whitehall Ceiling* (London and New York, 1958).
——*The Age of Charles I: Painting in England 1620-1649* (London, 1972).
——*Sir Peter Lely 1618-1620* (London, 1978).
——*Van Dyck in England* (London, 1982).
Murdoch, John, Murrell, Jim, Noon, Patrick J. and Strong, Roy, *The English Miniature* (New Haven, 1981).
Orgel, Stephen, *The Jonsonian Masque* (Cambridge, Mass., 1965).
Orgel, Stephen, and Strong, Roy, *Inigo Jones: The Theatre of the Stuart Court*, 2 vols (London, Berkeley and Los Angeles, 1973).
Parry, Graham, *The Golden Age Restor'd: The Culture of the Stuart Court, 1603-42* (New York, 1981).
Pevsner, Nikolaus, *The Buildings of England*, 46 vols (Harmondsworth, 1951-74).
——*The Englishness of English Art* (London, 1955).
Phillips, John, *The Reformation of Images: Destruction of Art in England 1535-1660* (Berkeley, California, 1973).
Praz, Mario, 'Baroque in England', *Modern Philology* LXI (1964): 169-79.
Rogers, Malcolm, *William Dobson 1611-1646* (London, 1983).
Saxl, Fritz, and Wittkower, R., *British Art and The Mediterranean* (London, 1948).
Stechow, Wolfgang, *Rubens and the Classical Tradition* (1968).
Summerson, John, *Sir Christopher Wren* (London, 1953).
——*Inigo Jones* (Harmondsworth, 1966).
——*Architecture in Britain, 1530-1830* (6th revd edn, Harmondsworth, 1977).
Tapié, Victor-L., *The Age of Grandeur: Baroque and Classicism in Europe*, trans. A. Ross Williamson (London, 1960).
Waterhouse, Ellis K., *Painting in Britain, 1530-1790* (Harmondsworth, 1953).
Whinney, Margaret, *Sculpture in Britain 1530-1830* (Harmondsworth, 1964).
——*Wren* (London, 1971).
Whinney, Margaret, and Millar, Oliver, *English Art 1625-1714* (Oxford, 1957).

Chapter 6

Conclusion: another pattern
Seventeenth-century Britain revisited

P.W. Thomas

I

A symbol perfected in death

Mr Dick in Dickens's *David Copperfield* is not quite right in the head. There he sits in his study 'working at his Memorial', 'still driving at it with a long pen, and his head almost laid upon the paper'. In a corner stands a paper kite 'covered with manuscript, very closely and laboriously written'; and 'when it flies high, it takes the facts a long way'. All about him is 'the confusion of bundles of manuscripts', numerous pens, and a quantity of ink 'in half gallon jars by the dozen'. 'Do you recollect the date', asks Mr Dick,

> looking earnestly at me, and taking up his pen to note it down; 'when King Charles the First had his head cut off?' I said I believed it happened in the year sixteen hundred and forty nine. 'Well', returned Mr. Dick, scratching his ear with his pen, and looking dubiously at me, 'so the books say; but I don't see how that can be. Because if it *was* so long ago, how could the people about him have made that mistake of putting some of the trouble out of *his* head, after it was taken off, into *mine*?' . . . In fact, I found out afterwards that Mr. Dick had been for upwards of ten years endeavouring to keep King Charles the First out of the Memorial; but he had been *constantly* getting into it, and was there now.

So the image of the long-dead king haunts and hampers Mr Dick's Memorials; and by doing so, as near as can be makes him whole, since his therapy, which is writing, can never be done. The memory of Charles's head shapes and sustains Mr Dick's identity. As Aunt Betsy Trotwood explains, 'he connects his illness with great disturbance and agitation, naturally, and that's the figure, or the simile; or whatever it is called, which he chooses to use. And why shouldn't he, if he thinks proper?' History, we know, is not all kings and few of us are holy simpletons: but the episode is a perfect paradigm of how past and present perennially intersect in our experience. As the figure of the real monarch and the novelist's figment meet in our minds, so history and imagination, fact and fantasy, life and literature, inform each other to enlarge our human sympathy. We are drawn into the solidarity of suffering.

More prosaically we recognize something of ourselves, too, in that laborious memorializer with his dates, his facts, his struggle to understand, his kite-flying, and his unerring eye for the key question: 'Do you recollect the date when King Charles the First had his head cut off?' He looks and sounds very like an historian. And of course we 'Remember': it was (whatever he meant exactly) one of the king's last words; and that date 1649 discloses more than any other, even 1660 or 1688, the character and meaning of the century.

What happened then, and how it was understood, unlocks a mentality very different, seemingly, and distant now from ours. For we no longer 'murder' monarchs; and we punish politicians, if at all, less finally. We have nothing in our more recent experience to match that execution. Staged on the verge of court in the capital city with a show trial preceding it in Westminster Hall, it was designed, not least, to demonstrate the power of Cromwell's army. Ringing down the curtain on the old order and ushering in a new, this act, even then without precedent or parallel in our history, was 'the greatest drama of the age'. And it misfired. Though leaving no one in two minds about Cromwellian *realpolitik*, it transformed the royal protagonist, at a stroke, into the most potent ikon of the century. On that bitter January day Charles conclusively took on the invincible power of myth and won, whatever one believes, an immortality of sorts. Passing from the stage of history he became, to borrow T.S. Eliot's phrase, 'A symbol perfected in death'. Long before Dickens fabricated Mr Dick, fact had merged into artefact. Somehow the rite of passage on the scaffold at the very last moment raised life to the level of art.

To focus on that dramatic figure (I mean the one Charles cut *and* the one I use) is not just modern hindsight. The role was of the king's own making: he knew in the first winter of Civil War that he must come out of it either 'a glorious King or a patient martyr'. And however he manoeuvred thereafter he accepted, from the moment his stage-managed trial began, that he would die on the block. He had studied his part minutely, some say beginning with Philogenes, the patient and forgiving ruler, in the last masque of his reign. He executed it now with immaculate timing. For he was the master of ceremonies of his own demise, and, as was customary, delivered his own obituary – 'I tell you . . . that I am the Martyr of the people' – from his scaffold. Within forty-eight hours John Cardell and John Owen had preached to the House of Commons to stiffen the weak-kneed with strong draughts of *Revelation*. Of the two, Owen is the more militant: now the way is open, he proclaims, through this unavoidable desolation and the overthrow of Antichrist, to the Kingdom of God. The language, the draconian figures of Apocalypse were invoked to exorcise the image and memory of the Royal Martyr.

Such conjurations were nothing new: not a few were convinced in 1642 that Christ had 'set up his glorious standard' against the king. Cromwell, Harrison, Overton, Rich and Goffe had all uttered millenarian war-cries. Theirs was the Army of Christ fighting to destroy the Antichrist, whose headquarters had long since removed from Rome to Whitehall. 'On the 23 day of October 1641 did the beast begin the war in Ireland . . . and in England untill the fifth day of April 1645', one wrote. Eventually this talk went too far for Parliamentary moderates and Presbyterians; but the Army pressed on, identifying the dead king in 1650 as 'one of the horns of the Beast'. In 1653 William Aspinall determined (more precisely) that he was actually the little horn of *Daniel* 7: 8. The High Court of Justice had done well to slay him; and John Canne for one was convinced that the act presaged the fall of Antichrist himself which must, by mathematical definition, ensue in 1666. Vavasour Powell, meanwhile, calculated that Charles was not the little horn after all; before long the attack had switched to the zealots' new villain-of-the-piece, Oliver Cromwell. The Fifth Monarchists, whose programme was violent revolution and the overthrow of all existing institutions, universities among them, predicted that *all* the rulers of the earth would soon 'sit bare breeched upon the Hawthorn bushes'. Cromwell did not warm to such images: urged to his face by John Rogers in 1655 to 'consider how neer it is to the end of the Beast's dominion' he silenced him, 'Talk not of that for I must tell you plainly, they are things I understand not.' He did not mean that *Revelation* was a closed book to him – far from it – but that Rogers's mystical mathematics cut no ice. Malcontents and fanatics are never easily deterred, however, and not long after that, John More made bold to send Cromwell an open letter identifying him in so many words – or rather numbers – with the Great Beast of the Apocalypse: REX OLIVER PROTECTOR he somehow added up, leaving the L out of account, to 666. Such calculations were not necessarily the work of cranks: Napier's *Logarithms* were originally devised primarily to help crack the number codes of *Revelation*. But Cromwell had a nation to govern and in any case was always led as much by common sense as godly intimations, though like most contemporaries he would scarce have recognized any absolute distinction between the two. So when Daniel Feake persisted in arguing that Oliver not Charles was the Beast, Cromwell tired of his whirligigs and packed him off to Windsor Castle where the prophet trained his little son to run around singing 'The Protector is a Foole.' The seventeenth century was not all high drama! Nor was the world yet done with Feake and friends.

Back in 1649, however, when visionaries saw the dead monarch as the Beast brought low and John Cook ranted about 'blood guiltyness' and 'justice, freedom, and mercy to the poor' as though this man had been the most terrible tyrant in history, bereaved royalists beheld a very different figure, spat on by rough soldiery as he accepted his crown of thorns and final agony, with scraps of blood-soaked linen (for the mysteries of the old faith had not all been jettisoned) duly effecting miraculous cures. Within a year some thirty reprints and editions of *Eikon Basilike* (purportedly the king's own prayers and prophecies) were produced, making it with the Bible and Foxe's *Book of Martyrs* one of the most powerful volumes of the period. Calvinist England may have turned its back on Catholic relics; and Milton, seeing idolatry as a sign of the latter days, was quick to poke fun at the frontispiece ikon of Charles, actor-like, before the altar at his devotions, but the image of royal saint and martyr was not so easily dislodged. For Protestantism – witness Foxe, Izaac Walton's *Lives* or Wotton's *Life* of his father, or Evelyn's of his – was not averse to hagiography.

Even godly folk, sparing of speech and gesture, wrought monuments of words to their dead. One such, characteristically absorbed with his sainted wife's exemplary life and providential death, fabricated 'a funerall banquet', a 'bookish coffin' wherein the 'elected innocent' lay 'anatomised and embalmed'. Of actual ceremonies, effigies, or petitionary requiems there is no need: his 'paper statue' made to 'cannonize' her, substitutes for all the obsequies it displaces. *Eikon Basilike*, recalling the anointed king whose death cannot but be a singular revelation of divine providence, was the apotheosis of this commemorative mode. Whatever Milton alleged, it was a thoroughly Protestant document, especially as prophecy, the prerogative of kings and dying men, was at the heart of the reformed Church and crucial to Britain's identity and sense of direction. So the king is revealed foretelling his own fate, that he would one day be killed 'in the midst of my Kingdom; my friends and loving subjects being helpless spectators'. He emerges not only as martyr but also as the great seer of his own and his people's destiny. So on all sides the momentous execution acquired a dense prophetic context. William Lilly, grand astrologer of the age, summed up: 'all or most of our ancient English, Welsh and Saxon prophecies had relation to Charles Stuart, late King of England'. He voices that belief in the British as the chosen nation, holy and elect, that was so vibrant in the 1640s and 1650s. Like all successful soothsayers he made the most of hindsight, not uttering his verdict till 1651. But people 'put more confidence in Lilly than they did in God'; what with his and other oracles the nation by 1652 was 'alarmed and even half dead with Prophecies'. Milton's *Ikonoklastes* had little chance of even denting the royal image. The removal from Whitehall of Le Sueur's bronze equestrian statue of Charles I proved equally futile: the piece was sold for scrap but the enterprising purchaser buried it on the quiet, and made a killing selling pocket-knives made, purportedly, from the melting. That effigy, too, emerged intact and in triumph at the Restoration, and still stands at the top of Whitehall.

Of all the images from 1649, however, Andrew Marvell's *Horatian Ode* most fully echoes the deep resonance, best catches the cataclysmic heroic implications of what happened. The poem, it has been said, holds 'in perfect balance' past and future, passive Charles and active Cromwell, the ancient rights and those greater spirits which displace them. Marvell's Cromwell is the instrument of providence, an apocalyptic leader sent to change the course of history: the desolation in his wake may portend a millenarian renovation, maybe a Machiavellian reconstruction. Charles, however decorous, must on both counts give way. Yet doing so he so adorns the 'tragic scaffold' that the surrounding troopers, like spectators at a play, cannot but clap their 'bloody hands'. Significantly the 'dismal groan' of horror that actually arose when the axe fell is not heard in the poem. Instead the focus rests on the Royal Actor, the 'comely' lover of his people dying, as he had lived, ceremoniously but at the last more publicly than had been his wont. The immediate effect, we know, was traumatic. Though John Owen, elated, spied the New Jerusalem at hand, and bright-eyed Fifth Monarchists expected King Jesus any day, most were aghast at the execution. James Harrington, who had come to know and love the king during his captivity, 'contracted a disease by it'; Ambrose Barnes said people were too stunned to speak to each other in the streets; 'women miscarried, men fell into melancholy, some with Consternation expired'. Lord-General Fairfax longed for the day to be blotted out; Archbishop Ussher, looking on from Wallingford House, blotted it out by fainting 'clean away as the axe was raised'. Vaclav Hollar, the engraver, returning from abroad soon after, thought people's expressions changed from former cheerfulness to something 'melancholly, spightfull, as if bewitched'. That was a more than metaphoric possibility in 1649.

Dying in style, in public, and to such effect was not, however, peculiar to princes. The Earl of Derby's case (though a king of sorts as hereditary ruler of the Isle of Man) is instructive. In 1651 he was brought to the block in Bolton: earnestly Calvinist, he agonizes more than Charles; but his ritualization of dying is no less deliberated. 'I draw near to the bottom of the ladder', he writes to his wife on the eve of execution, 'and I am drawing on to the grave, for presently I must away to the fatal stroke.' He prepares for bed: 'I can as willingly lay down my head upon a bed as ever I did upon a pillow.' He lies down: 'Methinks I lie like a monument in a church, and to-morrow I shall really be so.' And on that morrow he approaches the scaffold unkindly built in great part of timber from the ruins of Lathom House, so valiantly defended by his Huguenot wife against godly besiegers who had imagined it 'the great city of Apocalypse', no less! At the ladder's foot the Earl pauses: 'I am not afraid to go up here, though to my death; there are but these few steps between me and eternity.' He kisses the ladder and ascends. 'When I am got into my chamber [pointing to his coffin] I shall then be at rest, and no longer troubled with such a guard and noise as I have been.' The block faces the wrong way: he has it turned towards the church so that he can 'look towards thy sanctuary whilst I am here; and I know that in a few minutes I shall behold my God and my King in thy sanctuary above'. The block 'methinks is very low, and yet there is but one step betwixt that and heaven'. He kisses the axe; offers the axeman the usual sweetener, though the man is surly and unwilling to ask his victim's pardon as was customary. Derby lays his head on the block, and gives the signal. Nothing happens. 'Why', he reproaches his executioner, 'do you keep me from my Saviour?' And the second time the signal was not missed. So the Earl was given time (though not the sixty days of prayer and fasting Sir Simonds D'Ewes spent dwelling on the four last things, testing his election) to effect that final transformation into a 'saint'. Hence the earnest weeping and penitential prayers; the anxious private and public searching of conscience for signs of grace as he ponders, in due form, death, judgement, hell and heaven. There are other details too: the touching farewells with his children; the trooper shouting 'We have no King, and will have no Lords'; then the soldiers dispersing, and the sobbing women and children and the men whose 'grief was dumb, like their anger'. A familiar scene by now; its imagery here and there, consciously or not, recalls details of the king's demise. Yet it is so different from our way of death that we might think the witnesses have artfully improved on life. Not so. These were authentic ceremonies conducted according to the rules of the ancient craft of dying as laid down in medieval *ars moriendi* manuals and elaborated and dramatized in the fifteenth and sixteenth centuries, until in the very year of Derby's death the ritual achieved its noblest literary expression in Jeremy Taylor's *Holy Dying*.

All those verbal and symbolic gestures belong to the regular routines of deathbed and scaffold: they are the means whereby the individual orchestrates and takes control of the very crisis in which we might think them most vulnerable and passive. Every dying person becomes a battleground, the *locus* of a cosmic eschatological drama. Perhaps the process was especially intense for Protestants, with no last rites to fall back on and no purgatory to ease their passage; and arguably most urgent for those most recently reformed. For nowhere do we see the drama of dying acted out more completely than in John Donne: his *Hymn to God in my Sicknes* and, even more notably, his last sermon, *Death's Duel*, display his mastery of the art. Preaching in Whitehall for the last time in 1630 he

> Presented so to life that piece of death
> That it was feared and prophecied by all
> Thou hither camst to preach thy funeral.

Donne in the pulpit is literally a speaking picture. He is a corporeal and articulate emblem of the human condition at its moment of greatest peril and utmost significance and promise. As close as can be to addressing his congregation from the other side of the grave, Donne looks beyond the 'most deadly and peremptory nullification of man' to the Second Coming. But 'that piece of death' that Henry King refers to – the portrait Donne had painted of himself in his funeral shroud – is the most remarkable detail of all (see p. 143 and Plate 8). It was, or rather with its aid he turned himself into, his own *memento mori*: propping the picture where he could gaze on it the poet and divine returned to his sick-bed to die, that is, to become himself the finished artefact. So death was made the defining act of each secular biography. As Sir Henry Vane, facing his own execution and predicting that the end of the world would come in 1670, put it, 'Life is measured by the end.' When Charles I's enemies brought him to the block they gave him – indeed, as Christians dared not deny him – the one chance he needed to come up to the mark and fulfil his destiny.

How different Cromwell's end, private and unlooked-for, was. And Cavalier propaganda was quick to exploit its unheroic character, making much of the rapid decomposition of the corpse. Real saints do not rot! His laureate, Marvell, adroitly turned the tables on these scurrilities. He highlights the difference between the Protector's death and the king's: here are no 'Spectators vaine' to applaud the 'last Act'; here, for the mourning poet saw him dead, are displayed the mortal remains

> All wither'd, all discolour'd, pale and wan
> How much another thing, no more that Man.

The obliteration and nullification of that man of Machiavellian *virtu* acclaimed in the *Horatian Ode* is faced, lamented, and transcended:

> Yet dwellt that Greatness in his shape decay'd
> That still, though Dead, greater than death he layd.
> But in his alter'd face you something fayne
> That threatens Death he yet will live again.

The lines catch the sense, so powerful among the godly, of death as terrible and yet as a sallying forth towards the Resurrection and Judgement: 'It is not my designe to drink or sleep but to make what haste I can to be gone' were the Protector's own words as he lay dying. Here 'You . . . fayne' throws the onus on to the reader's power of imagination and belief: and we are transported into a beatific vision (more sublime than the *Eikon Basilike* frontispiece) where the 'greate soule'

> Despoyld of mortall robes, in seas of Blisse
> Plunging dost bathe, and tread the bright Abyss.

From this loftily baroque, Miltonic prospect we fall back to earth where our 'heavy Doome' is to 'Wander like Ghosts about thy loved Tombe'. The living survivors become half-hearted spectres, while dead Cromwell, now a Saint in heaven, more than ever lives. So Marvell reconstructs for us his great Christian hero's last rite of passage, his final metamorphosis. That done, he closes the poem – for true poets, too, like kings and dying men have the gift of foresight – with a prophecy of the hoped-for outcome of the son's succession. Meanwhile the Protector's actual obsequies were, after his style of government, monarchical. For his catafalque they used Inigo Jones's design for James I's. The old custom of exhibiting a life-size wax effigy of the dead ruler was upheld. Customary too was the stowing of the coffin beneath the Bed of State: but Cromwell's was empty because the embalming went wrong and even a double casket of wood and lead could not contain the stench of decomposition. Oliver's effigy lay decked in his most imperial robes: above was an imperial crown and alongside were four standards bearing the Protector's coats of arms. Half-way through the lying-in-state the simulacrum was stood upright to symbolize the passage of the soul from purgatory – which Cromwell did not believe in – to heaven. Such was the hold of customary ritual. The glass eyes (closed till now) were opened and the imperial crown was placed on the head, signifying the entry of the departed into after-life and the continuation of his line, in this case not destined to endure, on earth. Cromwell was posthumously king. Finally on 23 November his funeral procession bore the 'idoll crowned', as Cowley called it, in an open chariot draped in black velvet, on a seven-hour journey from Somerset House to Westminster Abbey where it was lodged in Henry VIII's Chapel without further ceremony, sermon or speech. John Evelyn meanly remarked that only the dogs cried. At the Restoration the effigy would be hauled out and hung by the neck in Whitehall. The actual corpse was dug up, too, and the head stuck on a pole on top of Westminster Hall. So Cromwell's destiny was acted out to the bitter end: he had died on the anniversary of his conclusive victories at Dunbar and Worcester; and was exhumed on 30 January 1661 – twelve years to the day from Charles I's decapitation. The regicide of 1649 was dead and gone for all to see, but what mattered most was the providential iconography: a head for a head, grim symmetry, capped all those coincidences and conclusively revealed the divine artist's hand. It is hard to think that the ironic riposte of history was lost on Andrew Marvell whose *Horatian Ode* had identified Charles's with the 'bleeding head' allegedly discovered at the founding of Rome's Capitol. That omen was retorted now with a vengeance. God, as General Fleetwood bitterly concluded, had demonstrably turned against the Republic. The only Caesar left was Charles II.

Little wonder, given a visionary politics that could inspire both Feake's tomfoolery and the grandest kind of enterprise, that poor puzzled Mr Dick got that bee about the king's head in his bonnet. Even now it is all, sometimes, decidedly bemusing. Those events and the figures of art that linked them to the past of Christian and classical revelation so as to shape a nation's future, express a way of ordering affairs and 'reading' history that is not exactly ours. We have (not least because desensitized by the habit of connecting politics with an essentially nineteenth-century materialist model of science) scant capacity for such public politico-literary celebrations and interpretations. Neither elegiac odes, nor high tragedies, nor providential epics sit naturally at the heart of *our* system of governance. In early Stuart society we see the power of those other modes of perception, of myth and ritual to animate a people, shaping and sustaining the individual and national identity. As we turn away from the scene of 1649 the isle seems to have been full of strange voices. They echo as from a distant shore. 'The past', we must conclude, 'is another country: they do things differently there.'

II

More than half medieval . . . More than half modern

Listen again, however, to Andrew Marvell's *Horatian Ode* closing on an apocalyptic possibility:

> And for the last effect
> Still keep thy sword erect;
> Besides the force it has to fright
> The spirits of the shady night,
> The same Arts that did gain
> A power must it maintain.

There is foreboding here, if not of Armageddon then of that moment just before Cromwell, 'war and fortune's son', marched off to Scotland; and the sword seems a Christian talisman, full of magic force against the powers of darkness. At the same time the close is a caveat much of a piece with Hobbes's 'Covenants without the Sword are but Words.' Marvell, accomplished Machiavellian, engages us as much with familiar *realpolitik* and the prospect of a classical republic as with the promise of a messianic leadership. His poem has the ring of cold steel in it, first and last. And at the dead centre of the ode – as of the century – the axe gleams. Charles tries (the word ironically reflecting his illegal trial) its edge with his keener eye: and about that edge, we perceive, the poem and the period pivot. On one side lie legitimacy and the long peace of Jacobean and Caroline Britain where the ancient rites and ceremonies of court proclaimed the sacred monarchy; on the other stands the New Model Army, *de facto* power, a headless body politic, and Cromwell who is a driven man and has no time for niceties.

One must not flatter the 1620s and 1630s, of course, nor condemn them out of hand because of the ensuing tragedy. But the England of Charles I *had* been in many ways more cosmopolitan, more modern, more prosperous too, more orderly and civil than James's realm. Jacobean melancholy (which when you think of cattle pests and failed harvests in the 1590s probably had its roots as much in the lack of dung as in the occult philosophy Frances Yates connected it with) had lifted. A festive, bucolic spirit was in the air when John Aubrey and friends took a trip to Bath in

1637, enjoyed some dalliance en route, and thought it all, looking back, 'the highth of a long peace and luxury'. The contrast with Europe, plunged in slaughter, rapine, pillage and plunder, starvation and confusion made English people acutely conscious of their happy lot. Thomas Carew, urged to trumpet the continental triumphs of militant Protestantism, declined. Not for him the role of Marvell's 'forward youth' compelled to don ancestral armour and leave 'numbers languishing' behind: in 1630 it was still possible – and much more pleasant – to stay at home, lyre in hand, beneath the boughs, languishing for all you were worth. The king's Arcadia, which tough-minded Marvell himself recalled with real nostalgia, was no mere fiction: but confronted with the killing of the king he knew it was done for. He sees in the *Horatian Ode*, as in his lines to Richard Lovelace, that the *coup d'état* and the cross-purposes of Civil War mark the end of an epoch. It is not bloodshed and physical danger that disturb him most: the Great Rebellion was less terrible altogether than the Thirty Years' War. His eye is fixed on something else – a loss of fineness.

Alone of the Cavalier poets of the late 1640s Marvell looks the future in the face. He records, in Blair Worden's words, 'the fundamental shift in English civilisation which the middle of the seventeenth century – even when our historian has made every conceivable qualification – did bring about'. 'The death of the King', writes Barbara Everett in the same vein, 'was also in some sense the end of ritual, of myth; it was the last Reformation, the final breaking of an icon.' We turn away from the old Monarchy to the new Republic, from Platonic kings to Machiavellian generals. Magic wanes and political science waxes. Prophets make way for statisticians. High Renaissance poetry with its sense of occult correspondences, its Platonic-Pythagorean impedimenta, its mystic numbers, emblems and hieroglyphs (which men like Hobbes, Butler, Temple and Dryden would laugh from fashion as fantastic obfuscations) will yield to a more prosaic literature, cooler, rational, regulated and restrained by common sense and carefully constructed codes of conduct. Maybe Marvell could not see all that in 1649; but he knew instinctively that it was a point of no return; and he accepted, reluctantly or not, the logic of history.

For systematic logic and hard-nosed realism Thomas Hobbes took some beating. So armed, he swept aside superstitious sacerdotalism and the spirit world of ghosts, hobgoblins and fairies, witches, demons, and dreams, along with the superfluous, misleading ambiguities of metaphor. John Aubrey thought he had single-handed 'pulled down all the churches, dispelled the mists of ignorance, and layd open their priest-craft'. Fittingly in 1651, the very year *Leviathan* was launched, the Countess of Derby found herself appalled – 'it makes one's hair stand on end to think of it' she wrote – to find 'The Koran printed with permission. It is common to deny both God and Jesus Christ, and to believe only in the Spirit of the Universe.' Rational deism, or something like it, was making headway. Hobbes's system, since matter and motion explained everything, could operate without even that: indeed his materialism, his 'scientific' thinking, seem very much part of our modern secular idiom. Aubrey's own work too, though less radical, witnesses to a changed mentality: his *Brief Lives*, the *Remaines of Gentilism and Judaism*, the pioneering archaeological investigations at Avebury, and so on, embody the new spirit of impartial inquiry and observation. For his money it was Civil War that had blown away the old 'Rites, or Customes' of the people. The phrase 'Before the Civil Wars' sounds time and again as he charts the shift of mind, of habit and fashion too, that had occurred. Even Welsh-speaking in South Wales was wearing out, he thought, 'especially since the Civill Warres'; and drum and trumpet had quite silenced the pipe and tabor of the old church bands. For 'Warres do not only extinguish Religion and Laws; but Superstition: and no *suffimen* is a greater *fugor* of Phantasmes, than gunpowder.' War, Aubrey believed, had helped people take hold of 'liberty of conscience and liberty of inquisition'. And things were the better for it: why, even the country poor now had glass windows!

This sense of shift, of passing from under the shadow of unfathomable arcana and an inscrutable providence into the liberty of 'true reason's light' appears in the careers of two very different men – John Ogilby and Edmund Ludlow. Beginning before the war as a tutor in Strafford's family, Ogilby went on to dance at Court, but 'endeavouring to doe something extraordinary' in the Duke of Buckingham's grand masque he injured himself and had to find a new occupation. Before long he pops up, a theatrical entrepreneur, in Dublin. Then he reappears in England in the later 1640s learning Latin and French for his next enterprise, which was to publish the most handsome, expensive edition of Virgil and Homer that money could buy. An edition of the Bible followed, the noblest of the century. Alas, sales flagged; Ogilby, ever the opportunist, launched a lottery with the books as prizes. He never looked back; indeed he moved swiftly into a new market with his greatest work, the grand survey of London and a series of substantial topographical and geographical surveys of home and abroad. In 1675, the year before he died, he compiled and published – at the king's request – a road atlas of Great Britain, the first ever of its kind. A self-made man, Ogilby embodies the expansion of the book trade in the second half of the century and, more generally, that entrepreneurial spirit, spurred on in him by loss of patronage, which was to carry the nation irresistibly forward. We travel with him the road from princely magnificence and dynastic display to useful and profitable national work founded, under a sympathetic royal eye, in the great metropolis. In 1683 Daniel Feake, sole surviving Fifth Monarchist, could safely be left preaching away on London Bridge: no one was listening to his kind of talk any more. The citizens went about their business.

The fate of Edmund Ludlow, incorruptible old warrior and unrepentant regicide, no less ironically discloses the change of tone and temper. In 1689, almost the sole survivor now of a mighty generation of revolutionaries, he hastened home from Swiss exile 'to strengthen the hands of the English Gideon' in the final battle against Antichrist. Outraged Tories called for his scalp, and not a Whiggish voice was raised in his defence. Sainted Ludlow had become an embarrassment and an irrelevance. No one wanted apocalyptic politics or rhapsodical republicanism now. Within a decade his editor John Toland, brilliantly conjuring away the uncomfortable bedrock of chiliastic ideology, transformed Ludlow's million-word *Voyce from the Watch Tower* with its fervent, bigoted and unforgiving haranguing of the Saints, into the thoroughly modern, abridged and refined *Memoirs* of a stolid country Whig. There, on the threshold of the Age of Reason, lies a vital evolution of the English mind. Canting Ludlow was no more. Freed from the past, society could proceed along the broad highway of improvement. Time, the old enemy, was on our side at last.

Charles II might have been made, or maybe fashioned himself, for this age of exorcism. From the first, when an old Royalist hearing the news of the Restoration laughed until he died, laughter of all kinds (and commonly the bawdier and more rakishly cynical the better) was the order of the day. Richard Flecknoe who complained in 1656 of those Cavaliers 'who never laughed since the king's death' had his answer now. Samuel Butler's burlesque *Hudibras*, a favourite poem of the monarch's, was an hilarious, inexhaustible 'Amen' to that. Scattering its fire like a Gatling gun across the available idiocies and pretensions, militant Presbyterians, lunatic sects, astrologers, alchemists, magicians, quacks and cranks of every kidney, the poem took the town by storm. Mockery and drollery (escapist, therapeutic, and subversive of old Puritan solemnities) and satire of all sorts ruled the roost. You hear the note in the merest chit-chat, as of the wit observing that the excessive cost of periwigs (more or less a post-war innovation) was 'sufficient *demonstration* of the weakness of the Brains they keep warm'. Even banter now ran QED. Actually cleanliness, not head-warming, was the beauty of the periwig: men could shave their heads and be rid of lice. Still the joke was worth making: raillery (like the rhyming couplet which in poetry ably abetted it), nonchalance, not taking oneself or one's enemies too seriously were the *modi vivendi*. Frenchmen, to their relief, found that his aristocracy so followed Charles's 'Patterne of Courtesie' that 'My Lord d'Angleterre' no longer 'look't comme un Mastif-dog'.

The Monarch made pleasure (foot-tapping light music, messing about in boats, gambling, jesting and amorous dalliance) the prime pursuit of high society. Typically Tom Killigrew, the poet, 'indulged himself in giving luxurious descriptions of Lady Shrewsbury's most secret charms and beauties, which above half the court were as well acquainted with as himself'. This was no place for prudes or Puritans. Ogling was a major pastime; the Duke of York, not to be wholly outdone by his prodigiously amorous brother, turned into 'the most unguarded ogler of his time'. Unguardedness was his *métier* and his eventual undoing. Charles, though open in his vices – for the kingly potency was both symbolic and engagingly human – was not so reckless politically. He got his own way with an adroit mixture of charm, ruthlessness and circumspection. His suavity, which he maintained to the last on his deathbed despite the torments of his treatment, was a marvellous political weapon. That engaging nonchalance should not disarm us. The accounts were balanced: expanding trade and a reasonable control of expenditure (despite what the mistresses got away with) saw to that. Cromwellian administrative reforms and naval patronage were maintained. From 1667 on (right up to 1870) the Treasury Minute Books were diligently compiled; public revenues were properly audited. Substantial taxation (what price ship money antics now!) had come to stay; and no one, as he wryly remarked, blamed the Merry Monarch.

Almost raffish at times, the king could also lose his temper formidably and was, like his father, icy to those who failed him. Perhaps he did not deploy art quite as Charles I had done: the masque gave way to masquerade. Nor did Lely invest him with the air of arcane power Van Dyck discerned in the father: even cast in the imperial role Charles II looks more tough unillusioned Machiavellian than aloof dynastic icon. Nevertheless, he knew how to put on the style when necessary. Above all, as 'Royal Actor' – and save in complete autocracies all successful leaders must act out the dominant aspirations and tendencies of their time and place – he displayed a range that leaves his father standing. Less private, less touchy too, he could tolerate the opening lines of *Absalom and Achitophel* acclaiming his 'heroic' promiscuity, and enjoy Marvell's *The Rehearsal Transprosed* not for its opinions, which he disliked, but for the sharp and witty way they were expressed. The second Duke of Buckingham, following suit, was 'too witty to resent' being satirically portrayed as Zimri: 'the jest went round, and he laughed at it in turn who began the frolic'. Better, as Dryden concluded in 1693, 'the fineness of a stroke that separates the head from the body, and leaves it standing in its place', than 'the slovenly butchering of a man'. He might almost have been thinking of James II's painless removal and replacement. Of course polishing satire is his subject, but another lesson learned (better the poet's rapier than the headman's axe) is at least hinted at. So in the 1680s a Stuart reigned supreme as though regicide had never been, as to the manner born. Passing from the Holy Martyr to Old Rowley is, to borrow the well-worn phrase, like moving from a mind and world more than half medieval to a world and mind more than half modern. It is a great mistake to underestimate the monarch who, schooling himself to speak his subjects' language, presided over that process and so artfully maintained his power. Unlike Charles I, Charles II kept his head.

III

> See, now they vanish,
> The faces and places, . . .
> To become renewed, transfigured, in another pattern.
>
> (T.S. Eliot)

So the way lay open from feudal darkness to the Enlightenment and beyond. It is a tale of progress in which human history took an irreversible turn for the better. The old high drama, opening in Eden and closing on Apocalypse, gave way to the familiar unending story of the state. The English Revolution carried our Stuart ancestors from the ancient world of myth and ritual towards the secular and scientific Utopia ahead. The tide of ever-increasing power, prosperity and pluralism runs straight from that moment to this.

If only such assumptions about then and now could hold. Sadly Utopia remains stubbornly over the horizon. Two world wars (compounded in Britain by loss of empire), a history of concentration camps and gulags, of holocaust and genocide, have more or less sunk the promised land. And once more Armageddon looms. The whole grinning ideology of progress, whether in the form of 'scientific' Marxist or of Welfare-State-Whig models of history, founders under the burden of our disillusionments, and fades from view. Science itself, shedding nineteenth-century certainties, finds even the laws of physics far from absolute and our capacity to explain not unlimited. Past and present can no longer connect in the old way; and things, from where we stand, look altogether less straightforward than they used to and too kaleidoscopic to fit the old design. Those shifting, uncertain fragments, memories we inherit of long-gone people and events, of old ideas and emotions, fall in changing light into another pattern.

Maybe no historical necessity, no evolutionary logic, no deep underlying causes brought Charles I, eventually, to the block: the *sine qua non* of that tragedy was the accident of his elder brother's premature death. Precocious Prince Henry had Renaissance magnificence at his fingertips: he, rather than Charles, first opened English eyes to all that. Unlike Charles, however, he was also actively interested in practical education, in shipbuilding and naval reform (as Charles II would be), in navigation and exploration and in history. At his court the study of Machiavelli and Tacitus was promoted; and Ralegh's dedication to him of the *History of the World* was altogether fitting. Henry had plans for an Academy Royal too, and for New World colonization. His Sidneyan zeal for internationalist military adventure, his Protestant expansionism was, if boyish, quite at odds with his father's and his brother's pacifism; though addicted to the cult of chivalry, there would surely have been no fond pursuit of popish princesses for him. Had he lived, his court might well have been more extrovert, less self-absorbed, less narrowly aesthetic, less Catholic too than Charles's.

This heir apparent's death at 18 from typhoid fever was a cataclysm: the poets from Donne to John Taylor the Water-poet poured out elegies singly and in droves. Two volumes of funeral sermons completed the literary rites. Who can say with certainty whether the young prince would have fulfilled his undeniable promise? Allowance must be made, after all, for the partiality of his disappointed protégés: to lose such a patron in an age when patronage was the key to success was to be made fatherless, leaderless, homeless, redundant and bankrupt at a stroke. But the grief and shock at the perverse providence which had snatched away a nation's brightest hope is heartfelt beyond the dreams of opportunism. In 1624, twelve years after he died, the prince was still being mourned, in John Webster's Lord Mayor's Pageant, as the City's lost hero who had understood

> that battailes
> Not the gaudy show
> Of ceremonies

or 'Court sport' were a king's 'Best Theatres' – good counsel there for the ceremonious young monarch in the wings. Surely Henry's reign would have been in tune with the national will as no ruler was till Cromwell – and of the latter there might have been no need. The might-have-beens and probabilities of the past, though dry-as-dusts disdain them, are reminders of the uncertainties of our lot, and of how large a part the unforeseen, which reading backwards we commonly overlook, plays in history. Prince Henry's death is one of the signal discontinuities of the century.

On the other hand, consider Dr John Dee. The great Elizabethan magus, accused of practising black arts, ended his days in disgrace and relative obscurity; there till quite recently he languished. Yet now he re-emerges from the shadows, disconcerting as ever, as an influential original thinker of European stature and a key figure in the absorption into British culture of that occult philosophy which, though anathema to Enlightenment and nineteenth-century rationalists, was a seed-bed of science. For Dee, cabalist, conjurer, spiritualist and astrologer, was also chemist, mathematician and instrument-maker. His *Elements of Geometrie* in 1570 opened English eyes to Euclid; at the Sorbonne students scrambled to hear him lecture; at Mortlake he had the finest scientific library in Britain; and without his great navigational treatises those epoch-making Elizabethan voyages of discovery could not have been undertaken. The conception he shared with Ralegh and Prince Henry of a Protestant Imperium in the western Atlantic was no fantasy, but a vital and practical vision of a national, international destiny which ultimately connects with the triumphant overseas adventures of Great Britain in the eighteenth century. Shake the kaleidoscope, then, and Dee turns in a twinkling from odd old relic and superstitious crank into a mighty innovator shaping the world ahead. He is part of a grand continuum.

Maybe no radical revolution, no metaphysical revulsion from myth to mathematics, no sudden transformation rendering old beliefs as obsolete as, say, Myddleton's Great Conduit of 1613 would be by 1673, need be conjured up to account for the way the seventeenth century unfolded. The innovating statistical work of Petty, Graunt, and King, for example, was no sudden *démarche* but the natural outcome of a constantly increasing need to take stock which was certainly not invented in 1649 or 1660. In 1600, nearly half a century before Samuel Hartlib, who took a systematic interest in such things, Sir William Vaughan of Golden Grove in Carmarthenshire published a treatise of progressive ideas on, among other things, estate management, crops, and dunging, liming and marling the land. Some twenty years later, troubled by poverty and unemployment in his county, and understanding the persuasive power of facts and figures, he backed his seemingly fantastic, semi-fictionalized propaganda for the colonization of Newfoundland with accurate assessments, supplied by Bristol merchants, of fish catches, shipping tonnages, and market potential. Long before the Civil War, in the aftermath of which there certainly was a multiplication of such things, mathematical, medical and agricultural treatises were appearing in steadily increasing numbers; and already by 1600 practitioners of mathematics and the mechanical arts had their established place in London.

Technology and science did not suddenly erupt, and Bacon's was not a voice crying in the wilderness: he caught, rather, and trumpeted an inclination of his age. Most of his ideas, in fact, were current among later-sixteenth-century English scientists; Gresham College was a vigorous centre well before he published; and the methods of observation, experimentation and quantification for the purposes of material improvement which he urged were advancing apace even as he wrote. Gilbert's work on magnetism and Harvey's discovery of the circulation of the blood – neither of which Bacon altogether grasped – were accomplished, the one in 1600, the other in 1630. Curiously, if coincidentally, that graph of scientific and practical publications actually begins to rise markedly in the mid-1620s when Charles comes to the throne. The young king was at least less dyspeptic about the new learning than his father; he recognized the importance of colonial settlements as enterprises beyond the private purse of individual adventurers; though not as devoted to maritime matters as his brother was, he did in 1636 become the first sovereign to grant a Royal licence for an off-shore lighthouse. He was no Emperor Rudolf-like patron of science and technology; but he did not obstruct advances. It was his habit of innovation (in artistic, ecclesiastical and fiscal policies) that would prove, for not a few, the rub.

Mathematical Henry Briggs, first Professor of Geometry at Gresham College from 1596 to 1620, proposed a more unmistakably forward-looking practical scheme, however: he suggested joining the Thames and the

Avon to speed goods traffic between London and Bristol. The idea, much modified, caught Charles II's imagination; but it took till 1810, when the Kennet and Avon canal was opened, to realize Briggs's dream. Surely this was a man before his time, as his dismissal of astrology as 'a system of groundless conceits' seems to suggest? Or does he prove his time more modern than we imagined; or (especially when we recall that his revered acquaintance, logarithmic Napier, endorsed astrology) is it that the present is always a mixture of old and new; and that scepticism and inventiveness are always in the air? Whichever, it was in the 1620s, too, that James Bovey, 'ever a great Lover of Naturall Philosophye' set down the 'prudentiall Rules' of commercial navigation, compiled tables of all Europe's Exchanges, surveyed trade, and expounded the art of retail. John Aubrey found thirty-two such treatises among his manuscripts and drew them to the Royal Society's attention. Even better known and more influential was Thomas Mimm's analysis of the regulation of the balance of trade, published in 1664 to great effect but actually worked out some forty years before. The taxation reforms of 1661 similarly hark back to the Earl of Bedford's pre-war 'Excise' proposal, which in turn was indebted to Salisbury's 'Great Contract'. Changes of practice, though they seem overdue once they have happened, depend on singular and precise coincidences of circumstance, personality, power and national mood; and, not least, on the palpable exhaustion of existing arrangements and old convictions. Equally the persistence through time of ideas and attitudes is remarkable: seemingly set aside, they revive phoenix-like when their moment, however long delayed, comes round once more.

No flight of fancy is needed to free the early seventeenth century from the grip of stereotype. From the Personal Rule to the Glorious Revolution useful and scientific pursuits ascend uninterruptedly both in volume and social regard. Nor was science inherently attached, as has been strenuously argued, to Puritanism and political radicalism – witness the cases of Elias Ashmole, Thomas Johnson, Walter Charleton, Ralph Bathurst and many others, to say nothing of that self-styled 'perfect and peremptory Royalist' Francis Bacon. So when the reformism which took up science with much millenarian zeal in mid-century ran out of steam, science emphatically did not. It was not suddenly sundered from 'outmoded' conceptions and indissolubly attached to our kind of secular materialism either: the later seventeenth century produced not only Hobbes, atomism, and co-operative science but also a powerful revival (signalled by the publication of Agrippa's *Occult Philosophy* in 1651) and a reinterpretation of hermetic, cabalistic and Neoplatonic thought. Boyle and Glanvill advocated demonological studies; Boyle and Petty went on believing in the transmutation of base metal into gold; Petty was intensely interested in judicial astrology; Ashmole believed in alchemy, ceremonial magic and talismans (as did the ill-starred young Duke of Monmouth); and if Bacon's interests took shape, as his *New Atlantis* suggests, in a sympathetic climate of Rosicrucian mysticism, Boyle's thinking too retained a mystical Utopian dimension as his admiration for a scheme along those lines concocted by Hartlib's young associate John Hall of Durham suggests. In any case, quantifying 'modernizers' were not automatically followed: in 1692 John Locke regretted that, despite Thomas Sydenham's heroic efforts, medicos had not really turned 'from Visions and Wrangling to Observation'. We catch Aubrey still preoccupied with 'Magic' and with dreams as spiritual revelations (an interest in common with Bunyan and Sir Thomas Browne) or credulously cataloguing the sequence of ill omens that marred James II's coronation. 'Credulously' is hardly the *mot juste*, however, when you think how the Great Fire, the Anglo-Dutch Wars, the Popish Plot, Exclusion Crisis and the Monmouth Rebellion were all commonly attributed to supernatural causes. Aubrey had a wonderful eye and ear, of course, and a knack for dramatizing, even overdramatizing his material: sometimes he turns the process of change into something much more abrupt and singular than it was; for he was not immune from the common tendency of later years to exaggerate the effects of Civil War, whether from fear of repeating or from some need to justify so drastic an experiment. Anyhow his contention that 'the searching into Naturall knowledge began but since or about the death of King Charles the First' was myth not fact.

Hanker as we may after the certitude of stasis or of irreversible change, life remains an uncertain affair of stops and starts, of unions and confusions, of best-laid plans and false alarms and unexpected outcomes amid the longer rhythms and persistencies. Few things, even in our private individual lives, are altogether straightforward – indeed they often look less so as they recede into the past. How odd, therefore, that the lives of others in earlier eras are somehow an open book! What is over and done with, we seem to think, ought to be cut and dried. The truth is altogether otherwise. Like childhood which is always part of us, the nation's past remains at once knowable and elusive. Even after Einstein, we cannot say we have done with Isaac Newton, let alone pinned him down. Was he, as honoured from the eighteenth century on, the first and greatest of rational scientists? Or was he, as Lord Keynes put it, with the physicist's Christian mysticism and intense alchemical and numerological preoccupations in mind, 'the last of the magicians'? On reflection, one must admit, he looks remarkably like a man sprung from the same stock as Dee.

Like the new philosophers, the old guard resist pigeon-holing. James I convinced himself that the sacred monarch could, as by magic, 'bestow peace where he will'; but he thought that 'neither he nor any other King can have power to heal scrofula, for the age of miracles is past'. Charles II, knowing which of those feats was easier, touched some

93,000 sufferers. William and Mary eschewed the practice; Queen Anne revived it. Court ceremonial similarly comes and goes: cut down in its Caroline heyday it reappeared gradually, though purged of 'mumbo-jumbo', with Cromwell who was not averse to diplomatic magnificence and would even indulge in an inexpensive masque or two; then under Charles II it bursts once more into full flower. His London coronation – for he had had enough of Presbyterian dourness at Scone in 1651 – was 'the most conspicuous solemnity ever seen in this nation', and more than ever steeped in the ikonography of mystical politics. The Restoration ceremony projects him as Roman emperor, Old Testament prophet, Neptune, the Sun, and the Messiah. And John Ogilby, who knew the old idiom, rigged a stupendous Roman arch for the royal entry. Hard-nosed Pepys thought it 'foolery' to take such things seriously; but that reaction, which recalls Bacon's and Dudley Carleton's earlier reservations about princely shows, was nothing new. And Charles II, no less than his forebears, thought sovereign and subject were clear different things. To Puritan Lucy Hutchinson understandably he was every inch the 'kingly idol'. And in the end he reigned supreme, without parliament, wielding a power no English sovereign had possessed since the death of Elizabeth. Then his brother threw it away. Nothing save death, it seems, is irreversible; sooner or later history more or less repeats itself, though what has passed is never exactly reproduced. The year 1649 was not, after all, the final shattering of the ikon, which in some sort survived for all the altered tone and temper of the later times.

So, too, a recurrent literary and political ambition is discernible connecting Sidney and Spenser, with Ralegh, Sylvester, Chapman and so with Milton and his vision of Protestant Britain as another Rome in the west. Even Marvell's perfect miniature, the lyric 'Bermudas' echoes the aspiration after godly empire 'beyond the Mexique Bay'. Devout George Herbert, too, had prophesied in 'Church Militant' and 'The British Church' the inexorable westward migration of God's people in pursuit of the millennium. The imperial note is struck again in Marvell's lines 'On the First Anniversary of Cromwell's Government', as on the coin minted for Oliver portraying him (like any Stuart) as England's Augustus. Cromwellian foreign policy, moreover, drove the image home. In the 1660s Dryden, in turn, turned dramatically westward. *The Indian Queen* and *The Indian Emperor* together appropriate Mexican history – the Christianization of pagan America by the Spaniards – as an analogue for the conversion of the Roman Empire which transformed Graeco-Roman civilization, and for that most recent shift from Commonwealth radical 'enthusiasm' and unmitigated power politics to Anglican science and a responsible monarchy. Dryden's Mexico, moreover, is a locus of occult as well as of missionary activities. Here magic, ghosts, demons, prophets and divinatory dreams – all those things that Hobbes and demystifying William Davenant aimed to cast out of nature – play a part in the unfolding pattern of history. Dryden, steeped in More and Glanvill, insists on the reality (indeed on the scientifically definable reality) of spiritual forces and intelligences in a world menaced by a materialistic and politicized order. The 'technology' has changed: for demonic magic cannot now intervene in the natural world, and the unfolding of providence is seen as an evolutionary not a revolutionary process; so Dryden proposes no radical dislocation but a development working itself out through natural human and psychological forces. But he remains committed to providence and to prophecy. He looks, albeit no wild-eyed chiliast, to the promise of the New World and to a national renovation too. In *Annus Mirabilis* he celebrates Britain's secular prospects, her commerce, science and naval power, with London, 'empress of the Northern clime', rising deified from the Great Fire

> more August
> Her widening streets on new foundations trust
> And, opening, unto larger parts she flies.

Wren was at hand! Momentarily, too, the image seems to glance back at Inigo Jones's grand scene 'The Suburbs of a Great City' at the end of *Salmacida Spolia* in 1640, even as it foreshadows the majestic panorama (specifically recollecting Jones, Palladio and Vitruvius) which in 1732 closed Pope's *Epistle to Burlington*:

> Bid harbours open, public ways extend,
> Bid temples, worthier of the god, ascend;
> Bid the broad arch the dangerous flood contain,
> The mole projected break the roaring main;
> . . .
> These honours Peace to happy Britain brings,
> These are imperial works, and worthy kings.

By the end of the seventeenth century Celia Fiennes (granddaughter of one of the old leaders of Rebellion, the severe Lord Saye and Sele) found Jonesian Palladianism, once contentious because seen as Italianate, extravagant and absolutist, simply the epitome of modern taste. It was old-fashioned Gothic Chester she jibbed at. So did dissenting Defoe at Westminster Hall, that 'heap of something' as he put it; but he too was all for keeping up with the Joneses and called for a British Versailles to be built. Such triumphalism is not what one expects of Thomas Traherne, who lived out of the mainstream, writing pious, visionary poetry that seems both a throwback to the Metaphysicals and, with its heterodox ideas of childhood innocence, a foretaste of Blake and the Romantics. Yet stirred by the prospect of abundance he uttered a Psalmic 'Thanksgiving and Prayer for the Nation' before he died in 1674. Published in 1699 it summed up the ebullient expansive mood of the era:

> Their Markets, Tillage, Courts of Judicature, Marriages, Feasts and Assemblies, Navies, Armies, / Priests and Sabbaths, Trades and Business, the voice of the Bride groom, Musical Instruments, the light of Candles, and the grinding of Mills / Are comfortable, O Lord, let them not cease.

Nor did they! Regular corn surpluses are one of the achievements of the century then ending. Flourishing cornmarkets ringed the capital; and by 1720 it took 1,100 horse-drawn grain wagons to service each Farnham market. Horticulture and agriculture prospered within a twenty- or thirty-mile radius of the city – even garlic was grown in the market gardens of Middlesex, Surrey, Kent and Essex. In the century up to the year 1700 the annual London consumption of beeves went from 38,000 to 88,000; of cheese from 2,750 to 6,417 tons; of butter from 111,600 to 256,680 tons. Pride of achievement and a sense of the capital's importance overtook the cliché of a swollen parasitic place. In reality London was all along the grand national stage: here the immemorial tensions between court, city and country, the attractions and repulsions which constitute the unending process of change and continuity, were most sharply focused; here the court acted out its rituals, while the country fretted in the wings, and the city went about its business – or so it seems when 'court' and 'country' are used as ideological poles, dramatically opposed embodiments of antipathetic values, even, in extremes, as though they were Antichrist and Christ respectively. And here, indeed, political and religious agitation did – as when Pym manipulated the mob or the Popish Plot shook the town – make its greatest stir. In reality, none the less, court, country and city were (though handy counters) never wholly separate, antagonistic entities; rather they were interactive and overlapping facets of national life. Ben Jonson and Walter Ralegh, for example, were court-based exponents of 'country' virtues, and Jonson's 'Penshurst' is a place where king and rustic are equally at home; the 'country' policy of European intervention had vociferous exponents in the Jacobean and Caroline court; the court's domestic policies could be implemented in the provinces only by courtesy of country gentlemen all too prone, if recurrent royal admonitions are anything to go by, to waste their time and substance on the fleshpots of court and city life, cluttering up the town and letting their estates go hang. The gentrification of suburban London was unstoppable; the demand for what the town had to offer grew exponentially as its theatres and, later, coffee-houses vied with the court not only as places of entertainment but also as a school of manners and morals for up-and-coming followers of fashion.

Nor was there in Britain, as abroad, any sharp division between the landed and the commercial classes – witness those merchants' houses ringing London in the 1620s and 1630s; witness the market gardens and idyllic groves as close in as Kensington; witness, not least, the milkmaids to be admired in Hyde Park. The pastoral was not a world apart, divorced from town or remote from court. In literature as in life, rural and urban experience constantly and variously mesh. Jacobean comedy parades city slickers ripping off rich country bumpkins; Caroline plays propose a harmony of rural taste with the pleasures of London's growing leisure industry; while Restoration rural dullness proves no match for city *joie de vivre*. Marvell too, though rather differently, explores the pastoral, civic, courtly 'interface', as in his lines on Richard Lovelace. It came naturally to Milton, London born and bred, to write a pastoral masque for a vice-regal court, to don the mantle of 'uncouth swain' (offspring of Spenser's Colin Clout), and eventually to reconstruct humankind's garden Paradise reflecting that but for the Fall an ideal city might have been raised there.

London was the engine of an astonishing, inexorable growth. What happened in seventeenth-century Britain cannot be understood solely in terms of some intellectual revolution overturning obstructive beliefs, even if some at the time imagined that had happened. Nor did civil war, however unforgettable, suddenly unlock a radically different future. Inertia, a fondness for known ways, the desire for stability are among us instincts too deep to be so overcome. Fundamental to the way things went is the capital: its unremitting expansion and the geographical and social mobility that generated far and wide. Here, and long before the Industrial Revolution, production and consumption were liberated from traditional guild regulation and restriction; what we call supply-side economics were given their head. Moreover Britain's capital, perhaps uniquely among European cities, had the whole realm as its economic hinterland and source of labour. For not only the gentry and aristocracy were free to migrate: Richard Gough's *History of Myddle* shows how readily, despite authorities' traditional disapproval, ordinary folk moved around the country, usually from north to south and from west to east, mostly to and from London and in and out of service, apprenticeship, and business. Country cousins were everywhere, and far from locked *in situ*. Knowing your place in the social hierarchy was not the same thing as staying put.

So the city population surged, plagues notwithstanding, from 200,000 to 490,000, doubling in size and as a proportion of total population between 1605 and 1661 while the national population was static. Sheer numbers exerted irresistible pressure: quantification, analysis, reorganization (as in the institutionalization of the treatment of poverty) were necessary; in such matters the city, inevitably, ran ahead of the country at large. And London went on growing till by 1700 she had outstripped

Constantinople and was the greatest city in Europe. An idea had come true.

The benefits of that expansion and centralization of demand, however, were not confined to town: they spread outwards even to the humble sheep- and cattle-drovers of Scotland and Wales. Transport and communications kept pace as part of the process. Waggons drove out packhorses, and a regular stage-coach and postal system took shape: by the 1680s there were, for example, four coaches a week on the London–Exeter run. By 1695 Charles Davenant could confidently assert (and others like Defoe concurred) that there was 'not an acre of land in the country, be it never so distant, that is not in some degree bettered by the growth of trade and riches of that city'.

Possibly the Civil War, when communications were crucial, helped accelerate this development, as it did the introduction of national taxation. What mattered most in the years of fighting, however, is that London, the very nursery of rebellion (as Clarendon called it), was spared siege and pillage, unlike its continental counterparts at war. Milton rightly celebrated that. London's coming through unscathed has a bearing on the sustained advances of trade and industry, even of agriculture, in the Commonwealth and Interregnum years, when Cromwell received and handed on an intact capital. Without that, perhaps, neither his administrative reforms nor his assertive foreign policies, nor the recovery from crisis after 1649 and again at the Restoration would have been sustainable. For the book trade, too, London's role as virtually the sole centre and mass market for journalism, as for more scholarly volumes, was vital. When censorship collapsed and the real and propaganda war broke out, anything and everything that would sell, from poetry and polemic to pornography, poured from the presses; there was scarcely any limit in a place like London to the range of opinion, interest and experience to be tapped. Censorship from the later 1650s on put a damper on things, but the flow and spread of printed material could never again be fully controlled.

Writers fed on the city. Between 1590 and 1630, for example, the output of epigrams doubled. Quick-witted, competitive, street-wise, they became as common on the town as ballads and graffiti; and they use city sites (St Paul's, Bedlam, the Exchange, and so on) as points of reference in their map of society. With its sharp antitheses, its balancing antagonisms, the epigram imposes, figuratively, a degree of order and shape on the bewildering, multitudinous cityscape where irrepressible energies threaten chaos. Dryden's mock-heroic *MacFlecknoe*, parading Shadwell's 'suburban' muse through the capital in a parody of imperial proclamation, entry and coronation, and ending in a farcical, theatrical send-up (or rather put-down) of the false poet-prophet, shares the technique. Even the most polished satire, we are reminded, rests on rugged foundations. 'He found it brick and left it marble' – the Augustan Roman tag – exactly locates Dryden's urbanity. Wittily, the poet made London the measure of things.

The Merry Monarch, too, since wit and merriment were properties of the town, prospered not least because, unlike his father and grandfather, he felt thoroughly at home there. Marvell's *Further Advice to a Painter* in 1671,

> And draw me in one scene London and Rome.
> There holy Charles, here good Aurelius sate,
> Weeping to see their sons degenerate:
> The Roman taking up the fencer's trade,
> The Briton jigging it in masquerade.

backhandedly acknowledged that rapport, even as it confirmed the city as yardstick of what is best and worst in history ancient and modern. Bias aside (for it was really no bad thing) Marvell was right, too, about the restless energy. Charles II sallied forth from court not simply to be seen – the kingly obligation – but to see and join in the fun. How easy it is to imagine him participating in the conversation in Dryden's *Essay of Dramatic Poetry*, where the little group of well-bred sophisticates, denizens of court and city, take the air on the Thames. They talk at ease, but learnedly enough, of English literature and their hope for it. In the distance rolls the sound of gunfire from Britain's fleet engaging the Dutch off Lowestoft, 'the two most mighty and best appointed fleets which any age had ever seen' disputing the 'command of the greater half of the globe, the commerce of nations, and the riches of the universe'. And when they disembark, their discussion done, these sober patriotic gentlemen of letters pass through an unheeding crowd of French people dancing 'merrily . . . in the open air'. In frivolous mood, no doubt, the king would have dallied with the dancers. But his real mettle showed in London's hour of need after the Great Fire of 1666 when 'His was the active, agitating mind. His hand was seen everywhere.' King and capital were made for each other.

The monarch in court, of course, was no less than the city a constant and decisive presence. He remained the supreme source of actual power; policy was moulded by his personality and personal relationships; he, for better or worse, set the style of the day. If, as the century unfolds, literature and the other arts dance to changing tunes and tempos, it has a deal to do with sovereigns' various inclinations. Above all, the life of the nation was legitimized by the idea of hereditary ruler. For the royal family, its line running unbroken from Adam and Eve, through Brutus, ancient Rome, and the Emperor Constantine to the crack of doom was literally the embodiment of legitimacy and continuity. Literature, in its way, followed suit. Poets, for all their dependency on patronage, trumpeted their own kingly role and lineage. The regal prototype shapes Carew's praise of Donne as the Monarch of Wit, as it does Dryden's of Jonson for invading other authors 'like a monarch'. It informs Lovelace's recollection of a golden age when

> Rome to her Bard, who did her ballads sing,
> Indifferent gave to Poet and to King

and Cowley's proclamation in *Davideis*

> I Sing the Man who Judahs Scepter bore
> Who from best Poet, best of Kings did grow,
> The two chief gifts Heav'n could on Man bestow

Poets, note, come first. And like kings they are priests and prophets, with god-like gifts: it was Amphion the poet who, Sidney noted, first raised cities, nations and empires out of chaos; and Orpheus whose song harmonized rude nature and well-nigh conquered death. Spenser as the Orphic singer of his own wedding-hymn, Milton rehearsing the legend in *Lycidas*, and Dryden demonstrating the virtuoso's power of words and music over the emperor in *Alexander's Feast*, successively invoke that central sustaining myth of poetry. The old humanist ideal of the writer's role and influence, counselling kings and leaders in plays, poems and masques, lived on through the century albeit not unaltered.

Honour, that most precious and precarious of commodities, was poetry's to bestow in encomium, elegy or epitaph. The making of monuments, inscribing for posterity names, deeds and qualities, is a major literary preoccupation. Equally, withholding praise or administering rebuke was a prerogative: the satirist might even steel himself, as Dryden's comparison of his skills with those of Ketch the famous headsman showed, to execute a guilty subject. Ben Jonson, holding court at the Mermaid Tavern with his subjects and 'sons' about him, receiving tribute and doing honour or opprobrium (as he does so notably in the *Epigrams* with their profound sense of Roman antecedence and presence) most deliberately – and amply – filled the monarchical, patriarchal role. Flecknoe, in Dryden's satire, aspires to the part but is absolute only in 'the realm of Non-sense'. The true line descends from Father Ben, whose memory and measure is dutifully invoked, just as Jonson himself acknowledged John Hoskyns, who 'polished him' as his 'Father', and Hoskyns's son therefore as his brother. These paternal, familial conceptions are no less active in Dryden's great elegy to Oldham, that powerful lament for the death of a young fellow satirist. The poem, charged with Virgilian, Catullan and Jonsonian resonances, is a model of how lineage links and authenticates literature down the ages, making it, like the family, an arrow through time as it bears beliefs, values, mores, attitudes and habits along the generations.

It is the task of the poet to carry forward his inheritance from his forebears into the modern world. So Dryden speaks of Milton as 'the poetical son of Spenser', and he himself tries to reincarnate, or translate,

Chaucer for another generation. Times and tastes had changed and the rough diamond 'must first be polished ere he shines': but he was essentially a 'Modern Poet' and in *The Canterbury Tales* are

> our Forefathers and Great Grand Dames all before us as they were in Chaucer's day; their general characters are still remaining in Mankind, and even in England, though they are called by other Names than those of Moncks, and Fryers, and Canons, and Lady Abbesses, and Nuns; for Mankind is ever the same, and nothing lost out of Nature, though everything is altered.

The same vision of history and art informs Dryden's farewell to his century as 'All of a piece throughout' its different reigns and moods.

Two centuries later Lord Salisbury observed that 'it is not schemes to improve our lot that sustain us in our human identity, nor the set design and forethought of some group of statesmen' but the 'convergence of many thoughts and wills in successive generations'. He might almost have been talking about seventeenth-century literature and society. So haunted and prophetic, so conscious of its ancestors and descendants, so rootedly familial and hierarchical, that world was composed of a network of kinship and obligation, a 'fabric of affective ties and strictly delineated social roles operating for the benefit of all'. The individual, whether poet or prince, commoner or king, male or female, adult or infant, was not an unencumbered being, a *tabula rasa* to be written on by mere contingency, but an identity inscribed by destiny and inheritance: hence, not least, the alarm at Hobbist atomism. Of course, the idea of the freeborn Englishman's liberty of life and limb was an inherent part of the pattern, but so was the key distinction between liberty and licence. Folk were not free to choose, without obligation, from some more or less unlimited, incoherent, supermarket range of possibilities; rather they found themselves born into and nurtured by an ongoing tradition, and significantly, though not absolutely, defined by their belonging to a close-knit, time-honoured community. 'The Family of Prince Henry', as his household was called, felt all that on the pulse when the blow of his sudden death shattered and scattered them. So did Charles I in *extremis*, bequeathing to posterity the episcopal Church of England 'as I found it left me by my father'. So in due course Charles II's tragedy, and his country's, was that he had, for all his prodigious potency, no legitimate child to carry the line forward: the consequence was the Succession Crisis and the Glorious Revolution in which, some say, a century-long constitutional struggle reached a climax and was resolved. That is one way of looking at it; another, less academic, is simply to observe that but for the accident of a queen's barrenness there might have been no 'Revolution' at all, glorious or otherwise.

Strange that in an age when offspring mattered so much children were treated so badly – or so we are sometimes told by *aficionados* of the when-did-you-stop-beating-your-wife school of history. Allegedly, in that pre-emancipated past, before the early modern era invented family life and parental feeling as we know them, even precious sons and heirs were coldly regarded by parents brutalized by the prevalence of disease and premature death. Marriage itself was commonly an exploitative arrangement, a nightmare of female oppression, male domination, and affectionless coupling. At the grass roots, in town and country, existence was generally ignorant, hag-ridden, feuding and violent. So the legend runs. Like Hobbes's hypothesis about life in a state of nature being 'solitary, poore, nasty, brutish and short', it has more to do with arbitrary axiom than discoverable fact. In reality most marriages, especially outside the aristocracy and gentry, were as much for love as now, and since at marriage men were usually in their late twenties and women in their mid-twenties, every bit as much the fruit of mature deliberation. Romeo and Juliet's teenage infatuation, all very well for exotic Italians and aristocrats, is the exception that proves the rule. The perinatal mortality rate too, contrary to stereotype, was lower than at any subsequent time till well into the twentieth century. Macduff's cry for his murdered 'pretty ones' is from the heart and as perennially poignant as Charles I's touching farewell to his 'sweetheart' children, or Ben Jonson's stoical laments for his first son and daughter. Parents typically took the same delight and anxious interest in their offspring as they do today. As Ralph Houlbrook shows in *The English Family*, the true history of marriage, sexuality, fertility, childhood, death and inheritance upholds the poets and our common instincts, not the cultural determinism of misanthropic antiquaries.

Allen Macfarlane in *The Justice and the Mare's Ale* no less successfully subverts the image of a vengeful crime-ridden society. Mercy was the prerogative of monarchs and their magistrates; automatically draconian penalties were unnecessary when hierarchy and deference inclined folk naturally to law and order. Save in the case of hardened offenders, leniency and rehabilitation were as often as not the order of the day even in handling capital offences. As for the old orthodoxy that England's social and economic development was uncertain and switchback, the country bedevilled by demographic crises, agrarian upheavals, and a stop-go pattern of urbanization, struggling and stagnating: that, thanks to the work of Joan Thirsk, Peter Clark, Wrigley and Schofield, and many another, no longer holds up. With a population steady at around 5 million while the capital grew apace, Britain did not suffer from the conditions that, allegedly, stunted European economic and social development. The time-honoured and all too easily despised idea of a rather distinctive island and people, providentially free from attitudes and conditions that constrained neighbour nations, rises once more; and this time with facts and figures to sustain it. How fascinating after all that wherever we examine the material conditions of life (and do so using the kind of quantification some think the seventeenth century pioneered, though looking at Domesday Book one wonders) we find some major myths of pseudo-scientific history dissolving. Wrigley and Schofield's powerful analysis is almost as great a *fugor* of *suffimen* as Aubrey's gunpowder!

Those foreigners were not deceived who, like the Venetian ambassadors, discerned in the British a people consciously steeped in tradition, with an ingrained sense of distinctive identity: hospitable and law-abiding, yet awkwardly independent, and distrustful of foreigners; and not averse to change, indeed ready to innovate, and highly adaptable to political and social flux. Gough's *History of Myddle*, essentially a record of the inhabitants and pecking order of a rural parish, shows both that people constantly came and went and that the village was animated by a strong and stabilizing sense of family and community, of individual liberty and common justice. Even its criminals (like its saints) ran in families; and when one child murderer ran off to London a posse following found him not far from the city, sleeping under a haycock, and brought him home to book. Laws and penalties may change; but the Law was, as it remains, a major continuum and bulwark of our life.

Myddle was what we think of as a typically homogeneous village community where hierarchy and differentiation (anathema to egalitarians who confuse freedom with uniformity) fostered social integration and adaptation. And London was no different in this respect; for it was composed, and still is in some degree, of a collection of villages, so that even the metropolitan topography was not class determined. Hence, perhaps, its remarkable vigour and resilience in the seventeenth century. For human society is not a machine but an organism, a complex natural growth full, unless moribund, of the vitality of variation. The metropolis, like Myddle where lesser dwellings were sometimes moved bodily from one site to another, was anything but immutable, and flourished therefore.

Maybe the actual landscape remained constant: recent archaeological and botanical research suggests that forest clearance and the field pattern may have been achieved as early as Roman times when the population more than matched the post-Black Death levels of the late Tudor period. But occupancy was decidedly unfixed: in some areas farmholdings rarely stayed in the same family for more than two generations. Some 60 per cent of the population, it seems, died away from their place of birth. We are not confronted by a stick-in-the-mud semi-feudal peasantry. Retracing *The Origins of English Individualism* back beyond the early modern period Macfarlane finds no proper peasants, no recessive yokels on the brink of starvation, groaning beneath an oppressive social and political system. Nor did visitors at the time, who saw a prosperous and pastoral land looking like some Garden of Eden. The natives concurred for once: Ralegh's *History of the World* begins in Paradise and ends in England, which Walter Blith was convinced in 1648 'might be made the paradise of the World'. Visitors also remarked on the lack of feudal deference, the bloodymindedness even, of quite humble people who seemed, unlike their European counterparts, not to know their place. When at the Putney Debates Colonel Rainsborough rousingly reminded the army grandees that 'the poorest he that is in England hath a life to live as the greatest he', he was not mouthing some shocking new revolutionary slogan but rehearsing a time-honoured sentiment, like Thomas Sydenham who, having fought against the king, still put 'the liberties of Englishmen' before 'privilege of Parliament'. Rainsborough was no ideologue, no commissar, but a man insisting that liberty of life and utterance does not depend on property or material power. That kind of radicalism has nothing to do with being 'left' or 'right': it was bred in the bone through countless generations of islanders who, however lowly, were in the habit of regarding their lives as their own. Some serfs!

We talk too often of continuity and change as though they were diametric opposites, alternatives locked in contention. In reality they need each other: change does not mean dislocation, and continuity entails adaptation. Burke, without benefit of Darwin, defined the process: 'a state without the means of change is without the means of its conservation'. Early modern Britain (as Marvell came to see) did not need a Revolution to make it new. The seventeenth century was not broken-backed after all: renewal was inherent in its life, as in its letters. How now, then, to locate amid the flux those turning-points we have been trained to treasure? How to lay one's hand with confidence on the beginning of the new or end of the old? History begins to look more sedimentary than linear, more geological than dramaturgical, more like an unremitting process of accretion and erosion. And layer upon layer it yields a mixture of what for convenience (though often misleadingly) we label 'innovation' and 'reaction', 'old-fashioned' and 'modern' – which is just as it is with us.

Men and women are not (never have been) mere paradigms of 'feudalism' or 'early modernism' or 'pre-' or 'post-industrialism'. Marxist-Leninism and bureaucratic Russian imperialism may have much to answer for in Stalin; but we miss the point if we fail to see him as one of nature's Tamburlaines. So, enemies alleged, was Cromwell; though others more generously cast him as Hannibal or Caesar. Either way the sense of the recurrences and persistencies of history and human nature was underlined alongside the no less potent idea that time was hastening towards some grand denouement. Naturally – because it is itself a constant of our condition – there was much talk of the outmoded and the forward-looking. Against that we must set the no less compelling evidence that old beliefs and attitudes did persist. So as the century passes the undergrowth of popular almanacs and millenarian tracts, instead of thinning out, grows denser. Avant-garde fashion, intellectual and otherwise, is not always broadly representative. Scientists and Hobbist philosophers might advocate plain language purged of ambiguity and metaphor and seem at times to have clipped the muse's wings. But Milton, Dryden and Clarendon together found Hobbes's aesthetic and political prescriptions impossible to swallow; and the poets insisted, against his rigid mechanistic definition of its workings, that poetry was essentially a 'heavenly gift'. Milton, of course, cared nothing for the merely *à la mode*; where others fled from inspiration, he kept faith.

Of course it is misleading to range writers along a scale of ascending modernity: that is not how we encounter and read them any more than it is how we really experience the past. Seventeenth-century letters do not fall into a tidy sequence. Obviously we can tell the difference between Donne and Dryden, even, with experience, locate them chronologically. Labelling Marvell's undated lyrics 'early' or 'late', however, is another matter: nor is his kind of debt to Horace confined to any one moment. Jonson (early) and Temple (late) set the same store by Horatian humanity, equanimity and common sense. In the theatre James Shirley's comedies of sexual manners, full of poised repartee and stratagems of seduction, seem to breathe the Restoration air: but they 'belong' to the 1620s and 1630s. Conversely Shirley's threnody of 1659

> The glories of our blood and state
> Are shadows not substantial things

prolongs an 'older' contemplative melancholy note. It might have been written at almost any moment of the era. The preoccupation with last things (not out of morbidity but to assert each and every life as part of the cosmic drama) is unabated in Bunyan. Almost the last words of the first part of *Pilgrim's Progress* remind us of the door leading straight to Hell from within view of Heaven's gate. In Part Two the Beast of the Apocalypse, since the Popish Plot had revived old anxieties, reappears as a lurking threat. *The Holy War* in 1682 vigorously reiterates apocalyptic themes, as does *Of Antichrist and His Ruine* which was stifled by the Catholic succession Bunyan so dreaded, and not published till 1692, four years after his death. If dissenters turned from the prospect of theocracy to the kingdom within, their godly convictions, like the fear of popery, ran on unchecked. So did hostility to them and to the Good Old Cause: the propaganda of forty years before was reprinted *en masse* in the late 1670s and early 1680s.

There were the enduring landmarks, too, the perennial texts available in increasing numbers as the market expanded and spread downwards. The popular appetite, at least, for improving treatises and books of devotion was well-nigh insatiable. Towards 1700 the output of such things (advice on how to prepare for the sacrament, for example) was more than double what it had been in the 1590s, and no less than 400 editions of the King James Bible, and some 700 of Sternhold and Hopkins *Psalms* had been published. Milton, still proclaiming the pre-eminence of 'Sion's songs, to all true tastes excelling', was not, after all, a voice crying in the wilderness in 1671. We must think again about the timing and pace of Britain's secularization.

People were not yet ready to dispense with the arts of holy living and holy dying; and to the end of the century public executions were conducted with all the old penitential, confessional and declamatory routines. The collaborative ritual, full of political and religious symbolism, which Bunyan rehearsed in *Grace Abounding*, might buckle in the Age of Enlightenment, for now the most hardened homicide died ceremoniously. Submission to the law and to properly constituted authority was demonstrated even as contrition was proclaimed; but the ceremony was an affirmation of individual identity, too, and of the essentially spiritual and moral nature of our being even in the most desperate of cases. If today (at least in western Europe) the public execution of a criminal, let alone of a king, in Whitehall is unthinkable it is not, paradoxically, because we are less brutal than our forebears (twentieth-century terrorism explodes that myth) but because we are more ill at ease with death, more uncertain of its significance, and more reluctant, therefore, to confront it. When that quintessential seventeenth-century aphorism 'Stone dead hath no fellow' stops us in our tracks, it is not just squeamishness but the fact that with us the individual at the point of death becomes, literally, a nonentity that unmans us. Bereft of a metaphysic of dying, the fact and the physical processes of death lose their significance. We take refuge in impersonal euphemism. 'Liquidation' and 'final solutions' reduce the experience that in the end defines us, to a scientific process or an impersonal, bureaucratic arrangement.

Even natural death is transformed as far as possible into a purely physical procedure: *in extremis*, on the life-support machine, we are unplugged; and the very last of us, most commonly, is a discreet puff of smoke. Death, once raised to the level of art, ceases to signify. What mourning ensues is, by a general agreement that finds grief more embarrassing than adultery, minimal. Inexorably, as Philippe Aries argued, we are desensitized therefore to the supreme value of life. Those euphemisms, that studied indifference masquerading as good democratic taste, betray an essential materialism and the callousness that goes with it. Our way of death is a dead end: a monument to nihilism.

Beyond 1700 the tide of urgent speculation about the date of the Apocalypse, far from ebbing in the wake of rational deism, materialist science and political pluralism, flowed on to 1750 at least. Thereafter, though checking awhile, it surges again, first with the French Revolution and then in the Russian Revolution. Even the *Communist Manifesto* in design and substance stands in the apocalyptic millenarian line. Tragically the hoped-for Utopia turned to living nightmare in Stalinist Russia, as did Hitler's short-lived 1,000-year Reich. Such dreams are dangerous. Yet without them, maybe, humans lack something to steer by; for even now they persist. Iran of the ayatollahs pursued the holy war, defying 'the great

Satan' America; while transatlantic televangelists prophesy Armageddon on the dried-up bed of the Euphrates where Israel will triumph in the last battle against International Communism. They intend, via satellite camera trained on the Mount of Olives, to be first with pictures of the Second Coming. What would uncrankish Cromwell make of that? There are moments when nothing seems to have changed.

There are moments too when Conrad's 'All passes, all changes' seems no less irrefutable. Perhaps in the nature of things only some provisional conclusion is possible: if for all the broad individual, familial and constitutional continuities of British life there *has* been in the last five hundred years some deep decisive break (spiritual, moral, intellectual, emotional, psychological) with the past – some crossing of the Rubicon – we would have to locate it now somewhere much nearer to our own pluralistic and totalitarian days than to the Stuart Age. Most men and women could have stepped with no great discomfort and certainly without trauma from 1600 straight into 1699. They would hardly feel so much at home in our world.

IV

> These fragments I have shored against my ruin.
>
> (T.S.Eliot)

We are not our ancestors. Indeed, whether we are still their true descendants or merely successors is a moot point. Unquestionably our relationship with them has ceased to be straightforward:

> We cannot revive old factions
> We cannot restore old policies
> Or follow an antique drum.

The sense of radical, if not irreparable disjunction is hard to resist. We flounder, intellectually and spiritually nonplussed, between conventional wisdom and modish modernity. The great rallying cry of the Renaissance, Petrarch's 'Back to Antiquity', falls on deaf ears. So does 'Onward Christian Soldiers'. Wondering what to make now of our record, we peer apprehensively ahead. Maybe our amnesia and loss of nerve will prove terminal. Meanwhile we can no longer compliment ourselves on having risen above the past.

Seeking a quickened sense of who we are and where we are heading, we *must* begin again with bygones; we must rebuild the relationship with our history and, free from *parti pris*, come to terms with whatever we discover. This is not to say we should affect indifference: rather we must learn to be (to use a sadly abused word) disinterested. For, as Joseph Conrad saw, 'It is not our business to sit in judgement on the past, to reprove mankind for what it is not, or generally to teach it how to behave.' He was not urging retreat from commitment – no one could be more free from the pretence of neutrality – but he rightly insists that history is not a school of virtue, where sitting in judgement or taking sides (as between 'progressive' or 'reactionary', victors or vanquished) is all that is demanded of us. We need, on the contrary, some more magnanimous approach; to remember that

> Whatever we inherit from the fortunate
> We have taken from the defeated
> What they had to give us – a symbol;
> A symbol perfected in death.

Samuel Pepys tells a story that perfectly embodies Eliot's perception: 'Pretty to see', he noted after visiting Swakeleys House near Uxbridge in 1665, 'over the screen of the Hall (put up by Sir J Harrington, a Long Parliament-man) the King's head.' Pretty indeed, since Harrington had been one of the Commissioners for the trial of Charles I and was currently in the Tower. But prettier even than that suggests: for there was, and still is, another head over the screen: the bust of Lord Fairfax, Parliament's great general and Marvell's patron who fought against Charles but dissociated himself from the execution. There in Harrington's house the two heads stand together wrapped in 'the constitution of silence'. So in the end, sooner or later, the dead (good and bad, friend and foe) are 'folded in a single party'. So the poet and the diarist join forces to suggest what history essentially is: not a dead letter, but a repository of experience, a stock of memories and images, a record and a revelation, and a form of self-knowledge; and therefore, above all, a source of solidarity.

Solidarity: the word is a favourite of Conrad. The ship with its captain and crew, as in *The Shadow Line*, facing the worst that the fates in the form of the elements and human frailty can do and somehow coming through together, is his great symbol of our life. It is the embodiment of what in practice solidarity means. At the end of that tremendous story Ransome the old hand, who has helped his young skipper come of age, ascends the companion-stairs step-by-step in morbid fear (for he has a weak heart) of starting into anger 'our common enemy' death. He is his own *memento mori*; yet he fares forward, quietly, heroically faithful to his calling and so to his fellows. He knows no religious consolation; he cannot turn to eschatology to see him through. The focus has shifted from dying into life to enduring unto death. Yet he stands with Donne in the pulpit, with Charles on the scaffold or with Cromwell on his deathbed. There Oliver recalled (rather as Conrad elsewhere invoked 'the national spirit' as a special source of strength and continuity) his dying mother's prayer for him and the words 'My dear son I leave my heart with thee.' And the Protector prayed in turn that our people might be granted 'consistency of judgement, one heart, and mutual love'. Across the centuries the sentiment rings true: there is nothing strange or remote in that voice. Oliver dying showed his true greatness when he spoke simply from the heart of the longing for solidarity.

The twentieth century and the Stuart Age in spite of everything that separates them, still connect. Marvell's vision (I paraphrase Barbara Everett) of the fusions and confusions of history with the self faring forward, ever hopeful, yet always betraying and betrayed, meets, however different the mode and scale of work, the world of *Lord Jim*, *Nostromo* and *Under Western Eyes*. Milton's contemporary and the modern novelist come surprisingly close, too, on the subject of human destiny. Twenty years of war and peace, of victory and defeat, of expectation and disappointment, on from his *Horatian Ode* Marvell wryly concluded:

> I think the cause was too good to have been fought for; men ought to have trusted God, they ought and might have trusted the King with the whole matter . . . men may spare their pains where nature is at work, and the world will not go the faster for our driving.

So much, it seems, for Cromwell's dynamism and the breakthrough of 1649. Yet Marvell is not adrift: neither defeatist nor dreamer, he would have men wait upon events. He chimes with Conrad's advice to our century: 'I think the proper wisdom is to will what the Gods will, without perhaps, being certain what their will is, . . . or even if they have a will of their own.' That, obviously, has additional depths of disbelief; yet the sense of an inscrutable providence, the instinct for patient endurance in the face of disillusionment, the refusal to abandon ship, unite the two writers.

So Milton's 'It is not so terrible to be afflicted as not to be able to endure affliction' salutes Conrad's unbowed 'I have looked at the worst of life – and am sure of myself.' Milton the seer would have stirred, too, at the undaunted heroism of Conrad's apocalypse:

> I am inclined to think that the last utterance will formulate, strange as it may appear, some hope now to us utterly inconceivable. For mankind is delightful in its pride, its assurance, and its indomitable tenacity. It will sleep on the battlefield among its own dead, in the manner of an army having won a barren victory. It will not know when it is beaten.

That looks well beyond the doom-laden prophecy in Matthew Arnold's 'Dover-Beach' of a

> darkling plain
> Swept with confused alarms of struggle and flight
> Where ignorant armies clash by night.

Conrad, no mistake, has gone over the brink where the despondent Victorian teetered. His vision of humankind destined to perish from the cold, its lot determined by a fate indifferently knitting us in and out of an existence that is simultaneously poignant, intensely interesting, and not of the slightest consequence is altogether bleaker. The ache of nihilism is in his bones – that *angst* which, though no age lacks torment, is peculiarly ours. Yet there is a resistance in him too, an indefatigable fortitude, the will to *face* things (another favourite word), an exhilaration even. He marches with Milton and Marvell rather than with Victorian recessionals.

Conrad, who like Eliot and all true artists was both historian and prophet, helps renew our relationship with past, present and future. At one point he comes curiously close to antiquarian John Aubrey: at least the latter's claim that

> the retriving [sic] of these forgotten Things from Oblivion in some sort resembles the Art of a Conjuror, who makes those walke and appeare that have layen in their graves many hundreds of yeares: and to represent as it were to the eie, the places, Customes and Fashions, that were of old Times

has something in common with Conrad's conviction that his calling as an artist was to snatch experiences from the 'remorseless rush of time' and to 'hold up unquestioningly the rescued fragment before all our eyes . . . that at last the presented vision . . . shall awaken in the hearts of the beholders the feeling of unavoidable solidarity'. Can we propose a better definition of the historian's role than, between them, those two conjure up? If an old model of history, having served us well, has come to pieces in our hands we need not capitulate. Maybe even now another dynamic paradigm is taking shape, in Britain's case perhaps some more John Bullish myth of patriotic capitalism to steer our affairs and plot the past anew. Meanwhile, however, our freedom from fixed schemes and grand scenarios may actually be tonic. Getting the record straight, facing the facts and keeping faith with them, however alien or uncomfortable, becomes, if possible, more than ever imperative – a greater challenge, even, in a world where illusion and lying are not unknown and a sense of direction harder than before to find and fight for. When much of the nation's past (its indispensable guide and inspiration) is overlooked or even withheld from a rising generation, memory, which is not the same thing as nostalgia, matters more than ever.

It is important to be able to recognize in the past, and come to terms with, those worlds (like seventeenth-century Britain) which are in some respects quite different from ours – so much so that sometimes we must wonder whether we can relate to them other than *à la* Vico as part of a succession of discontinuities. Above all we need the readiness to respond unquestioningly, that is to say spontaneously, to the 'vibration . . . colour . . . form' of what we find in the record that still binds this time to that and that to this in the 'feeling of an enduring existence'. The king on the scaffold remains one of those authentic fragments rescued from the rush and shipwreck of time which still exerts a hold on us, is part, you might say, of our human and national identity. So humble, haunted Mr Dick, Dickens's holy simpleton, found, who could not but remember King Charles's head. Unable to explain himself, he found in it 'the figure, or the simile; or whatever it is called' that connected with his own condition and somehow made sense of it. As Betsy Trotwood said, he puts us all right. Admittedly there is no turning Mr Dick into a brave new model; but while we stand doubting – as in some degree we always must – he represents a reassurance. A kind of wholeness despite congenital weaknesses and fragmentary knowledge – this is what history and literature can give us even now to hand on to others. 1649 and all that, however you look at it, still counts.

Index

Page numbers in **bold** refer to illustrations

Act of Oblivion and Indemnity, 41
Act of Settlement, 49, 50
Act of Union, 49
Adamite, 59
Agrippa, Cornelius, 11; *Occult Philosophy*, 167
alchemy, 86
Anabaptists, 61, 82
Ancients and Moderns, 5–6, 13–15, 102–4
Andover, Dorothy Howard, Viscountess, 138
Andrewes, Lancelot, Bishop, 66, 70
Anglican biography, 79
Anglican Church, 65, 66
Anglicanism, 54–64, 66, 73, 74
Anne, Queen, 42, 48, 169; Anne of Denmark, Queen Consort, 112, 113, 116
anti-Catholicism, 57
anticlericalism, 57
antinomianism, 62, 63
Archimedes, 104
Argyll's rebellion, 46
Aries, Philippe, 181
Aristophanes, 5
Aristotle, 5, 104
Arlington, Henry Bennet, 1st Earl of, 44
Armada, the, 57
Arminianism, 20, 55–6, 60
army, 29, 31, 38, 39, 40, 153; Army Council, 29, 31, 56; New Model Army, 28, 76, 159 Standing Army, 41;
Arnold, Matthew, 1, 184
Artisan Mannerists, 113
Arundel, Aletheia Howard, Countess of, 110, 136

Arundel, Thomas Howard, 14th Earl of, 109–10, 112, 135, 136, 138, 143, 149
Arundel Marbles, 110, 113
Ashmole, Elias, 167
Aspinall, William, 153
Assembly of Divines, 28
Astell, Mary, 83, 84; *A Serious Proposal to the Ladies*, 83
Aston Hall, Birmingham, 112–13
Aubrey, John, 99, 159, 167, 168, 185; *Brief Lives*, 79, 161; *Remaines of Gentilism and Judaism*, 161
Augustanism, 15, 114, 169
Augustine, St, 13, 93
Augustus, Caesar, 16

Bacon, Francis, 14, 16, 70, 86, 91, 92, 98, 101, 102, 104, 105, 106, 166; *Advancement of Learning*, 13; *Novum Organum*, 100, 104
Bacon, Sir Nathaniel, 135
Baker, Thomas, 112, 143
Banqueting House, 112, **118**, 134
Baptists, 59
Barebone's Parliament, 35
Barnes, Ambrose, 155
baroque, 107, 108, 145, 147, 148, 149, 157
Barry, Edward, 116
Barry, Elizabeth, 8
Bathurst, Ralph, 167
Baxter, Richard, 70
Beaumont, Sir John, 15
Bedford, Francis Russell, 4th Earl of, 115, 167
Behn, Aphra, 7, 8
Belton, 144

Benlowes, Edward: *Theophila*, 73
Bentley, Richard, 88
Bernini, Gian Lorenzo, 112, 143, 145, 146
Bible, 2, 5, 30, 180
Biblical exegesis, 2, 5
Biddle, Hester: *The Trumpet of the Lord Sounded Forth*, 72
Birch, Colonel John, 48
Bishops Wars, 22
Blake, William, 170
Blazing World, The, 8
Blenheim Palace, 112, 148, 149
Blickling Hall, Norfolk, 113
Blith, Walter, 178
blood, circulation of the, 16; transfusion, 96
Booth's rising, 39
Borromini, Francesco, 147
Bovey, James, 167
Boyle, Robert, 86, 97, 104, 167, 168; *Sceptical Chemist*, 97
Boyne, Battle of the, 49
Bracegirdle, Anne, 8
Brecht, Bertholt, 9
Briggs, Henry, 166
Brontë, Charlotte: *Villette*, 107
Brooke, Robert Greville, Lord, 59
Browne, Sir Thomas, 71, 72, 87, 89, 168; *Pseudodoxia Epidemica*, 71; *Religio Medici*, 71
Buckingham, George Villiers, 1st Duke of, 19, 82, 110, 136, 161; assassination of, 19
Buckingham, George Villiers, 2nd Duke of, 163; *Rehearsal*, 9
Buff-Coat, 31
Bunyan, John, 11, 12, 62, 64, 68, 74, 76, 79, 84, 168, 180, 181; *Of Antichrist and His Ruine*, 180; *Grace Abounding to the Chief of Sinners*, 69–70, 84, 181; *The Holy War*, 180; *Pilgrim's Progress*, ix, 4, 68, 69, 180; *Pilgrim's Progress* II, 76
Burke, Edmund, 179
Burlington, Richard Boyle, 3rd Earl of, 149
Burnet, Elizabeth: *Reasonableness of Religion*, 84
Burnet, Gilbert, Bishop: *Some Passages in the Life and Death of John, Earl of Rochester*, 79

Burnet, Thomas: *Sacred Theory of the Earth*, 103
Burton, Robert, 87
Bushnell, John, 144
Butler, Samuel, 92, 160; *The Elephant in the Moon*, 100; *Hudibras*, 62, 63, 162
Byron, George Gordon, Lord, 107

Cabal, 44
Cage, Arthur, 96
Calvinism, 54, 55, 56, 63, 69
Cambridge Platonism, 73, 74, 76
Campbell, Colen: *Vitruvius Britannicus*, 114
Canaletto, Antonio: *The Thames from Somerset House Terrace*, **121**, 148
Canne, John, 153
Caravaggio, 138
Cardell, John, 152
Carew, Thomas, 81, 160, 174; *To Saxham*, 77
Carleton, Dudley, 169
Carpenter, Edmund, 144
Casaubon, Isaac, 10
Catullus, 6, 92
censorship, 23, 173
Chapman, George, 169
Charles I, 11, 18–32, 33, 42, 55, 56, 57, 58, 66, 67, 110, 111, 112, 114, 116, 136, 143, 151–5, 157, 159, 163, 164, 168, 176, 183
Charles II, 12, 33, 40–6, 57, 58, 64, 66, 67, 69, 71, 82, 102, 109, 158, 162–3, 168, 169, 174, 176
Charleton, Walter, 167
Chatsworth, 144, 148
Chaucer, Geoffrey: *The Canterbury Tales*, 176
Chelsea Hospital, 109, 147, 148
children, attitudes to, 176–7
Cibber, Caius Gabriel, 144
Cicero, 16, 103
Civil War, 8, 18, 26–9, 32, 41, 57, 161, 168, 173
Clarendon, Edward Hyde, 1st Earl of, 19, 24, 33, 41, 42, 64, 110, 173, 180; *History of the Rebellion*, 42
Clarendon, Henry Hyde, 2nd Earl of, 46
Clarendon Code, 41, 64, 76
Clarendon House, 144
Clarkson, Lawrence 62

Cleyn, Francis, 111
Clifford, Thomas, 44
Clifford of Chudleigh, Thomas, Lord, 140
Coke, Edward, Sir: *Institutes*, 30
Coleshill, Berkshire, **119**, 134, 144
Colonialism, 24
Columbus, Christopher, 96
Committee of Both Kingdoms, 28
Commonwealth, the, 32–40, 61
communications, 173
Communist Manifesto, 181
compass, mariner's, 16
conceptions of language, 104–6
Conrad, Joseph, 182, 183, 184, 185; *The Shadow Line*, 183
Conventicle Act, 65
Cook, John, 153
Cooper, Samuel, ix, 12, 33, 108, 109, 111, 112, 139–41; *James Scott, Duke of Monmouth and Buccleuch* **132**; *Oliver Cromwell* **131**, 140
Copernicus, Nicolaus, 87
Coppe, Abiezer: *A Second Fiery Flying Roule*, 62
corn surpluses, 171
Cotterell, Sir Charles, 139
Cotton, Charles, 6, 92; *Scarronides*, 3; trans. of Montaigne's *Essays*, 92
Council of Officers, 34–5
Council of State, 35
Country, 49
Court, 49
Court, Inns of, 4
Covent Garden, 117
Cowley, Abraham, 6, 71, 84, 86, 87, 90, 158, 175
Cranfield, Lionel, 16
Crashaw, Richard, 81
Creech, Thomas, 3, 104
Cromwell, Oliver, ix, 12, 28, 30–9, 58, 59, 61, 73, 74, 109, 111, 112, 152, 153, 155, 157, 159, 169, 173, 179, 182, 183, 184
Cromwell, Richard, 39
Cudworth, Ralph, 10
Culpepper, Sir John, 4, 25
Curwen, Alice, 82
Cusa, Nicholas of, 86

da Cortona, Pietro, 147
da Vinci, Leonardo, 110, 145
Dahl, Michael, 142

Danby, Thomas Osborne, 1st Earl of, 42, 44
Darwin, Charles, 179
Davenant, Charles, 173
Davenant, William, 9, 170
Davies, Lady Eleanor, 82
de Caux, Isaac, 117
de Caux, Salomon, 117
de Keyser, Hendrik, 143
de Sangallo, Guiliano, Villa Medici, 116
death, attitudes to, 181
decimation tax, 37
Declaration of Breda, 40, 41
Declaration of Indulgence, 47, 65
Dee, Dr John, 10, 11, 12, 168; *Elements of Geometrie*, 165
Defoe, Daniel, 170, 173
Dekker, Thomas, Ford, John and Rowley, William: *The Witch of Edmonton*, 75
Democritus, 104
Demosthenes, 103
Denham, John, 15, 145
Derby, Charlotte, Countess of, 160
Derby, James Stanley, 7th Earl of, 155
Descartes, René, 86, 91, 98, 101, 104, 105, 106; *Dioptrique*, 97
D'Ewes, Sir Simonds, 156
Dickens, Charles, 151, 186; *David Copperfield*, 151
Dieussart, Francois, 143
differential calculus, 16, 96
Digby, George, 25
Diggers, the, 31
Digges, Thomas, 87
Directory, 60
Dobson, William, 108, 109, 111, 138–9, 140; *Charles II as Prince of Wales*, 139; *The Artist with Sir Charles Cotterell and ?Nicholas Lanier* **130**
doctrine of decay, 93
Donne, John, 11, 12, 14, 15, 16, 66, 72, 90, **125**, 165, 174, 180, 183; *Death's Duel*, 156; *Hymn to God in my Sickness*, 156; *Ignatius His Conclave*, 93,
Drayton, Michael, 148
Dryden, John, 3, 6, 11, 12, 15, 17, 42, 62, 80, 84, 90, 92, 102, 103, 160, 163, 170, 174, 175, 180; *Absalom and Achitophel*, 4, 45, 67, 163; *Aeneid*

(tr. of Virgil), 3; *Alexander's Feast*, 175; *Annus Mirabilis*, 170; *Astraea Redux*, 58; *Essay of Dramatic Poetry*, 174; *MacFlecknoe*, 4, 6, 173, 175; *The Indian Emperor*, 169; *The Indian Queen*, 169
du Jon, Francois: *The Painting of the Ancients*, 110
Dunbar, victory at, 35, 158
'Dutch House', Kew Gardens, 113
Dutton, John, 56
Dyrham Park, 148

Education: classical, 5–6; women's, 6–8
Edwards, Thomas: *Gangraena*, 30, 62
Egerton, Sarah Fyge, 83; *The Female Advocate*, 83
Eikon Basilike, 66, 154, 157
Einstein, Albert, 10, 97, 168
Eliot, T.S., 12, 152, 164, 182, 183, 185
Eltham Lodge, 145
emblem-books, 78
enthusiasm, 61, 81
epigrams, 173
Erasmus, Desiderius, 11
Escorial, 116
Essex, Robert Devereux, 3rd Earl of, 28
Etherege, Sir George, 11
Euclid, 165
Euripides, 5
Evans, Edith, 8
Evelyn, John, 8, 64, 144, 145, 153; *Discourse of Forest-Trees*, 99; *The History of Religion*, 78; *The Life of Mrs Godolphin*, 78; *Sylva*, 78
Everett, Barbara, 11, 160, 184
Exclusion Crisis, 42, 43, 45, 57, 168

Fairfax, Sir Thomas, Lord-General, 28, 56, 155, 183
Familists, 59, 82
Fane, Mildmay, 'To Retiredness', 73, 77
Fanelli, Francesco, 143
Fanshawe, Sir Richard, 20, 58; *Ode Upon Occasion of His Majesty's Proclamation*, 20
Farnham market, 171
Feake, Daniel, 153, 158, 161
Fell, Margaret: *Womens Speaking Justified*, 82

Felltham, Owen, 13
Ferrar, Nicholas, 73
Fiennes, Celia, 170
Fifth Monarchists, 34, 59, 60, 61, 153, 155, 161
Filmer, Robert: *Patriarcha*, 45
Flecknoe, Richard, 162
Fleetwood, General George, 158
Florio, John, 92
Fontenelle, Le Bouvier de: *Entretiens Sur la Pluralité des Mondes, 103*
Ford, John: *'Tis a Pity She's a Whore*, 9
Foucault, Michel, 2
Fox, George, 62, 64, 79; *Journal*, 76
Foxe, John: *Book of Martyrs*, 153
France, 19, 32, 37
French Revolution, 11, 181
Freud, Sigmund, 1
Fuller, Isaac, 142

Galen, 104
Galileo, 86, 93, 96, 104, 105
Gardens, 77–8
Gauden, John, 66
Gentileschis, Artemisia and Orazio, 111, 112
Gibbons, Grinling, 144, 147
Gilbert, William, 166
Glanvill, Joseph, 87, 88, 103, 167, 170; *Plus Ultra*, 96; *Scepsis Scientifica*, 87; *Vanity of Dogmatizing*, 87
Glorious Revolution, 48, 176
Goffe, William, 153
Gonzaga Collection, 110, 111, 136
Goodman, Arthur, 137
Goodman, Godfrey, 98; *Fall of Man*, 13, 93
Gough, Richard: *History of Myddle*, 172, 178
Gould, Robert: *A Late Satyr Against the Pride, Lust and Inconstancy of Women*, 83
Grand Remonstrance, 24, 138
Graunt, John, 99, 166
Great Fire of London, 57, 109, 115–16, 143, 146, 168, 170, 174
Greenhill, John, 142
Greenwich, 112, 143, 145, 147, 148
Gresham College, 87, 166
Grew, Nehemiah: *Anatomy of Plants*, 96
Gunnersby, Middlesex, 134
gunpowder, 16

Gunpowder Plot, 57
Gwyn, Nell, 8

Hakewill, George, 103; *Apology*, 13, 94
Halifax, George Savile, Marquis of: *The Character of a Trimmer*, 45
Hall, John, of Durham, 168
Hamilton, James, 1st Duke of, 135
Hampden, John, 20
Hampton Court, 112, 134, 143, 147
Hampton Court Palace, **122**, 148
Hardwick Hall, 108, 112
Harley, Sir Robert, 111
Harrington, James: *Oceana*, 17, 39
Harrington, Sir James, 183
Harrison, Thomas, 153
Hartlib, Samuel, 71, 166
Harvey, William, 104, 166
Hawksmoor, Nicholas, 145, 148, 149; Castle Howard, 149; Mausoleum, 149; Mausoleum at Castle Howard, **124**
Heads of the Proposals, the, 31, 35
Hearth tax, 41
Heisenberg's Uncertainty Principle, 88
Henrietta Maria, Queen, 8, 9, 22, 66, 137
Henry, Prince of Wales, 110, 117, 164, 176
Herbert of Cherbury, Lord Edward, 79
Herbert, George, 21, 55, 68, 73, 75, 89, 105, 169; *The British Church*, 169; *The Church Militant*, 169; *The Country Parson*, 74, 77; *Temple*, 79
Hermetic philosophy, 10, 13, 73, 102
Herrick, Robert, 6, 15, 135; *The Ceremonies for Candlemass Day*, 64; *A Country Life*, 77; *Hock-cart*, 64; *A Pastorall upon the Birth of Prince Charles*, 58
Hesilrige, Sir Arthur, 32, 39
Hilliard, Nicholas, 16, 108, 109, 135, 138, 139
Hindmarsh, Joseph, 4
History of Insipids, The, 67
Hitler, Adolf, 181
Hobbes, Thomas, 12, 26, 86, 87, 96, 101–2, 105, 140, 159, 160, 169, 180; *Leviathan*, 33, 68, 101, 160
Hogarth, William, 139, 143
Holbein, Hans, 110
Holland, Henry Rich, 1st Earl, 138

Hollar, Vaclav, 110, 155
Holles, Francis, 143
Holles, George, 143
Homer, 5, 15, 16, 103, 161
Hooke, Robert, 87, 97, 146; *Micrographia*, 96, 102
Hooker, Richard: *Laws of Ecclesiastical Polity*, 54
Hoole, Charles: *A New Discovery of the Old Art of Teaching Schoole*, 5
Hopkins, John, and Sternhold, Thomas: *Psalms*, 180
Horace, 5, 6, 16, 17, 103, 180
Hoskins, John, the elder, 108, 139, 140
Hoskins, John, the younger, 111, 139–40
Houlbrook, Ralph: *The English Family*, 177
Howard, Sir Robert, 62
Humble Petition and Advice, The, 38
Hutchinson, Colonel John, 81
Hutchinson, Lucy, 8, 67, 70, 81, 169
Huygens, Christian, 87, 96, 97

Iconoclasm, 63–4, 107, 111–12
imitation, 17
Independence, American War of, 11
Independency, 60
Independents, 29
Industrial Monopolies, 23
Inns of Court, 4
Instrument of Government, 35–6
Ireland, 21, 24, 29, 33, 36, 49
Ireton, Henry, 31

James I, 18, 45, 66, 67, 110, 114, 158, 159, 168
James II, 49, 57, 168
James, Duke of York, 43, 44, 65
James, Henry, 1, 2
Janssen: *see* Johnson, Cornelius
Jeffrey, George, Judge, 46
Johnson, Cornelius, 108, 135
Johnson, Dr Samuel, ix, 75, 90, 134
Johnson, Thomas, 167
Jones, Inigo, 16, 17, 107, 108, 109, 110, 111, 112, 113–17, 134, 145, 149, 158, 170; Wilton House, 117
Jonson, Ben, 6, 11, 14, 16, 17, 62, 77, 80, 103, 114, 116, 135, 171, 174, 175, 180; *Epicene*, 103; *Masque of Augurs*, 114; *Penshurst*, 171; *Poetaster*, 4; *Volpone*, 15

judiciary, 50
Junius: *see* du Jon
Justices of the Peace, 22
Juvenal, 17, 103
Juxon, William, 20

Kempster family, masons, 147
Kentish Petition, 26
Kepler, Johannes: *Dioptrice*, 97
Killigrew, Thomas, 8, 9, 137, 142, 162
King, Henry, 156, 166
Kingston Lacey, 144
Kircher, Athanasius, 96
Kneller, Godfrey, 112, 142; *Admirals at Greenwich*, 142; *Hampton Court Beauties*, 142; *Kit Cat Club*, 142

Ladurie, Emmanuel Le Roy: *Montaillou*, 88
Laguerre, Louis, 112, 142
Lamport Hall, Northamptonshire, 134
Lanhydrock, Cornwall, 112
Lanier, Nicholas, **139**
Larkins, William, 135
Lathom House, 155
Laud, William, 19, 20, 21, 22, 55, 65, 66
Lauderdale, John Maitland, 1st Duke of, 44
Laudianism, 21, 23–4, 55–6, 60, 63
Le Sueur, Hubert, 143, 154
Lee, Mary: *The Ladies Defence*, 83
Leibniz, Gottfried Wilhelm, 87, 96
Leicester, Rupert Sidney, 2nd Earl of, 141
Lely, Sir Peter, 12, 33, 108, 109, 111, 112, 140, 141–2, 163; *Flagmen*, 142; *Self-Portrait*, **133**, 141; *Windsor Beauties*, 142
Lemery, Nicholas: *Course in Chemistry*, 97
Lemon, Margaret, 140
Leonardo: *see* da Vinci
Levellers, the, 30, 31, 33, 43
Ley, John: *A Discourse Concerning Puritans*, 54
Licensing Act, 45
Lilburne, John, 21, 23, 30, 31, 82
Lilies Grammar, 5
Lilly, William, 154
Lindsey House, 113
literacy, female, 7

Little Gidding, 73
Livy, 6
Locke, John, 26, 84, 92, 105, 168; *Essay Concerning Human Understanding*, 91, 102; *Letter on Toleration*, 65; *The Reasonableness of Christianity*, 68; *The Two Treatises of Government*, 45, 48
Lollards, 55
London, 25, 26, 28, 31, 171–4
Longinus, 16
Longleat, 108
Louis XIV, 44, 47, 50, 148
Lovelace, Richard, 26, 160, 172, 175
Low Church Tradition, 41
Lower, Richard, 96
Lucian, 8
Lucretius, 3, 8, 104; *De Rerum Natura*, 3, 16
Ludlow, Edmund, 48, 161; *Memoirs*, 162; *Voyce from the Watch Tower*, 161, 162
Lurting, Thomas, 60

Macfarlane, Allen, 177; *The Justice and the Mare's Ale*, 177; *The Origins of English Individualism*, 178
Machiavelli, Niccolo, 164
Magna Carta, 30, 31
Maine, Jonathan, 147
Major-generals, 36–7
Makin, Bathusa, 7
Malpighi, Marcello, 96
Manchester, Edward Montagu, 2nd Earl of, 28
Mantegna, Andrea, 111
Mantua, Dukes of, 110
mariner's compass, 16
Marlborough, John Churchill, 1st Duke of, 149
Marlowe, Christopher: *Doctor Faustus*, 75
Marshall, Edward, 113
Marshall, Joshua, 147
Marshall, Stephen, 70
Marston, John, 4
Martin, Richard, 16
Marvell, Andrew, 11, 12, 13, 77, 80, 84, 155, 158, 160, 169, 172, 179, 180, 183, 184, 185; *An Account of the Growth of Popery*, 72; *The First Anniversary of the Government*, 58, 61, 169; *Further Advice to*

a Painter 174; *An Horation Ode upon Cromwell's Return from Ireland* 1, 32, 154, 157, 158, 159; *The Mower Against Gardens*, 71; *The Rehearsal Transprosed*, 163; *Upon the Victory Obtained by Blake*, 57
Mary, Queen, 46, 148
masques, 9, 66
Matisse, Henri, 145
May, Hugh, 145
Maynard, Serjeant John, 48
Mennes, Sir John and Smith, Dr James: *Musarum Deliciae: or The Muses Recreation*, 4
Mercurius Aulicus, 23
Mercurius Pragmaticus, 23
Methodist Revival, 74
Michelangelo, 143
microscope, 96
Middleton, Thomas, 74
Millenarianism, 11, 12, 13–14, 34, 54, 58, 68, 153, 155, 181
Milton, John, ix, 6, 10, 11, 12, 13, 17, 23, 31, 56, 59, 60, 71, 74, 75, 76, 78, 80, 84, 87, 92, 93, 169, 172, 175, 180, 184, 185; *Areopagitica*, 23; *Ikonoklastes*, 154; *In Quintum Novembris*, 57; *Lycidas*, 175; *Paradise Lost*, ix, 56, 68, 71, 75, 82; *Ready and Easy Way to Establish a Free Commonwealth*, 17, 39; *Tractate*, 17
Mimm, Thomas, 167
misogyny, 83
Molière, Jean-Baptiste Poquelin, 9, 17
Moncada, Marquis of, 136
Monck, General George, 40
Monmouth, James Scott, Duke of, 45, 140, 168
Monmouth's rebellion, 46, 48, 168
Montaigne, Michel 17, 92
More, Henry, 73
More, John, 153
More, Sir Thomas, 11, 170
Muggleton, Lodowick, 60
Muggletonianism, 59
Myddleton, Sir Thomas, 166
Mytens, Daniel, 110, 135; *Algernon Percy, 10th Earl of Northumberland*, **127**, 137

Napier, John, 167, 153; *Logarithms*, 153
Naseby, Battle of, 28
Navigation Act, 33
Nayler, James, 38, 65
Needham, Marchmont, 23
Neoplatonism, 13, 66, 102, 113
Newcastle, Margaret Cavendish, Duchess of, 8, 70, 81; *Memoirs*, 70
Newton, Isaac, 10, 13, 50, 68, 71, 86, 87, 96, 98, 104, 105, 168; *Opticks*, 86, 97; *Principia*, ix, 86, 87, 97, 102
Nineteen Propositions, 25, 27
Northumberland, Algernon Percy, 10th Earl of, 109, 111, 112, 135, 138, 141
number symbolism, 89, 160

Oates, Titus, 44
Ogilby, John, 161
Oldham John, 6, 15, 84, 92, 103, 175; *Satyrs upon the Jesuits*, 80; *Upon the Works of Ben Johnson*, 15
Oliver, Isaac, 108, 135, 139
Oliver, Peter, 108, 139
optics, 97
Organon, 104
Orinda: *see* Philips, Katherine
Overton, Richard, 30, 153
Ovid, 16
Owen, John, 152, 155

Palladianism, 149
Palladio, Andrea, 112, 113, 114, 116, 170; *I Quattro Libri Dell 'architettura*, 114; Palazzo Chiericati, 116
Paracelsius, 11, 12, 71
Parker, Samuel, 105
Parker, Henry, 25
Parliament, 19, 25, 27; Cavalier Parliament, 41; Convention Parliament, 40–1; Convention Parliament (1689), 48; House of Lords, 38, 40, 42, 43; Long Parliament, 22, 33, 37, 40, 41; Short Parliament, 22
patronage, 42, 109–12
Peace of Ryswick, 50
Peake, Robert, 135
Pearce, Edward, 117
Pellegrini, Giovanni Antonio, 142

Pembroke, Philip Herbert, 4th Earl of, 109, 112
Pembroke, Philip Herbert, 5th Earl of, 141
Pembroke College, Cambridge, 146
Penruddock's rising, 36
Pepys, Samuel, 8, 139, 169, 183
perpendicular style, 112
Persius, 17
Petition of Right, 19
Petrarch, Francesco, 182
Petty, Sir William, 142, 166; *Political Arithmetic*, 99; *Treatise of Taxes*, 99
Petworth, 144
Philips, Katherine, 8
Philosophical Society, John Wilkins's, 87
Picasso, Pablo, 145
Pierce, Edward, 144, 147; *Sir Christopher Wren*, **126**
Pindar, 5
Pirkheymer library, 110
Plato, 16
Platonism, 105
Pope, Alexander, 6, 86, 98; *Epistle to Burlington*, 170
Pope, Mary: *A Treatise of Magistracy*, 84
Popish Plot, 42, 44–5, 57, 168, 171
Post Office, 36, 173
Powell, Vavasour, 153
Pratt, Sir Roger, 12, 109, 117, 134, 144, 145
Prayer Book, 60, 64
preaching, 20–1, 66, 70
Prerogative courts, 19, 23
Presbyterians, 28, 29, 54, 55, 59, 60, 61
Pride's Purge, 32
progress, 92, 98, 103, 164
Prynne, William, 8, 21, 22–3, 66, 40; *Histriomastrix*, 8
psychology, 97
Puritanism, 54–66, 69, 72, 79
Putney debates, ix, 31
Pym, John, 22, 24, 27–8, 55–6, 171; *Grand Remonstrance*, 138
Pyrrho, of Elis, 92

Quakers, 31, 39, 59, 60, 61, 64, 65, 82
Quarles, Francis, 78
Queen's Chapel at St James Palace, 114–15
Queen's House, Greenwich, 116–17, 148

Rainsborough, Colonel Thomas, 179
Ralegh, Sir Walter, 164, 165, 169, 171; *History of the World*, 164, 178
Ranters, 31, 59, 61, 62, 64
Raphael, 111
Rationalism, 53, 68, 74, 81
Ray, John: *Historia Plantarum*, 96
Redford, Elizabeth, 84
Reformation, 53, 57
Religious toleration, 34
Republicanism, 56, 57
Restoration, 40; settlement, 12
Revolution of 1688/9, 43, 46
Reynolds, Edward, 61
Ricci, Marco and Sebastiano, 142
Richmond, James Stuart, 1st Duke of, 137
Riley, John, 142
Rochester, John Wilmot, 2nd Earl of, 6, 75, 80, 84, 92
Rochester, Lawrence Hyde, 1st Earl of, 46
Rogers, John, 153
Roman Catholicism, 54, 55, 57, 64, 65
Rosicrucian, 168
Rota, The, 39
Royal Society, the, 12, 70, 71, 78, 87, 99, 100, 101, 104, 105, 106, 145
Rubens, Peter Paul, 110, 111, 112, 116, 134, 136
Rump, the, 32, 33, 34, 35, 39, 40
Rump Parliament, ejection of by Cromwell, 34
Russian Revolution, 11, 181
Ryswick, Treaty of, 50

St Lawrence Jewry, 144
St Paul's Cathedral, ix, 107, 115, **120**, 143, 144, 146, 147, 148
St Paul's Church, Covent Garden, 114–15
Salisbury, Robert Arthur, 3rd Marquis of, 176
Satire, 4, 16
Savile, Henry, 6
Savoy Declaration, 61
Saye and Sele, William Fiennes, 1st Viscount, 170
Scamozzi, 113, 116
Scarburgh, Sir Charles, 145

Scarron, Paul: *Virgile Travestie*, 3
scepticism, 53
Schama, Simon, ix
Scotland, 21, 24, 28, 29, 33, 26, 40, 49, 63; Act of Union with, 49
Seaton Delaval, Northumberland, **123**, 149
Sedley, Sir Charles, 11
Seekers, 59
Selden, John, 110
Self-Denying Ordinance, 28
Seneca, 16
Serlio, 113
Seymour, Sir Edward, 42
Shadwell, Thomas, 4, 6, 92, 173; *The Virtuoso*, 100
Shaftesbury, Anthony Ashley Cooper, 1st Earl of, 4, 42, 44, 45, 92; trial of, 4
Shakers, 61
Shakespeare, William, 11, 17
Sheldonian Theatre, Oxford, 146
Shepherd, William, 36
Sheppard, William, 142
ship money, 19, 22, 23
Shirley, James, 180
Shrewsbury, Anna-Maria, Countess of, 162
Siddons, Sarah, 8
Sidney, Sir Phillip, 169; *Defence of Poetry*, 80
Simmonds, Martha, 84
Simon, Thomas, 33
Smith, Maggie, 8
Smythson, John, 16, 113
Smythson, Robert, 16, 112, 113
Soest, Gerard, 141
Solemn League and Covenant, 60
Sophocles, 5
Spain, 19, 32, 37
Spenser, Edmund, 169, 175
Spragge, Sir William, 99
Sprat, Thomas, 78, 101, 105
Sprint, John, 83
Stalin, Joseph, 179
Stapleton, Sir Robert, 4
Sterry, Peter, 73
Stone, Nicholas, 113, 117, 143, 147; *John Donne*, St Paul's Cathedral, **125**
Strafford, Thomas Wentworth, 1st Earl of, ix, 21, 22, 23, 27, 137, 138
Strong family, masons, 147

Suckling, Sir John, 81
Surveyorship of the King's Work's, 145
Sussex, Anne, Countess of, 137
Swakeleys House, 113, 183
Sydenham, Thomas, 168, 179
Sylvester, Josuah, 169

Tacitus, 164
Talman, William, 145
Tassoni, Alessandro, 102; *Dieci Libri di Pensieri Diversi*, 103
taxation, 38, 37
Taylor, Jeremy, 54, 89, 90; *Ductor Dubitantium*, 54; *Holy Dying*, 156
Taylor, John, 165
telescope, 16, 96
Temple, Solomon's, 116
Temple, Thomas, 70
Temple, Sir William, 103, 160, 180; *Essay on Ancient and Modern Learning*, 103
Terence, 9
Test Act, 45, 46, 65
theatre, 8-9; and women, 8
Thimbleley, Elizabeth, Lady, 138
Thirty Years War, 20, 160
'Thirty-Nine Articles', 55
Thomason, George, 23
Thornhill, Sir James, 143
Thorpe Hall, 134
Thurloe, John, 36
Tijou, Jean, 147
Tillotson, John, Archbishop, 74
Tintoretto, 110
Titian, 110, 111, 136, 145
Toland, John, 162; *Christianity Not Mysterious*, 68
toleration, 41, 47, 61, 71
Toleration Act, 49, 65
Tom Tower, Oxford, 148
Tonson, Jacob, 3
Tories, 43, 46, 47, 49
Traherne, Thomas, 12, 76-7, 89, 170; *Centuries*, 102
transport, 173
transubstantation, 54
Trapnel, Anna, 82
Treaty of Dover, 44
Trienniel Act, 23, 42, 49
Trinity College chapel, Oxford, 144
Trinity College library, Cambridge, 144, 147, 148
Tyttenhanger, 134

Ulster rebellion, 24
Ussher, James, Archbishop, 79, 155

Van Dyck, Sir Anthony, 20, 107, 108, 109, 110, 111, 112, 135–8, 139, 140, 141, 143, 163; *Algernon Percy, 10th Earl of Northumberland*, **128**, 137; *The Five Eldest Children of Charles I*, **129**, 138; *The Lommellini Family*, 137
Vanbrugh, Sir John, 145, 148, 149
Vane, Sir Henry, the Younger, 56, 157; *A Healing Question*, 57
Vaughan, Henry, 13, 73
Vaughan, Thomas, 73
Vaughan, Sir William, 166
Venice, 17
Verney, Sir Ralph, 7, 141
Veronese, Paolo, 138
Verrio, Antonio, 112, 142
Versailles, 148
Vico, Giambattista, 185
Vine, The, Sherbourne, 134
Virgil, 3, 16, 92, 103, 161; *Aeneid*, 5, 6; *Eclogues*, 5; *Georgics*, 5
Vitruvius, 113, 114, 170
Voltaire, 39

Wadham College, 87
Walker, Clement; *History of Independency*, 34
Walker, Robert, 111, 141
Waller, Edmund, 'Of His Majesty's receiving the news of the Duke of Buckingham's Death', 66
Walton, Izaac, 79, 143, 154
Walwyn, William, 23, 31, 39; *A Still Soft Voice*, 30; *A Whisper in the ear of Mr Thomas Edwards*, 30
Warwick, Robert Rich, 2nd Earl of, 137, 138
Watson, Samuel, 144
Webb, John, 12, 109, 117, 134, 145; King's block, Greenwich, 148
Webster, John, 80, 165; *The White Devil*, 80

Westminster Assembly, 29, 60
Wharton, Philip, Lord, 112, 137
Whigs, 43, 46, 47, 49
White, Dorothy, 84
Whitehall, Palace of, 109, 116, 134
Whitelocke, Bulstrode, 32, 36
Wildman, Sir John, 140
Wilkins, John, 71, 74, 87, 96; *Essay towards a Real Character and a Philosophical Language*, 105; *Of the Principles and Duties of Natural Religion*, 74; Philosophical Society, 87
William III (William of Orange), 46, 47–50, 57, 65, 148; William and Mary, 169
Willis, Thomas: *Cerebri Anatome*, 96
Willoughby, Francis, 96
Wilton House, 109, 147
Wimborne St Giles, 134
Winde, William, 145
Winstanley, Gerrard, 23, 31, 33, 62, 72, 81; *A New-Yeers Gift*, 72
Wisbech Castle, 134
Wissing, Willem, 42
witchcraft, 73
witches, 71
Wither, George, 78, 90; *Collection of Emblems*, 90
Wolsey, Cardinal, 148
Woman's Sharpe Revenge, The, 6
women, role of, 82–4
Worcester, victory at, 35, 158
Worden, Blair, 160
Wordsworth, William, 87
Wotton, William, 103, 154; *Reflections upon Ancient and Modern Learning*, 103
Wren, Sir Christopher, 16, 96, 107, 109, 116, **126**, 145–9, 176; Greenwich Hospital, plans for, 149
Wright, Michael, 141

Yates, Frances, 159
York, James, Duke of, 43, 44, 65, 162

For Product Safety Concerns and Information please contact our EU representative GPSR@taylorandfrancis.com
Taylor & Francis Verlag GmbH, Kaufingerstraße 24, 80331 München, Germany

www.ingramcontent.com/pod-product-compliance
Lightning Source LLC
Chambersburg PA
CBHW061443300426
44114CB00014B/1813